This book is dedicated to the memories of:

Harry Bader and Fern Ransom

A WORD ABOUT THE AUTHOR

Dr. Myles H. Bader known by many as "Doctor Of Food Facts" has been heard on over 1200 radio and television talk shows, throughout the United States and Canada. Television appearances include: The Oprah Winfrey Show, Mike and Maty, America's Talking, The Discovery Channel (Home Matters Show), and The Morning Exchange to name just a few.

Dr. Bader received his Doctorate Degree from Loma Linda University and is board certified in Preventive Care. He has practiced in major clinics in California and is presently presenting lectures and seminars worldwide.

During the last 20 years Dr. Bader has established numerous prevention programs for Fortune 500 companies and senior organizations. These programs were in the areas of executive health, weight management, diabetes, fitness, school health and biofeedback.

Celebrity host Robin Leach says "a fun and useful book that should be on every kitchen counter in America."

Lendon Smith, M.D., better known as the Good Morning America Doctor for many years has this to say of Dr. Bader, "He is highly knowledgeable in the areas of health, nutrition and preventive medicine."

TABLE OF CONTENTS

Chapter 1:   Fun Miscellaneous Facts 1
Chapter 2:   It's Party Time 17
Chapter 3:   Fruits of the Bloom 25
Chapter 4:   Vegetables, The Old and The New 53
Chapter 5:   Spud Facts 89
Chapter 6:   Vitamin and Mineral Facts 97
Chapter 7:   Egg Knowledge 117
Chapter 8:   Cold and Freezing Facts 129
Chapter 9:   Lets "Not" Chew the Fat 137
Chapter 10: Cheese Facts 153
Chapter 11: Meat Facts 167
Chapter 12: Fowl Facts 187
Chapter 13: Fathoms of Fish 197
Chapter 14: Beverage Facts 223
Chapter 15: Grain and Nut Facts 231
Chapter 16: Bread and Muffin Facts 249
Chapter 17: A Cup of Joe, A Spot of Tea 257
Chapter 18: Cake, Pie and Cookie Facts 271
Chapter 19: Fast Food Facts 287
Chapter 20: Food Safety Facts 297
Chapter 21: Food, Not for Eating 305
Chapter 22: Packaging and Food Nutrient Facts 313
Chapter 23: Soft Drink Facts 319
Chapter 24: Supermarket Facts 325
Chapter 25: Restaurant Facts 329
Chapter 26: Consumer Awareness Facts 333
Chapter 27: Cooking Facts 343
Chapter 28: Herb & Spicy Facts 355
Chapter 29: Food Additive Facts 373
Chapter 30: How Sweet It Is 383
Chapter 31: The Travelers Food Facts 403
Chapter 32: Frosting and Topping Facts 407
Chapter 33: Sauce and Gravy Facts 411
Chapter 34: Soup and Stew Facts 415

Chapter 35:   Food Canning Facts 421
Chapter 36:   Substitution Facts 425
Chapter 37:   Statistical Facts 429
Chapter 38:   Dairy Facts 435
Chapter 39:   Vegetarian Facts 447
Chapter 40:   Water Facts 453
Appendix A: Food Terminology A to Z 465
Index 483

Chapter 1

Fun Miscellaneous Facts

BATTLE OF THE BUGS

"INTO THE WILD BLUE YONDER"
Basil plants will repel mosquitoes and flies, just keep a plant or two around the house.

"KEEPING THE CRITTERS AT BAY"
Bay leaves should be placed in all kitchen drawers and in the flour and sugar containers to keep crawling insects away.

"Le Pew"
Mice can't stand the smell of fresh peppermint. Plant it around the outside of the house to keep them away. Oil of Peppermint placed on a piece of cloth and placed in their favorite location will also work.

"GETTING METHODICAL"
Ants - *Method 1:* To keep ants away, place whole cloves or sage around the windows and doors or anywhere else they appear. This works great!

Ants - *Method 2:* For a quick ant kill, mix two cups of borax with one cup of sugar in a quart jar. Punch holes in the lid and sprinkle around the outside of the house.

Ants - *Method 3:* To get rid of ants, pour Ivory Liquid Soap around. This is the only liquid soap that seems to work.

Ants - *Method 4:* To eliminate ants from your kitchen counters, try washing the counter with equal parts of water and white vinegar.

Ants - *Method 5:* If you have an area that ants travel most, just sprinkle a small amount of baby powder in that area. They will never cross the powder.

Ants - *Method 6:* Cucumber peelings will repel ants outside the house.

If all of the above fails to rid your premises of ants, try renting an Aardvark from the local zoo.

Roaches hate cucumber peels as well, just place a few in their favorite areas and you will never see them again.

A good roach killer can be made from 35% borax, 15% white flour, 10% powdered sugar and 40% cornmeal.

If you want to keep weevils and other crawling insects out of your grits and legumes, try placing a hot dried red pepper in with them.

A solution of weak tea, ammonia and dish soap placed in a spray bottle and sprayed on plants will keep most bugs away.

If you have a roach problem, fill a large bowl with cheap wine and place it under the sink. The roaches will drink the wine, get drunk, fall in and drown. Go ahead and laugh, but this is for real.

STAIN REMOVAL WITH FOODS, ETC.

Fruit berry stains can be removed by pouring hot water with salt added on the stain as soon as possible after the stain occurs, then wash the area with milk before placing it in a washing machine. Milk will provide a natural bleaching agent.

Cornstarch will remove blood stains. Use as a paste, then wash in warm soapy water.

If your dishwasher has stains in it, try filling your dispenser with powdered Gatorade and run it through a cycle.

Egg stains will respond to cold water only, hot water will only set the stain.

Water in which onions have been cooked will clean brass bottomed pots.

To make your porcelain sink look like new, place paper towels on the bottom and sides of the sink, then saturate with household bleach. Clean after an half-hour to one hour.

"RHUB-A-DUB-DUB"
Rust stains on clothing can be removed with rhubarb, Use the hot juice from 5-6 stalks.

Egg yolk mixed with warm water should remove most coffee or tea stains on fabrics.

"THE BUNDY SOLUTION"
If your shoes have an odor, treat them to a shot of baking soda. It does wonders.

Fruit juice can be removed from fabrics by pouring at least 3 quarts of boiling water slowly on the stain.

To remove most grease stains from cloth, try rubbing the stains with lard before washing with a detergent.

Carpet stains from oil or grease may be removed by rubbing cornmeal into the stain and allowing it to stand for 12 hours.

Keep an empty plastic soda bottle handy, in case you ever need a hot water bottle. Just fill it up with hot water and wrap it in a towel.

VINEGAR, THE ALL AROUND HELPER

"BE-WARE"
Never use a painted plate for serving with vinegar dressing. Vinegar will corrode the paint off the plate. This will not only ruin the plate, but may release harmful toxins into the foods.

To de-crud a flower vase or wine bottle, try using a solution of 1 tablespoon of salt and 1 cup of white vinegar. If you still have some residue left, add some rice and shake.

White vinegar will remove coffee or tea stains.

Sour wines may be used in place of vinegar.

To remove water spots from stainless steel place alcohol or white vinegar on a cloth.

Lime deposits can be removed from teapots by filling the kettle with equal parts of vinegar and water, bringing to a boil and letting it stand overnight.

Use warm vinegar to remove old decals. Just allow the vinegar to soak in for a few minutes then sponge off the decal.

"DO THE TWIST"
Pour oil and vinegar into the remains on the bottom of a ketchup bottle, shake vigorously to make a great salad dressing.

To control the mold in your breadbox, try washing it occasionally with a mild solution of vinegar and water.

White vinegar will help eliminate the odor from a dog's accident on the carpet.

To make your hair shiny, try a teaspoon of vinegar in your final rinse.

CLEANING UP

"HI YO SILVER"
Wash silver or silverplate soon after it comes into contact with eggs, salad dressing, olives, vinegar and other foods that have been seasoned with salt. These will cause silver to tarnish faster.

To remove grease spots try using talcum powder.

Your oven can be cleaned easily with baking soda.

Corningware cookware can be cleaned by filling them with water and by dropping in two denture cleaning tablets. Let stand for 30-45 minutes.

"ANTI-FREEZE"

In winter, add denatured alcohol to your window cleaning solution to prevent freeze-ups.

Woodwork is easily cleaned with cold tea.

Silver polish will remove coffee stains from plastic cups.

To clean an oven spill, sprinkle the area with salt immediately; then when the oven has cooled, clean with a damp cloth.

Oven Guard used on a clean car bumper will make it easier to get the bugs off next time.

Left over cola drinks poured into your toilet, adds cleaning power to your cleaner as well as giving it a brilliant shine.

If you have problems cleaning a grater after grating cheese, rub raw potato over it before washing.

Use an old toothbrush to clean the grater.

A few drops of ammonia should be dropped into greasy pots before hot water is poured in. This will make them easier to clean.

An excellent way to clean butcher blocks is with a plastic window scraper.

Place a piece of chalk in a silver chest to absorb moisture and slow tarnishing.

"A LITTLE DIP WILL DO YA"
If you want your fingernails to be whiter, dip them in lemon juice. The acidic nature of the lemon juice will bleach them.

Always keep a clean small plastic baggie handy when you have both hands in any food you are mixing. If the phone rings, just slip your hands in the baggie.

To keep plant-eating pets out of your garden or from potential poisonings, place red or black pepper on the leaf tips of plants and especially African violets and other toxic houseplants.

"FOILED AGAIN"
To keep animals away from your plants, try placing tin foil around them. Most animals will stay clear.

The reason you can place your hand into a 500 degree oven and not into a pot of boiling water at 212 degrees is that air doesn't transfer heat well.

A FEW HELPFUL HEALING FACTS

Place an ice cube on a splinter a few seconds before removing it. This will deaden the area.

A slice of cold onion placed on a bee or insect bite should stop the pain and swelling.

To cure hiccups, try a cup of dill leaf tea sipped slowly.

Run a warm iron over contact paper and it should peel right off.

"SEASON YOUR CARPET"
Carpet colors will be more livelier if you sprinkle a small amount of salt on before vacuuming.

Empty ketchup or mustard containers are great for decorating cakes or cookies.

"KITCHEN KOPTER"
To get the last drop out of a ketchup bottle, grasp the bottom of the bottle firmly and swing it in a circular motion from your side. The remaining ketchup will go to the top.

"CRUMBY SECURITY"
Keep a jar handy for leftover crumbs from empty cereal boxes or cracker boxes. When you need bread crumbs they will be there for you.

Spray Pam on your snow shovel and the snow will slide right off.

Milk cartons make excellent kindling. Fill with wood chips for a great fire starter.

A "SINKING" FEELING

To unclog a drain, try using a cup of salt mixed with a cup of baking soda (no liquid). Pour the dry solution into the drain followed by a pot of boiling water.

ODOR EATERS

To eliminate refrigerator odors, try a small amount of vanilla on a cotton ball.

If you boil several cloves in a cup of water, it will rid the house of unwanted food odors.

Cloves can also be combined with cinnamon, wrapped in a piece of cheesecloth and placed in boiling water. It will give off a pleasant fragrance.

Coffee grounds kept in an open jar will help absorb odors.

For an efficient refrigerator deodorizer, try using a few charcoal briquets on a small plate.

"AN UPLIFTING EXPERIENCE"

To raise the nap of carpeting after heavy furniture has matted it down, place one or two ice cubes on the area overnight. In the morning the carpet should be back up.

"A PERKER UPPER"

Dry eggshells in the oven them pulverize them in the blender and make a high calcium meal, which is excellent for plant fertilizer.

Club soda, that has lost its fizzle, has just the right chemicals left to add vigor and color to your plants.

To save washing extra cups and spoons, first measure all dry ingredients, place them on waxed paper, then use the same cup or spoon for measuring the liquids.

Save all microwave food containers, place leftovers in them and freeze them for later use.

"MICROWAVE SAVVY"

To check to see if a container is safe for use in the microwave, place the container next to a cup that is half-full of water. Use full power for one minute. If the container is hot to the touch, it cannot be used in the microwave, if its warm it may be used to reheat, and if its cool its OK.

To grease a pan easily, try using a soft bread crust spread with the butter or ?

FOR THE KIDS

'CHILD'S PLAY"

Formula for playdough: mix together ½ cup of salt, 2 tablespoons alum, 2 tablespoons cooking oil, then add the mixture to 2 cups of boiling water and knead.

Use natural food coloring for different colors.

"A BUBBLE TO BURST"

Formula for children's bubble solution: mix 1 tablespoon of glycerin with 2 tablespoons of a powdered detergent in 1 cup of water. Add food coloring if desired.

"GET A GRIP ON IT"

Wide rubber bands placed around drinking glasses give children a better grip.

"PLUG THE DIKE"

If you place a marshmallow on the bottom of an ice cream cone, the ice cream will not leak through.

When traveling with small children, carry a bottle of powdered milk instead of regular milk which spoils, all you have to do is add water and shake.

"REJUVENATION"

To bring ping pong balls back to life that have been dented, just place them in hot water for 15-20 minutes.

"COLD STORAGE"

Keep plastic wrap in the refrigerator to prevent it from sticking to itself when handled.

Hydrogen peroxide won't lose its fizzle if kept in the refrigerator.

Nail polish should be stored in the refrigerator. It will go on smoother and have a longer life.

"MIXER UPPER"

Keep a shaker of mixed salt and pepper near the stove. Use 3/4 part salt to 1/4 part pepper.

FOOD FIXER UPPERS

If food is scorched, place the pot immediately in cold water to stop the cooking action, which will eliminate the burnt taste from the food that was not scorched.

If you overdo the mayonnaise, add bread crumbs to absorb it.

"REVIVAL"

To bring the bounce back into tennis balls, place the can in the oven with the lid removed overnight. The heat from the pilot light will revive them.

If plastic has burned on an appliance, clean with lighter fluid.

To remove cigarette burns or coffee stains, rub the stain with a damp cloth dipped in baking soda.

To remove stains from enamel pots, mix bleach with water and boil in the pot until the stain is gone.

Stainless steel pots will remain shiny if you rub them with a piece of lemon rind, then wash in warm soapy water. If you have a problem, try adding a small amount of salt to the lemon.

BAKING SODA FACTS

Juice, coffee, and tea stains may be removed by scrubbing them vigorously with a paste made of baking soda and water.

Clean crayon marks off walls with baking soda on a damp cloth. Has just enough abrasive action to do the job without causing damage.

A thin layer of fresh baking soda should be placed on the bottom of a litter box before adding litter.

THE "NOSE" KNOWS
A small amount of baking soda applied to your armpits will replace your deodorant.

Baking soda works great in place of toothpaste.

To repair a nail hole on woodwork, just mix a small amount of instant coffee with spackling paste or starch and water and voila.

Mirrors can be brightened by rubbing them with a cloth dampened with alcohol.

"TROUBLE WAKING UP? TRY THIS ON"
Pantyhose will last longer if you freeze them before wearing. It strengthens the fibers.

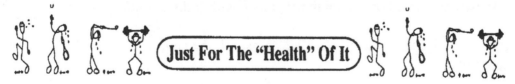

Just For The "Health" Of It

Water from boiled vegetables should be saved and mixed with your cat or dog's food to give them additional nutrients.

"TASTE BUD ALERT"
To check your salt intake, eat a piece of bacon, if it doesn't taste salty you're probably eating too much salt.

Aged wine and cheeses contain the substance tyramine, that in sensitive individuals can cause migraine headaches.

Tin coffee cans make excellent freezer containers for cookies.

Mayonnaise will remove dead skin on your elbows. Rub briskly.

"BRRRRRRRRRRR!!!"
To cool a hot dish more rapidly, place it in a pan of salted cold water. It will cool faster than if placed in cold water.

To keep milk from sticking to a pot, massage a little butter on the bottom of the pot.

Lightly grease gelatin molds before using. It will make it easier to remove the mold.

Add raw rice to the salt shaker to keep the salt free-flowing.

"SHOW STOPPERS"
To prevent carbonated beverages from fizzing over, try rinsing the ice-cubes with water first, before pouring the soda in. This will work for all sodas except root beer.

Place a hot dog in plastic wrap, then put it into a thermos of soup or coffee. When lunchtime arrives, put it into a bun for a real hot dog.

If you coat the bottom of pots used over an open fire with shaving cream before using, the black marks will come off easier.

Sugar bags can be used to store ice cubes. Much thicker than plastic ones.

Small marshmallows can be used for candle holders on cakes.

Sandwiches will not become limp and soggy as readily if you spread the butter or mayonnaise to the edge of the bread.

Many sandwiches can be frozen for up to two weeks. Best fillings are cold cuts, meat loaf, chicken, peanut butter (no jelly), tuna, and beef.

Floor tiles should be used instead of contact paper on kitchen shelves. They last longer and are easier to clean.

"SLICK IDEAS"
To prevent mildew from forming in the refrigerator, try spraying the insides of it with vegetable-oil spray after you defrost it. It will make the job much easier next time.

Blenders and egg beaters should be lubricated regularly. Use mineral oil instead of vegetable oil. Vegetable oil may cause corrosion.

If you use a small amount of oil on the threads of syrup bottles, it will stop the syrup from running down the sides of the bottle.

When you measure sticky liquids, try wiping the inside of the measuring cup with a small amount of oil. The liquids will flow freely.

To prevent ice-cube trays from sticking to the bottom of the shelf, place a piece of waxed paper underneath the tray.

A hair dryer will help defrost a freeze-up in the ice-maker.

When glasses are stuck together, just fill the top one with cold water and dip the bottom one in hot water.

 Chef's Secrets

The secret to keeping butcher blocks in good shape is to wash then dry, then cover with salt to draw the moisture out of the wood. Then treat with mineral oil for a smooth surface.

For clear ice cubes, just boil the water first.

When grating, chefs always grate the softest items first, then the firmer ones. This will keep the grater clean.

"STUCK UP"

When postage stamps have stuck together, try placing them into the freezer for 10 minutes, they should come apart without damaging the glue.

Any cloth material that has chewing gum stuck to it can be placed into the freezer. After about an hour the gum should break off easily.

WASHING DISHES

"A PENNY SAVED"

Save money by purchasing the least expensive dishwasher soap, then add a few teaspoons of vinegar to the dishwater. The vinegar cuts the grease and leaves the dishes spot-free and sparkling.

When washing greasy dishes, add a half-cup of baking soda to the water to cut the grease faster.

To clean an electric coffee pot, place one teaspoon of dish soap into the pot and boil.

Washing greasy dishes, add a half-cup of baking soda to the water to cut the grease faster.

When you want to fill a thermos bottle or small mouth container, try using a funnel.

To help a semi-solid soup slide right out of its can, try shaking the can first and them opening it from the bottom.

"NUKED"

Never lean on a microwave door. It may become misaligned and leak radiation.

Crisco can be used as a makeup remover.

Chapter 2

It's Party Time

ENTERTAINING FACTS

"FILLER UPPERS"
Use a large green pepper as a cup for dips. Cut off top, scrape pepper clean of ribs and seeds, then fill with dip.

Cucumbers make an excellent holder for dips. When cutting, leave a handle in the middle, like a basket.

Use halved or hollowed-out melons, oranges or grapefruits as a cup to fill with cut-up fruit bits.

THE "NOSE" KNOWS"
Before your guests arrive, give your home that "something's bakin'" fragrance. Just sprinkle cinnamon and sugar in a tin pie pan and cook it on high heat slowly on the stove for a few minutes.

 Chef's Secrets

When making small finger sandwiches, use an electric knife to cut them and the filling won't run all over the counter.

To keep your pizza crust crispy, try placing the cheese before the tomato sauce.

To keep ice from melting, place a container of dry ice underneath the ice.

Champagne is best if not chilled for too long a period in the refrigerator.

To save leftover wines, freeze them in your ice cube trays. They can be used for any dish that you would season with wine or use in coolers.

"SPRINKLER HEAD ALERT"
For a flaming pudding, soak sugar cubes in orange or lemon extract. Place them on the pudding and light.

Cottage cheese can be used in place of sour cream when making dips. Just place it in the blender until it is creamed.

Cream cheese can be colored with powdered or liquid food coloring as a filler for dainty rolled sandwiches. Try a different color for each layer and slice as you would a jelly roll.

To stop hard candy from sticking together, just sift a little cornstarch on it.

"PARTY CUBES"
Freeze red and green maraschino cherries in ice cubes. Also, cocktail onions, mint leaves or green olives for martinis.

Freeze different colors of grapes to use in punches.

Freeze lemon peels in ice cubes for use in water glasses.

Use large ice cubes made from milk cartons for punches. The larger the ice cube the slower it melts.

"A CHILLING SUBJECT"
If you ever wondered how much ice you will need for a party, the rule of thumb is one pound per person.

"JOLLY GOOD SHOW"
Use crescent dinner rolls as a quick and easy pastry to prepare a Beef Wellington.

To make a quick and unusual dip or spread, try pureeing a can of well drained white beans and a package of herb flavored soft cheese together.

"FOILED AGAIN"
Place a piece of aluminum foil under your napkin or paper towel in a bread basket to keep the bread or rolls warm longer and protect the bread basket from stains.

Leftover sandwiches can be brushed with butter and cooked in a shallow pan.

"IT'S ZOO TIME"
When making sandwiches for the children, try using your animal shaped cookie cutters on them for a unique treat.

Place a damp paper towel over Hors d'oeuvres, meat or cheese platters to help retain the moistness and slow the drying out time.

"A REAL DE-CORKER"
To remove a cork from inside an empty wine bottle, pour some ammonia into the bottle, set it in a well ventilated location. In a few days the cork will be disintegrated.

Make your own Easter-egg dyes. Boil the eggs with grass for green, onion skins for yellow and beets for red.

For attractive individual butter servings, squeeze butter through a pastry bag or plastic bag onto a cookie sheet; set into refrigerator to harden.

"MEDICAL MIRACLE"
To preserve a Halloween pumpkin, just spray the inside and outside surfaces with an antiseptic spray to kill bacteria and keep the pumpkin in better shape.

"DOUBLE DECKER"
Salads and dips can be kept chilled by using two bowls. Place the salad or dip in the smaller bowl, partially fill the larger bowl with water and freeze. Then place the smaller bowl onto the larger one and serve.

When using a tray, place a damp napkin under the dishes to stop them from moving around.

"A LITTLE DAB WILL DO YA"
If red wine is spilled on a carpet, it may be cleaned with shaving cream, then sponged off with water. Club soda may also work.

After the holidays, purchase the large eggs and bunnies made from chocolate at half price or less. Use for any recipes to save dollars.

If vodka is kept in the refrigerator, it will be more flavorful.

Champagne should only be ice-chilled up to the neck of the bottle, any higher and the cork may be more difficult to remove.

Since most dips for chips contain a milk product that may spoil easily, it would be wise to place 1/2-1 inch of water in a bowl that is slightly larger than the dip bowl, then freeze the water and place the smaller bowl on top of the ice when serving. This will slow down the spoilage time.

"PEEK-A-BOO"
If a watermelon needs to be removed from the refrigerator and sit for a while before being cut, try placing it in a double brown bag to keep it cool longer.

To fancy up the top of a cake, cookies or pie, try placing a wide-patterned doily on top the sprinkle powdered sugar over it and remove.

"SMART MOVE"
If your table is set with candles, it would be wise to place a small amount of salt around the top to eliminate wax droppings on the tablecloth.

Chapter 3

Fruits of the Bloom

"The Words Out"

Sales of fruits and vegetables have increased significantly in 1994, while meat and cigarette sales have dropped.

"PEELING IT OFF"

To peel thin-skinned fruits and vegetables easily, place in a bowl and cover with boiling water, let stand for one-minute then peel with a sharp paring knife or spear the fruit with a fork and hold over a gas flame until the skin cracks.

To peel thick-skinned fruits, cut a small amount of peel from top and bottom, set fruit on a cutting board, cut off the peel in strips from top to bottom.

If the box is available that the fruit came in be sure to look for a government stamp such as "U.S. Grade No. 1" or that they have a USDA stamp.

For an easy dressing for fruit salad, try a grated orange rind and orange juice added to sour cream.

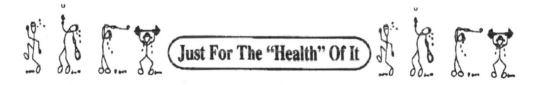
Just For The "Health" Of It

Canned pumpkin is one of the best sources of beta-carotene, it has approximately 27,000IU in a 40 calorie 8oz. serving.

Two of the most nutritious fruits are papaya and cantaloupe.

Wash all fruits and vegetables in cold water to remove any chemicals, but never soak or store them in water. Vitamins B and C are easily lost. Dry all fruits and vegetables After washing.

The more surface of a fruit or vegetable you expose, the more nutrients will be lost to oxidation.

Enzymes needed by the body will be completely destroyed by cooking.

Never allow your fruits and vegetables to be placed in the same bag with meats. Juices may leak and contaminate the fruit and vegetables.

"IT'S THE PITS"

Certain fruits such as apricots, apples, pears, cherries and peaches contain a small amount of the chemical "amygdalin" which tends to release cyanide, a deadly poison. Best advise is not to chew or ingest the pits, problems are rare and you would have to eat about 60 apricot pits to get a lethal dose.

Coconut water found inside a coconut is almost fat-free and high in vitamin K.

Coconut oil is made from the meat and is very high in saturated fat.

Maraschino cherries contain red dye #2, which, according to studies by the United Nations Food and Agriculture Report, may cause birth defects.

To preserve the nutritional value of fruits and vegetables, it is best to leave them in their original wrappings.

Excessive consumption of acidic fruit juices can wear away tooth enamel.

Order of nutritional quality of fruits - 1. Fresh, if grown properly, 2. Dehydrated Grade A, 3. Freeze Dried, 4. Frozen, 5. Canned.

Some of the best sources of pectin are figs, oranges, apples, bananas, pears and soybeans. Pectin is being studied as a significant factor in assisting the body to increase its good cholesterol (HDL) levels.

Dried fruits loses most of its vitamin C when dried, however, it does retain almost all of the minerals and is high in beta-carotene.

Dried fruits may contain sulfites as a preservative. Sulfites have been known to cause allergic reactions in susceptible individuals. It would be best to dehydrate your own.

Dentists are advising that dried fruits may stick to your teeth increasing your risk of tooth decay. Best to brush after eating dried fruits.

Chef's Secrets

Toasting intensifies the flavor and adds crispness to nuts.

Raisins won't stick to a food chopper if they are soaked in cold water for a short period of time.

Cream won't curdle when poured over fruits if you add a pinch of baking soda with the cream before serving.

"BROWN-OUT"''
To reduce the amount of food discolorization, slice bananas, apples, pears, plums and peaches with a stainless steel knife, then either combine them with any citrus fruit or sprinkle them with lemon or pineapple juice. Refrigerate as soon as possible.

Keep the rinds of oranges and grapefruits. Grate them and store in a tightly sealed jar in the refrigerator. They will make excellent flavorings for cakes and frostings.

For the best flavor cook dried fruit in the same water it was thawed in.

If you add a small pat of butter when cooking fruit for jams and jellies and you won't have any foam to skim off the top.

If you have any problems with fruit jelly not setting up, place the jars in a shallow pan half-filled with cold water, then bake in a moderate oven for 30 minutes.
To make ripe olives taste better, soak them overnight in olive oil with a clove of garlic added.

When making fruit compote, try adding some herbs, such as sweet cicely, mint or basil to bring out a sweeter flavor.

To ripen fruit, place it in a brown paper bag in a dark place for a few days.

If whole citrus fruits are warmed in the microwave or oven for a few minutes, they will yield more juice.

Lemons, limes, and grapefruits will not wilt or shrink if stored in water in the refrigerator. Place a small saucer on top of the fruits if necessary, to keep them submerged.

Prunes are a natural laxative due to the ingredient diphenylisatin.

To make dry raisins plump again, wash them, place them in a shallow dish and bake them covered in a preheated 350° F oven for no more than 10 minutes.

THE "WILD" SIDE
The Aborigines' favorite fruit in Australia is the "green plum." A 3 ½ ounce portion contains 2,300 to 3,150 milligrams of vitamin C. Oranges, which we purchase fresh only contain 50-80mg. of vitamin C, if we are lucky enough to buy them freshly picked.

The Hadza hunters in Tarzania enjoy the "kongoroko fruit." A 3 ½ ounce serving contains 526 milligrams of calcium. The U.S. RDA is 1,000 milligrams per day for the average adult.

The South African cape buffalo contains 1.5% of its fat in the form of omega-3 fatty acids. One of the best sources we consume is usually from fish oil. Our beef contains hardly a trace. Cod liver oil which is considered one of the best sources contains only 5%.

Ouch!

To test fruit for ripeness, stick a toothpick in the fruit at the stem end. If it goes in and out clean and with ease the fruit is ripe and can be eaten.

Chef's Secrets

Dried fruits are graded: Extra Fancy, Fancy, Extra Choice, Choice or Standard. These gradings are based solely on size, color, condition and water content, not nutrient content.

Dried fruits kept in an airtight container will keep up to 6 months in a cool dry place or up to 1 year if placed in the refrigerator.

To easily chop raisins, place a small amount of butter on both sides of the knife.

APPLES

Certain apples will taste different depending on the time of year purchased. If you are buying large quantities, it would be best to purchase a few and taste them. They should be firm, have no holes, be unbruised, and have a good even color. If the apple is not ripe, leave at room temperature for a day or two. Apples are capable of lasting 3-5 weeks in the refrigerator, and will still retain vitamin C content. Most apples are tart flavored. The best and sweetest eating apples are the Red and Golden Delicious varieties. There are many varieties of apples which make them available year round.

Apples will spoil 10 times faster at room temperature. After they are ripe, be sure to refrigerate them.

Apples will float because 25% of their volume is made up of air between the cells.

The soft texture of cooked apples is caused by the heat collapsing the air spaces between the cells.

Apple butter contains no fat if prepared properly with cinnamon and allspice.

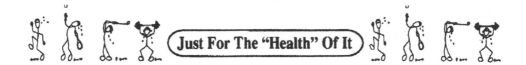

Pare apples by pouring scalding water on them just before peeling them.

Cut apples into quarters before peeling, it will be easier.

To give applesauce a different flavor, add sliced unpeeled orange in the last few minutes of the cooking.

To avoid wrinkled skins on apples when baking, cut a few slits in the skin to allow for expansion.

Apples will store for a longer period if they do not touch one another.

For winter storage, wipe apples dry and pack in dry sand or sawdust. Keep in cool, dry place.

Fresh apple juice will only last for a few weeks, even if under refrigeration.

Most of an apple harvest ends up being made into pasteurized apple products or frozen in order to preserve it. When pasteurized at temperatures of 170° to 190°F. microorganisms are destroyed and the juice has a stable shelf life of up to one year.

If you purchase frozen apple concentrate, it will only last for a few weeks after it is thawed.

The tartness of an apple is derived from the balance of malic acid and the fruit's natural sugars.

Commercially prepared sweetened applesauce can contain as much as 77% more calories than unsweetened varieties.

Nutritionally there is no difference between "natural" and "regular" apple juice, even the fiber content is the same.

Apple juice is not high on the nutrient scale. It contains no vitamin C unless it has been added.

FDA testing can only detect 50% of the approved 110 pesticides that are used on apples. The worst ones are; Captan and Phosmet, both can be removed with washing or cooking.

Apple juice and cider should not be purchased unless you are sure that the whole apple was not used in their preparation. The pits contain a poison.

Americans eat approximately 22 pounds of apples per year per person. 33% of apples in one government study contained residues of pesticides. 43 different pesticides were detected in apples.

If you store apples along with green tomatoes, they will ripen at a faster pace.

There are 150 strains of Red and Golden Delicious apples.

APPLE VARIETIES

Akane - Do not store well. Have sweet-tart flavor. Skin is thin and usually tender. They retain their shape well when baked and have a tart flavor.

Braeburn - Store exceptionally well. Skin is tender, moderately tart. They keep shape well when baked and retain their tartness.

Cortland - Fragile and needs to be stored carefully. High in vitamin C and resists browning. Thin skinned with slight tart-sweet taste. Keeps shape well when baked.

Criterion - Yellow apples that are difficult to handle without bruising. High in vitamin C and resists browning. The skin is tender but flavor is bland when baked.

Elstar - Store well with their tart flavor mellowing when stored. They have tender skin and retain their flavor and shape well when baked.

Empire - Do not store well and tend to get mealy easily. High in vitamin C and will resist browning. Thick-skinned and bake well retaining flavor.

Fuji - Store well with tangy-sweet flavor. Will retain shape well when baked, but take longer to cook than most apples. Looks like an Asian pear.

Gala - Choose apples with pale-yellow background and light-reddish stripes Sweet with slight tartness and have tender skin. Hold shape well when baked but does not retain flavor.

Golden Delicious - Stores well but spoils fast at room temperature. Should be light yellow not greenish. Skin is tender and flavor is sweet. High in vitamin C and resists browning. Retains shape well when baked.

Granny Smith - Best color is light green not intensely green and could even have a slight yellow tint. High in vitamin C and resists browning. Nicely balanced sweet-tart flavor. Cooks into excellent thick applesauce, but is not recommended for baking.

Gravenstein - Comes in both red and green. Excellent sweet-tart flavor and very juicy. Good for applesauce but not a good baking apple.

Idared - They keep exceptionally well and become sweeter during storage. Resembles Jonathans, skin is tender. When cooked they will retain full flavor.

Jonagold - Has good sweet-tart balance. A very juicy apple with tender skin. For best applesauce, cook with peel then strain.

Jonathan - Found in California around mid-August. They become soft and mealy quickly. Thin skinned, cook tender and make good applesauce. Retain shape well when baked.

McIntosh - Most come from British Columbia. Be careful when selecting, they get mushy and mealy easily. Skin is tough and will separate from flesh. Tend to fall apart when baked in pies.

Melrose - Normally found in the Northwest. Store very well and flavor actually improves after one or two months of storage. Well-balanced sweet and tart flavor. Retains shape well when cooked in pies.

Mutsu - (Crispin) Looks like Golden Delicious, but is greener and irregular in shape. Store very well. Has sweet but spicy taste with fairly coarse texture. For applesauce, cook with peels and strain.

Newton Pippin - Sometimes picked too green, wait until light green for sweetest flavor. Crisp, sweet-tart flavored apple. They keep shape when baked or used in pies. Makes a thick applesauce.

Northern Spy - A tart red/green apple, excellent for pies

Red Delicious - Ranges in color from red to red- striped. Store for up to 12 months. Will not last long at room temperature. Avoid any bruised ones. Normally are sweet and mellow with hint of tartness. When cooked they do not hold flavor well.

Rhode Island Greening - Best choice for pies, but not very available. Only available October and November on the East Coast.

Rome Beauty -If stored for long periods Rome Beauty apples will develop a bland flavor and get mealy. They are very mild and have a low acid level. The skin is thick, but tender. It is an excellent baking apple.

Spartan - Will not store for long periods and get mealy easily. Sweet flavor and very aromatic. Flavor is weak when cooked.

Stayman Winesap - Stores well. Spicy-tart flavor and good crisp apple. Have thick skins which separate easily. When cooked they will retain flavor well. Good for baking or pies.

APRICOTS

Usually the first fruit of the summer season. A relative of the peach and in one ounce they contain enough beta carotene to supply 20% of your daily vitamin A requirements. Astronauts ate apricots on the Apollo moon mission.

Apricots originally were grown in China over 4,000 years ago and were brought to California by the Spanish in the late 18th century.

California is the largest producer of apricots.

Over half the apricots grown are canned due to their short season.

3 ½ ounces of dried apricots can supply 4 million grams of beta carotene.

Dried apricots are over 40% sugar.

Try and purchase unsulphured dried apricots.

BANANAS

Available all year round. They should be plump. The skin should be free of bruises as well as black and brown spots. Bananas should be purchased green and allowed to ripen at home. They may be ripened at room temperature until they reach the desired stage, then refrigerated and used in a short period of time. Refrigeration may darken the outside of the bananas, but this will not effect the fruit on the inside. In fact, refrigeration allows for longer storage of bananas.

If you want to ripen bananas even more quickly, wrap them in a wet paper towel and place them into a brown paper sack.

The new size of miniature bananas now appearing in supermarkets has more taste than many of the larger ones.

Banana chips are usually fried in coconut oil and is not a good nutritious snack like a banana or air-dried banana chips. One ounce of fried chips can have as much as 150 calories and up to 10 grams of fat, much of which is saturated.

American consume 25 pounds of bananas per person annually.

Bananas contain less water than most other fruits.

Bananas are a type of berry from a tree classified as an herb tree which can grow up to 30 feet high.

They are the largest plant in the world without a woody stem.

VARIETIES INCLUDE:

Cavandish - This is the standard banana that we normally purchase and for the most part is grown in South America.

Manzano - Called finger bananas and turn black when they are ripe.

Plantains - Very large green bananas, high starch content and are usually cooked like a vegetable. Sometimes substituted for potatoes.

Red Bananas - Not usually curved, they turn a purplish color when ripe. Sweet tasting.

 Chef's Secrets

If a green banana is placed next to a ripe banana, it will ripen more quickly.

Unpeeled bananas will last longer if stored in the refrigerator in a sealed jar.

If you slice bananas with a sterling silver knife they will not darken as fast. Old wives tale??

BERRIES

Should be fairly firm. Color should be good and not faded. Berries should all be refrigerated and should not be allowed to dry out. Use within 2-3 days after purchase for best flavor and nutritional value. Berries do not ripen once picked. Choose only bright red strawberries and plump firm blueberries that are light to dark blue.

Always check the bottom of berry containers to be sure they are not stained from rotting berries or if they show any mold.

Mold on berries spreads quickly. Never leave a moldy berry next to a good one. This goes for all fruits.

Chef's Secrets

Never hull strawberries until they have been washed or they will absorb too much water and become mushy.

Just For The "Health" Of It

Blueberries are higher in vitamin A then most berries.

By adding 1/4 teaspoon of baking soda to the cranberries when they are cooking, you will use less sweetener.

Fresh cranberries has 86% more vitamin C than canned cranberries.

One cup of strawberries contains only 55 calories and much more calcium, phosphorus, vitamin C, and potassium than blueberries, and raspberries.

Raspberries, strawberries, cranberries and loganberries contain "ellagic acid" a substance which is now being studied as a natural preventive for certain types of cancer.

Blueberries and blackberries are better if cooked since cooking will deactivate an enzyme that effects your absorption of vitamin B1.

Strawberries should be stored in the refrigerator in a plastic colander allowing the air to circulate around them.

A V-shaped can opener is ideal for hulling strawberries.

CANTALOUPES

Best June through September. They should be round, smooth, and have a depressed scar at the stem end. If the scar appears rough or the stem is still attached, the melon will not ripen well. Cantaloupes are best if the netting is an even yellow color with little or no green. Melons can be left at room temperature to ripen. The aroma will usually indicate if it is ripe and sweet. Refrigerate as soon as ripe. Whole melons will last for a week if kept cold. Cut melons, wrapped in plastic with seeds in and refrigerated, are best eaten in a few days.

If cantaloupe is ripe you should be able to hear the seeds rattling inside. It should also give off a sweet fragrance. The "belly button" should be somewhat soft, but if the melon is soft all over, it's probably overripe.

CHERRIES

Cherries are one of the most popular fruit and are grown in 20 countries worldwide. The United States grows approximately 150,000 tons of cherries annually.

The best known varieties are the Montmorency and the Bing. Available from May to August. Bings should be a dark purplish color and somewhat firm.

Europeans enjoy a chilled cherry soup as a summertime treat.

CRANBERRIES

A good cranberry will bounce. Buy berries that are hard, bright, light to dark-red. Sealed in plastic bags, they keep refrigerated for a month; frozen, they will keep up to one year.

 Chef's Secrets

Cook cranberries only until they "pop". Further cooking makes them taste bitter. When cooking cranberries, always add one teaspoon of butter to each pound to eliminate over boiling and excess foam.

DATES

These are one of the sweetest fruits and may contain up to 70% sugar. California and Arizona are the major suppliers for the United States, however, Africa and the Middle East have been growing them for 4,000 years.

A date cluster can weigh up to 25 pounds. Supplies 250% more potassium than an orange and 64% more than a banana ounce for ounce.

FIGS

Figs are one of the oldest known fruits. 90% of all figs grown are dried. They were brought to California by the Spanish and most are still grown in California. The most popular fig is the Calimyrna. Size is not an indicator of the quality.

They are uniquely pollinated by small fig wasps.

GRAPEFRUIT

As with all citrus, the heavier the fruit, the juicier. Florida grapefruits are juicier than those from California and Arizona. However, Western fruit has a thicker skin which is easier to peel. If refrigerated, grapefruit will last for a few weeks. Grapefruit should be firm and not discolored. Fruit that is pointed at the end tend to be thicker skinned and have less meat and juice. White fruit has a stronger flavor than pink fruit. Available all year, but best January through May.

Grapefruits were developed from crossing an orange with a shaddock. Shaddock's are not usually found in the supermarkets since they have almost no juice, a thick skin, a sour taste and many seeds.

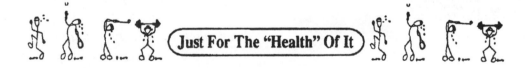

Just For The "Health" Of It

Recent studies show that grapefruit may be more effective in lowering cholesterol than any other pectin source.

Shredded grapefruit will be a great addition to any fish salad.

Chef's Secrets

If you allow a grapefruit to stand in boiling water for a few minutes it will be easier to peel.

"BELIEVE IT OR NOT"

Salt will make a grapefruit taste sweeter.

GRAPES

Should be plump and firmly attached to a green stem. Good color for type of grape, not faded. Grapes do not ripen off the vine, so be certain that they are ripe when chosen. Buy small quantity and taste. When refrigerated, grapes will last 5-7 days.

All grapes are really berries and are native to Asia Minor where they were cultivated for 6000 years.

Grapes are grown on 6 continents.

California produces 97% and Arizona produces 3% of all European varieties grown in the United States.

COMMON VARIETIES

Black Beauty - The only seedless black grape.

Calmeria - Large dark red grapes with a light gray finish. Has very few seeds.

Champagne - Used to make currents. Usually a gourmet product.

Concord - major variety of American grape. Blue/black with a sweet but somewhat tart flavor.

Delaware - Small pink-colored grape with a tender skin.

Emperor - One of the most popular small grape. Reddish/purple in color and seedless.

Exotic - Blue/black in color and have seeds.

Flame Seedless - Deep red and seedless, about the same size as the Emperor, but somewhat more tart.

Italia - Muscat, mainly for wine making. Green/gold grape with seeds.

Niagara - Large amber-colored grape, may be somewhat egg-shaped. Not as sweet as most other varieties.

Perlette Seedless - Green grape imported from Mexico.

Queen - Red, large grape that have a mild sweet flavor.

Red Globe - Very large grape with large seeds and a delicate flavor.

Red Malaga - Thick-skinned reddish somewhat sweet grape.

Ribier - Large blue/black grape with tender skins.

Ruby Seedless - Deep red grape, very sweet.

Steuben - A blue-black grape similar to the Concord.

Thompson Seedless - Everybodys favorite. The most common grape sold in the United States. Small green sweet grape. Common raisin grape.

Tokay - Sweeter version of the Flame Seedless.

HONEYDEW MELONS

The best are creamy white or pale yellow with a silky finish. They are best if purchased between June and October. A faint sweet smell indicates ripeness. Blossom end (the end opposite the stem) should be slightly soft. Like most melons, honeydews taste better if left unrefrigerated for a few days. Whole ones keep fresh for up to one week when refrigerated. Store cut melons with seeds in plastic bags. Eat within a few days.

KIWI

Firm kiwis, left at room temperature, soften and sweeten in 3-5 days. Ripe kiwis feel like ripe peaches. Refrigerated, they stay fresh for weeks. Average size 2-3 inches long. Has a furry brown skin which is peeled off before eating. The inside should be lime green. Kiwi may be used to tenderize meat. They are available June to March. When ripe, kiwi will give slightly to the touch. They are low in calories and are an excellent source of vitamin C.

Sometimes called a Chinese gooseberry, but is not related to the gooseberry.

2 kiwis = the fiber in 1 cup of bran flakes.

Peel with a vegetable peeler for less waste.

"RIPENS FASTER WITH FRIENDS"
To ripen faster, place them in a paper bag with an apple or a banana.

Excellent meat tenderizer when pureed and used in a marinade. Contains the chemical "actinidin" which also is the chemical in kiwi that causes the gelatin not to gel if you add kiwi to gelatin. Cooking the fruit even for a short period of time, however, deactivates the chemical.

LEMONS

If sprinkled with water and refrigerated in plastic bags, lemons (as well as limes) will last a month or more frozen, both their juices and grated peels last about 4 months. Look for lemons with the smoothest skin and the smallest points on each end. They have more juice and better flavor. Also, submerging a lemon in hot water for fifteen minutes before squeezing it will yield almost twice the amount of juice. Or, try warming lemons in your oven for a few minutes before squeezing them. If you need only a few drops of juice, prick one end with a fork and squeeze the desired amount. Return lemon to the refrigerator and it will be as good as new.

Lemons will keep longer in the refrigerator if you place them in a clean jar, cover them with cold water and seal the jar well.

After using one-half a lemon, store the other half in the freezer in a plastic baggie.

When lemon is used for a flavoring it tends to mask the craving for salt.

Lemon and lime peelings may cause skin irritation on susceptible persons. They contain the oil "limonene."

LIMES

Originated on the island of Tahiti. Key limes are a smaller variety with a higher acid content. The California variety is called "Bears" and is a seedless lime.

MANGOES

Available late December through August. Excellent source of Vitamin A & C. Should be eaten when soft, and will ripen at room temperature. Mangos are becoming a problem fruit. They are imported into this country with traces of a carcinogenic fumigant, ethylene dibromide (EDB). Purchase only mangos and papayas grown in Hawaii or Florida.

Mangos are one of the best sources of beta-carotene, they contain 20% more than cantaloupe and 50% more than apricots.

Mangos contain as much vitamin C as an orange.

Only 10% of all mangoes are grown in the United States.

NECTARINES

Their peak season is in July and August. They combine a peach and a plum characteristics. Color should be rich and bright. If too hard, allow to ripen at room temperature for a few days. Avoid very hard dull-looking nectarines.

There are 150 varieties of nectarines worldwide.

ORANGES

The color of an orange is no indication of its quality because oranges are usually dyed to improve their appearance. Brown spots on the skin indicate a good quality orange. Pick a sweet orange by examining the navel. Choose the ones with the biggest holes. If you put oranges in a hot oven before peeling them, no white fibers will be left on them.

Oranges that look green, have undergone a natural process called "regreening." This is due to a ripe orange pulling green chlorophyll pigment from the leaves. They are excellent eating and usually very sweet.

Chief food crop of the United States.

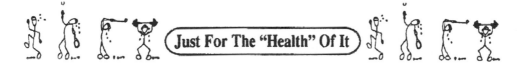

Orange juice is not necessarily high on the nutritional scale. While it may contain vitamin C and potassium, it provides little more than a source of carbohydrates in the form of a natural sugar.

Orange juice will lose more vitamin C content when stored in an open container or one with a plastic lid. Always store in a glass container with a screw cap.

Oranges that need to be peeled for dishes should be soaked in boiling water for at least 5-7 minutes before peeling. This will make it easier to peel and remove all the white pulp.

PAPAYAS

When ripe, they will be completely yellow. Papaya and kiwi both have tenderizing properties. They take 2-5 days to ripen at room temperature.

Papaya seeds are edible, wash them first. Similar flavor as that of pepper. Can be dried and ground for seasoning.

PEACHES

Peaches ripen quickly by placing them in a box covered with newspaper. Gases are sealed in. Skins come off smoothly if peach is peeled with a potato peeler. Remember when peaches had all that peach fuzz? Well, today peaches are defuzzed by a mechanical brushing process before shipment.

Peaches won't mature or get sweeter once picked.

PEARS

Ripen pears quickly by placing them in a brown paper bag along with a ripe apple. Place in a cool, shady spot and make certain a few holes are punched into the bag. The ripe apple will give off ethylene gas which will stimulate the other fruit to ripen. (This ripe-apple hint will also have the same effect on peaches and tomatoes).

Most of the vitamin C is located in the skin.

PERSIMMONS

Available October through January. They have a smooth, shiny, bright, orange skin, which is removed before eating or they will be sour. High in vitamins A, C, and potassium. May be ripened overnight by wrapping them in tin foil and placing into the freezer. Must be thawed at room temperature and eaten the next day.

PINEAPPLE

Available year round. Best March through June. Buy as large and heavy as available. Leaves at top should be deep green. Do not buy if they have soft spots. Refrigerate and use as soon as possible.

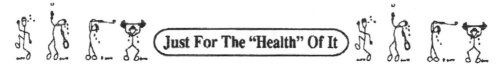

Fresh pineapple contains an enzyme that causes gelatin not to set-up. Canned is best.

Studies have shown that the chemical bromelin in pineapple may help keep arteries clean.

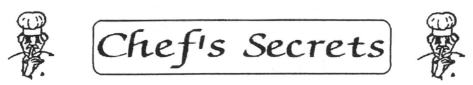

To ripen a pineapple, cut off top, remove skin and slice. Place in pot and cover with water, sweeten to taste, boil for five minutes, cool and refrigerate.

Never use fresh pineapple in a gelatin mold or the protein will be broken down and the gelatin will not gel. This is caused by the chemical "bromelain" a potent protein tenderizer.

PLUMS

Available June through September. Buy only medium firm to slightly soft plums. Hard plums will not ripen well. To ripen, let stand at room temperature until fairly soft. May take 2-3 days. Refrigerate after ripe.

The traditional "English Plum Pudding" never contained plums, only currents and raisins.

California French is the most common plum variety used for prunes.

POMEGRANATES

Available September through December. Contain many seeds surrounded by red pulp, which are both edible. The sponge-like membrane is bitter and usually not eaten. Pomegranate juice is used to make grenadine syrup. Excellent source of potassium.

UGLI FRUIT

A close relative of oranges and grapefruit. Yellowish, pebbly skin with green blotches that turn orange when the fruit is ripe. Makes excellent eating and is high in vitamin C. Looks Ugli!

WATERMELON

The ground-based side of a perfect watermelon is yellow. The rest of the rind is smooth, waxy, green, with or without stripes. If cut, pick bright, crisp, even-colored flesh. Whole melons can stay unrefrigerated for a few days. Once they are cut, they must be kept covered and cold.

To test for ripeness in watermelon, snap thumb and third finger against the melon. If it says "pink" in a high, shrill tone, the melon isn't ripe. If you hear "punk" in a deep low tone, the melon is ready to eat.

The following is a list of salad bar items I encountered on a trip to a Palm Springs restaurant, it is the best I have ever seen:

Lettuce	Cabbage	Celery Carrots	Cauliflower
Broccoli	Radishes	Cucumbers	Raisins
Grapes	Cantaloupe	Honeydew	Cheeses
Tomatoes	Watermelon	Sprouts	Mushrooms
Peppers	Seeds	Avocado	Strawberries
Beans	Olives	Beets	Onions
Boiled Eggs	Anchovy	Pimentos	Nuts
Shrimp	Apple	Oranges	Cranberry
Jicama	String Beans	Snow Peas	Croutons
Coconut	Zucchini	Cottage Cheese	Lunch Meats
Macaroni Salad	Coleslaw	Caviar	Dates
Bacon Bits	Papaya	Kiwi	Spinach
Chestnuts	Ginger Root	Capers	Bananas
Breads	Tuna Salad	Seafood Salad	Pickles
Smoked Fish.			

Since nobody likes mushy fruit many recipes ask you to add sugar to the recipe. This strengthens the cell walls and brings the water back into the cells that the cooking has removed.

Fruit consumption in the United States has risen from 101 pounds per person in 1970 to 124 pounds in 1994.

Chapter 4

Vegetables, The Old and The New

Sea vegetables are becoming a new food experience. They may be called "wakame" or "kombu" and they are derived from seaweed which is high in minerals.

"BEST TO GET A 4.0"
There are three grades of canned, frozen and dried fruits and vegetables: U.S. Grade A (fancy), U.S. Grade B (choice or extra standard) and U.S. Grade C (standard). Grades B and C are just as nutritious but have more blemishes.

"FANCY THAT"
Most fresh fruits and vegetables have three grades: U.S. Fancy, U.S. Fancy No. 1 and U.S. Fancy No. 2. The grades are determined by the product's color, size, shape, maturity and the number of defects.

"SAY GOODBYE TO SOGGY SALADS"
To prevent soggy salads, place an inverted saucer in the bottom of the salad bowl. The excess liquid drains off under the saucer and the salad stays fresh and crisp.

Never salt any vegetable during cooking, the salt will draw the liquid out and they will not cook evenly.

Try freezing different fruits and vegetables for kids snacks, such as peas, blueberries, etc.

July is National Baked Bean Month.

A new category of foods is now known as the "fruit-vegetables" and includes eggplant, squash, peppers and tomatoes. These are all the seed-bearing bodies of the plants they grow on.

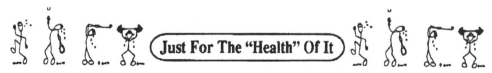

Just For The "Health" Of It

The chemical, solanine, has been associated with arthritis pain in a study by Rutgers University. Foods that contain high amounts of solanine are green potatoes, tomatoes, red and green peppers, eggplant and paprika.

Never eat home-canned vegetables before cooking them.

Cabbage, turnips, kale, rutabaga, watercress and rapeseed contain a harmful chemical called a thioglucoside, which may adversely affect the thyroid gland, but is destroyed by cooking.

Parsnips contain a chemical group called psoralens, which cause cancer readily in laboratory animals. They should be peeled and cooked to get rid of these toxins.

Vegetables high in beta carotene may interfere with menstruation. Women having problems should refrain from eating too many carrots, squash, broccoli and any vegetable high in carotene according to RN Magazine. It was also noted that their protein intake was increased.

Plants high in oxalic acid should be avoided as you approach middle age and beyond. These include; spinach, rhubarb and especially coco bean (chocolate). Studies have shown that they interfere with calcium absorption.

Parsley may make your skin sensitive to sunlight.

Wax coatings on fruits need to washed off or cut off. Check with your produce manager to find out which ones are waxed to increase their shelf life.

"SCRUB'EM OR PEEL'EM"
The FDA during a routine sampling of domestic and imported foods found pesticide residues in 31% of the 3,699 domestic vegetables. However, the FDA only tests 1% of all vegetables sold in the U.S.

It is best to save liquids from vegetables that you have cooked and use the liquids in soups, stews, etc.

Wash all fruits and vegetables in cold water, but never store them in water. If you do they will lose a large percentage of their nutrients.

Keep all produce wrapped loosely, especially if wrapped in plastic. Air must be allowed to circulate around them to reduce spoilage.

Order of nutritional quality (in most cases) (1) Fresh if grown properly, (2) Dehydrated Grade A, (3) Freeze Dried, (4) Frozen, (5) Canned.

Avoid baking soda around vegetables, many vitamins are acidic and turn into a salt.

Processing and storage times affect the nutrient content of both fruits and vegetables.

We have reduced our purchase of fresh vegetables 12% since the 1950's and have increased our use of canned and frozen vegetables by 50%.

If cut up greens need to be crisped up, place them in a the freezer in a metal bowl for 5-10 minutes. If they are wet, remember to place an inverted small saucer on the bottom to drain off the excess liquid.

"GREAT CAESARS SALAD"
Caesars Salad was named after a restaurant owner in Tijuana, Mexico. Caesar Cardini was in trouble and was running out of food, so he used the only ingredients left, and invented Caesars Salad.

Chef's Secrets

Try placing a few unshelled pecans in your saucepan when cooking greens, kale or collards, it will help keep the odor down.

THE "NOSE" KNOWS
When cooking onions or cabbage, boil a small amount of vinegar in a pan to remove the odors.

The best method of cutting parsley is to use a scissors.

To place some life into your salads, try adding sorrel, cress or nasturtium to it.

If you sprinkle salt into the water when you are washing vegetables, it will draw out insects.

To caramelize vegetables and make the flavors and colors more intense, take carrots, celery, parsnips, onions or tomatoes and toss with olive oil then roast in a 500 degree F. oven for 30-40 minutes or until dark brown.

If you add a small amount of sugar to vegetables, it will bring out more flavor.

All leafy vegetables such as spinach, kale, greens and chard, should be cooked in water that clings to their leaves for the best flavor.

When boiling greens, add a pat of butter to the water. This will prevent them from boiling over without constant stirring.

"PERKER UPPER"
If you cook with a small amount of milk, it will help to retain the color of the vegetables.

Wilted vegetables can be freshened by soaking them for an hour in cold water with the juice of one lemon.

If you add salt to the water when washing vegetables, it will help remove any sand that is left.

Always line your refrigerator drawers with a double piece of paper towel to absorb the excess moisture.

Vegetable stains can be removed with a slice of wet potato or vinegar.

Tomatoes, cucumbers and carrots rank as the most popular salad fixings. The least popular are beans and peas.

Use a well-greased muffin tin to bake tomatoes, apples or bell peppers. They will keep their shape better.

"GETTING PICKLED"

When making pickles, cut off 1/4 inch from each end. The ends contain an enzyme that may cause the pickles to soften.

Pickle juice should be saved and used for making cole slaw, potato salad, etc.

If you will add a small piece of horseradish to the pickle jar, it will keep the vinegar active while keeping the pickles from becoming soft.

Choosing The Most Nutritious Greens:

1. Dandelion - Use young leaves.
2. Arugula - Slight mustard green flavor.
3. Kale - Use young leaves.
4. Parsley - Helps bring out the flavor of others.
5. Romaine - Somewhat strong taste.
6. Spinach - High in nutrients but contains oxalates.
7. Beet - Best if you use young and small leaves.
8. Butter - Lettuce.
9. Endive - Contains oxalates. May affect calcium absorption.
10. Iceberg - Most popular lettuce, least nutritious.

Never salt the water when cooking turnips, it will remove the sweetness.

The top 10 Fruits and vegetables in overall nutritional content:

1. Broccoli
2. Cantaloupe
3. Carrots
4. Kale
5. Mango
6. Papaya
7. Pumpkin
8. Red Bell Peppers
9. Spinach
10. Sweet Potato

Spinach should be washed quickly in warm water.

Chives need to be refrigerated and used within 3-4 days after purchase for the best flavor.

A new plastic wrap is being developed that will breathe and extend the life of wrapped vegetables. It is being developed by the U.S.D.A.

Vegetables are best steam cooked. The faster the better.

Coleslaw will taste better, if you use sweet pickle juice instead of vinegar.

Sour wines may be used in place of vinegar.

When taking salad greens on a picnic, wrap them in a damp towel and the dressing in a jar.

To crisp up salad greens, add 1 teaspoon of vinegar to a pan of water, then let the greens soak for 15 minutes.

If vegetables and salad are dry when served, the dressing will adhere better.

Parsley will cure bad breath.

CHOOSING THE "CREAM" OF THE CROP

ARTICHOKES
Best to purchase March through May. California is the main supplier. Choose from compact, tightly closed heads with green, clean-looking leaves. Their size is not related to quality. Avoid ones that have brown leaves or show signs of mold. Leaves that are separated, show that it is too old and will be tough and bitter.

There are 50 varieties of artichokes grown worldwide.

A single artichoke is an unopened flower bud from a thistle like plant.

Best to wear rubber gloves when working with artichokes.

Artichokes should never be cooked in aluminum pots. They tend to turn the pots a gray color.

Artichokes will burn unless kept completely covered with water while they are cooking. However, they are easy to overcook.

When cooking artichokes you can obtain a better flavor if you add a small amount of sugar and salt to the water. They will be sweeter and will retain their color better.

ASPARAGUS
Stalks should be green with compact, closed tips and tender. Avoid flat stalks or stalks that have a lot of white in them. Do not buy them if they are soaking in water. Asparagus toughen rapidly, and should be used soon after purchase. The best time of year to purchase is March to June. Refrigeration will help retain the B and C vitamins, but wrap the ends in moist paper towel, then seal in a plastic bag.

White asparagus is planted under mounds of soil, blocking sunlight and reducing the plants ability to produce chlorophyll.

If ridges form on stems, this is a sign of age and soaking in ice water will help revive it.

The water that vegetables are cooked in will be high in vitamins and minerals. Use for soups and stews.

To revive limp asparagus, try placing them in a tall pot with ice water in the refrigerator for thirty minutes.

"WHOOPS"

Always open asparagus cans from the bottom or you may break the tips. However, read the can carefully as they may be canned upside down.

To tenderize the asparagus stalks, try peeling the stalks with a potato peeler up to the bottom of the tips.

Asparagus contains a sulphur compound that may cause a strange odor in a persons urine. This happens in approximately 40% of the population and is harmless.

AVOCADOS

Available all year round. They should be fresh in appearance and the color should range from green to purple-black. They should feel heavy for their size and be slightly firm. Avoid ones with soft spots and discolorizations. Refrigerate and use within 5 days after ripening.

Avocados ripen quickly when placed in a brown paper bag and set in a warm place.

Avocados have a higher fat content than most other vegetables, but are still a good source of protein.

Avocados of the Florida (Trapp Type) is not recommended for persons watching their fat intake. They contain 22.1% palmitic acid. The California type (Fuerte Type) has only 9.1% palmitic acid.

California avocados that are picked in November to March have 1/3 less fat than those picked September and October. They are less mature and have only 2 grams of fat compared to 6 grams of fat.

Another method of ripening avocados is to place them in a plastic bag with a piece of banana peel.

Leaving the pit in a guacamole dip will not keep the dip from turning black. The only area that won't turn black is the area under the pit which protects the dip from oxygen and the color change.

Avocados will not ripen if placed in the refrigerator.

To ripen avocados quickly, place them into a wool sock, then set them in a dark place.

Ripe avocados should be stored in the refrigerator for longer life.

An avocado is ripe when it gives slightly to finger pressure.

The fat in avocados is mostly monounsaturated, which is one of the fats most preferred by the body.

BEANS, GARBANZO (chick peas)

Has a nut-like flavor and will puree easily to make dips.

BEANS (Edible Pods)

May be green, purple or yellow in color. They should have no scars or discolorizations. When broken, they should have a crisp snap. Available year round, but are best May through August. Store without slicing and refrigerate to retain vitamin content. Do not soak in water.

Varieties include:

Chinese long beans	Snap Beans	Haricots verts
Italian	Purple wax beans	Scarlet runners

Snap beans are found in green and yellow varieties.

Purple wax beans turn green when cooked.

Haricot verts are also called French Beans.

Chinese long beans may be up to 18 inches long.

Cooked beans will stay fresh in the refrigerator for approximately 5 days.

For a different taste, add celery soup to the green beans.

Boiling whole green beans instead of cut-up ones will retain 50% more of the nutrients.

BEANS (SHELL)

Higher in vitamin C than snap bean varieties. varieties include cranberry beans, fava beans and lima beans.
Shell beans should have a bulge and a tightly closed pod. If the pods are not opened they should last for 2-3 days.

BEANS, LIMA

Pods should be dark green and bright in color. Best May through October. When shelled, should appear green or greenish white. Very perishable and should be used as soon as purchased.

To help retain color, add a small amount of baking soda to the cooking water.

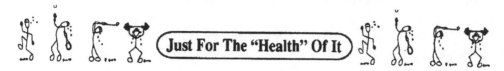

Just For The "Health" Of It

Gas-free lima beans are now being grown. They will contain less of the hard-to-digest sugars that cause the problem.

BEANS, SOY

The only natural food to contain all the essential amino acids that the body needs to synthesize all the other amino acids. Should be stored in their original package or in a covered container.

Soybeans and white beans are the highest in calcium of any bean.

Chickpeas have the most calories, however, beans for the most part are low in calories and contain hardly any fat. The only exception is soybeans which are high in polyunsaturated fat.

BEANS, PINTO

Should have a bright uniform color, fading is a sign of aging and long storage. Small beans cook faster and should not be mixed with large ones or they will be mush. Do not buy if they are cracked or if too much foreign material is found in the bin, especially small stones.

Beans can be stored in an airtight container and should last up to a year and still retaining a good nutrient level.

Beans contain 22% protein. Beef only 18% and eggs 13%.

To prevent beans from becoming mushy, try adding a small amount of baking soda to the water while they are cooking.

Cooked beans will store for up to six months in the freezer, but only 4-6 days in the refrigerator.

If beans get too salty, try using a small amount of brown sugar.

"OH, WHAT A RELIEF IT IS"
To eliminate gas in beans, try using "Beano", you can get a FREE SAMPLE by calling 1-(800)257-8650. It can neutralize the sugar in the beans that causes gas production in the body.

Gas production from beans can also be eliminated by adding a teaspoon of fennel seed to the water the beans are soaking in.

"NUTRITIONALLY SPEAKING"
Beans are one of the best sources of protein. The following gives their quality of nutritional content on a scale of 1-10. 10 being the best.

Kidney beans.....10   Lentils.....7.0
Navy beans.......9.5   Chickpeas...6.5
Lima beans.......8.5   Split peas..5.5
Tofu........4.0

BEETS
Buy only small or medium-sized beets. Large beets are usually not very tender. Do not purchase if they look shriveled or flabby. Beets should be firm. They are high in vitamins and minerals. Greens should be used immediately and roots within 5-7 days.

Beets should be cooked whole to retain their red color.

Beets contain a chemical pigment called betacyanin which gives the beets their reddish color. Some people cannot metabolize this pigment and it may turn their feces and urine a red color for a few days after ingestion.

Sugar beets are approximately 20% sucrose by weight, twice the sugar content of standard beets. Approximately 100 pounds of sugar beets are needed to produce 5 pounds of sugar.

BROCCOLI

Available year round. Best from October to May. Stems should not be too thick. Wilted leaves may indicate old age. Do not buy if buds are open or yellowish. Bud clusters should be firm, closed and of good green color. Use as soon as purchased. Refrigeration will help retain the vitamin A and C content.

Broccoli (one cup chopped) contains 90% of RDA of vitamin A, 200% of vitamin C, 6% of niacin, 10% of calcium, 10% of thiamin, 10% of phosphorus and 8% of iron. It also provides 25% of your fiber needs and to top it off, five grams of protein.

The EPA has registered more than 50 pesticides that can be used on broccoli. 70% of these pesticides cannot be detected by the FDA. 13% of broccoli, in a study showed that pesticides residues remained. The worst one is Parathion and even after washing and boiling some reside may remain.

THE "NOSE" KNOWS
To eliminate the smell of broccoli, add a slice of bread to the pot.

Broccoli consumption has risen over 50% since 1983 to approximately 18 servings per person in 1994.

"EXTRA, EXTRA- BROCCOLI PARDONED"
Hillary Clinton places broccoli back on the White House menu after it was removed by President Bush.

Broccoli florets have about eight times as much beta-carotene as the stalks.

Broccoli that has been cooked still has 15% more vitamin C than an orange and as much calcium as milk.

To retain the nutrients in broccoli, either steam it, stir-fry it or boil it in a very small amount of water. Most other methods will cause a nutrient loss of about 25-35%.

Cruciferous vegetables such as broccoli tend to release strong-smelling chemical compounds when cooked. These ammonia and hydrogen sulfide compounds will smell up the kitchen. Steaming or cooking in a small amount of water and as fast as possible will reduce this problem.

BRUSSELS SPROUTS

When cooking Brussel sprouts, add a few pieces of white bread to the cooking water to reduce the odor.

Brussel sprouts are one of the better vegetable protein sources. Approximately 30% of their calories are from protein.

Best to refrigerate Brussel sprouts or the leaves will turn yellow quickly. Should be a bright green color.

CABBAGE

Available all year. There are three main varieties; red, green and savory which has crinkly leaves. Avoid cabbage with worm holes. Smell the core for sweetness. Green and red cabbage should have firm tight leaves with good color. Cabbage should be refrigerated in plastic bag and used within 7-14 days.

Present research shows that ½ head of cabbage a day may help to prevent certain types of cancer. The chemical indole may prove to prevent breast cancer.

THE "NOSE" KNOWS

Cabbage odors can be contained if you place a piece of bread on top of the cabbage when cooking in a covered pot.

When you need cabbage leaves for stuffed cabbage, try freezing the whole cabbage first, then let it thaw, and the leaves will come apart easier.

To keep red cabbage red, try adding a tablespoon of white vinegar to the cooking water.

CARROTS

Available all year. Should have smooth skins, good orange color and be well formed. Do not purchase if wilted, cracked or flabby or if tops are green. Keep refrigerated. High in vitamin A if not kept soaking in water.

Chef's Secrets

To slip the skins off carrots, drop them in boiling water, let stand for 5 minutes, then drop them into cold water.

To curl carrots, peel slices with a potato peeler, then drop them in a bowl of ice water.

The tops of carrots should be removed before storing them in the refrigerator. Tops will drain the carrots of moisture, making them limp and dry.

For the best results when cooking frozen vegetables, cook them directly from the freezer (except, corn on the cob and spinach).

Keep carrots away from apples and tomatoes, these fruits give off higher amounts of ethylene gas and may make the carrots bitter.

When grating carrots, leave part of the green top on to use as a handle. Keeps your fingers intact.

"THE YOUNGER, THE BETTER"

If you wish to freeze vegetables, try to purchase "young" ones. They will be higher in nutrients and less starchy. Do not store for more than 10 hours before using for the best results.

"CARROT TOP"

Carrot greens are high in vitamin K which is lacking in the carrot itself.

Carrot skins contain 10% of all nutrients found in carrots.

Recently the USDA completed studies showing that 7 ounces of carrots consumed every day for 3 weeks lowered cholesterol levels by 11%. This was probably due to calcium pectate, a type of fiber found in carrots. A good percentage of which will be lost in juicing.

CAULIFLOWER

Best if purchased September through January, but available year round. Should have compact flower clusters(florets or curds) with green leaves. Do not purchase if flower clusters are open. If there is a speckled surface, this is a sign of insect injury, mold or rot. Store in the refrigerator.

To keep cauliflower white during cooking, add lemon to the water. Overcooking tends to darken cauliflower and make it tougher.

Due to certain chemicals in cauliflower it is best not to cook it in an aluminum or iron pot. Contact with these metals will turn the cauliflower yellow, brown or blue-green.

 Chef's Secrets

When you boil cauliflower, add a piece of white bread to eliminate the odor. Another method is to replace the water after it has cooked for 5-7 minutes.

Prior to cooking cauliflower, you should soak it head down for approximately 30 minutes in salted water to remove the grit and insects.

CELERY

Available year round. Stalks should have a very solid feel, since softness indicates pithiness. Do not purchase if there are any wilted stalks, even if all others are firm. Store in refrigerator. Lasts 7-10 days if not placed in water for prolonged period.

Don't discard celery leaves; dry them, then rub the leaves through a sieve turning them into powder that can be used to flavor soups, stews, salad dressings, etc. Also, can be made into celery salt.

Celery and lettuce will crisp up quickly, if you place them into a pan of cold water and then add a few slices of raw potatoes.

To prevent celery from turning brown, soak it in cold water with lemon juice before refrigerating.

Celery juice may be used as an effective stress reducer.

Celery may be bleached, using ethylene gas which will give it a clearer color. Also, it causes reduced vitamin potency.

CELERIAC

A root vegetable that looks like a turnip and is prepared like any other root vegetable.

CELTUCE

A combination of celery and lettuce which is prepared similar to cabbage.

CORN

Best May through September. Kernels should be a good yellow color. Do not buy if husks are straw colored, since they should be green. Straw colored husks and silks indicate decay or worm damage. Corn should be refrigerated. Yellow corn usually taste better than white corn and is higher in vitamin A content.

The best way to remove kernels from an ear of corn is to use a shoehorn or a spoon.

Corn contains 5-6% sugar by weight.

Americans eat about 25 pounds of corn per year.

There are more than 200 varieties of sweet corn.

When wrapping corn in tin foil for barbecuing, try adding a sprig of marjoram next to the corn.

Florida grows the most sweet corn and the best sweet corn is known as "Florida Sweet."

"PILED HIGHER AND DEEPER"

When storing corn, keep it cool. When corn gets warm the sugar tends to convert to starch. In fact, when corn is piled high in the markets and is allowed to stay for days, the bottom ones will be less sweet due to the heat generated by the weight of the ones on top.

The kernels at the tip of corn should be smaller. Larger kernels are a sign of over maturity.

If the kernels are shrunken away from the tip, the corn may be older and not as sweet.

Pop a kernel, the juice should be milky not a clear liquid.

Corn should not be stored more than a few hours after husking and should be refrigerated or cooked as soon as possible.

Never add salt to the cooking water, it toughens the corn.

Steaming corn for 6-10 minutes is one of the preferred cooking methods.

Yellow corn usually taste better than white corn and has a higher vitamin A content.

To store corn longer, cut a small piece off the stalk end, leave on the leaves, then store in a pot with about an inch of water, stems down.

 ## Chef's Secrets

To cook better tasting corn, add a little milk and sugar to the water.

A food brush will remove silk from corn.

To lighten the color of dark yellow corn, try adding a small amount of vinegar to the boiling water.

CUCUMBERS

Should be long and slender for best quality. Should be a good green color, either dark or light, but not yellow. Purchase only firm cucumbers and refrigerate. Available all year. Large ones are usually not the better ones and may be pithy.

Old cucumbers look shriveled and spongy.

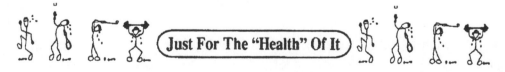

Do not store cucumbers near fruits, many fruit surfaces may contain ethylene gas to enhance ripening and looks. This will cause the seeds to become hard.

Cucumbers have the highest water content of any vegetable and have only 13 calories per 3 1/2oz. serving.

"PICKLED CALORIES"
Dill or sour pickles contain about 3 calories per ounce, but sweet pickles have 30 calories per ounce.

EGGPLANT
Available all year. Best in August and September. Should have smooth, glossy, purple black skin, free of scars and must be firm. Soft eggplants are usually bitter. Keep cool and use in 2-4 days after purchase.

Never eat raw eggplant since it contains the toxin solamine. Solamine is destroyed by cooking.

Varieties of eggplant are Chinese purple, globular, Japanese and Italian Rosa Bianco.

"THE FAT SPONGE"
When eggplants are fried they tend to absorb four times more fat than an equal amount of potatoes. Studies have shown that eggplants will absorb 80 grams of fat in approximately 70 seconds which adds 700 calories to the eggplant. Best not to fry eggplant.

FENNEL
Has a rounded pale green bulb with a short stem and feathery green leaves. Looks like a "fat" bunch of celery. The bulbs should be firm and clean with fresh looking leaves. If any brown spots are seen avoid the fennel. Dries out quickly and should be wrapped and used within 3-4 days.

Fennel can be substituted for celery in all recipes or in salads.

JICAMA
A root vegetable similar to a potato. It has a slightly sweet flavor and is an excellent source of vitamin C. Only 45 calories in 3 ½ ounces.

LEEKS

Purchase between September through November. Tops should be green with white necks 2-3 inches from roots. Do not purchase if tops are wilted or if there appears to be signs of aging. Refrigerate and use within 5-7 days after purchase.

LETTUCE

Available year round. Should be heavy and solid with medium green outer leaves. Inspect for insects. Store in plastic bag in refrigerator. Remove all damaged leaves. Use within 4-6 days. The greener the leaves, the higher the vitamin and mineral content. Romaine is one of the best, while iceberg is the worst.

The outer lettuce leaves can be cooked like any type of green instead of throwing them away. Most are very nutritious except iceberg.

Varieties include:

butterhead	*iceberg*	*looseleaf*	*romaine*	*red oak leaf*
boston	*bibb*	*green leaf*	*stem*	

"OLD WIVES TALE"

Lettuce should always be torn, never cut or the edges will turn brown faster. Can't find out who started this rumor.

Never add salt to a lettuce salad until you are ready to serve it. The salt tends to wilt and toughen the lettuce.

Lettuce will not rust as quickly if you line the bottom of the refrigerator's vegetable compartment with paper towels or napkins. The paper absorbs the excess moisture.

To stop the lettuce from getting rusty, for a longer period of time hit the bottom of the lettuce hard against the counter and remove the core.

Americans eat approximately 11 pounds of lettuce per year, per person.

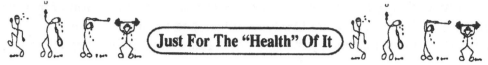

Just For The "Health" Of It

Romaine lettuce has six times as much vitamin C and eight times as much vitamin A as iceberg lettuce.

The greener leaves on the outside of lettuce contain more nutrients than the inner leaves. Try to save as much as possible.

Over 60 chemical agents can be applied to lettuce. Most can be removed by washing, but tests show that some cannot be removed by washing. The EPA can only detect 60% of these chemicals. However, the worst one is Permethrin, which can be reduced or removed totally by washing.

MUSHROOMS

Available year round. Best November through March. Caps should be closed around the stems. Avoid black or brown gills as this is a sign of old age. The tops are more tender than the stems. Refrigerate after purchase and use as soon as possible.

Never immerse mushrooms in a pan of cold water when cleaning, since they will absorb too much water. This will also make it more difficult to cook them, without losing flavor.

Mushrooms contain the same flavor enhancing substance found in MSG, glutamic acid.

Mushrooms are 90% water and do contain some natural toxins. Best not to eat too many raw ones, cooking tends to kill the toxins.

There are 38,000 varieties of mushrooms, some edible, some very poisonous.

"SNIFF, SNIFF, SNIFF"

Truffels grow underground, are an oak or hazel tree fungus and are found by pig or dog sniffing truffellors. There are two types, black and white. They have a distinctive taste and are prized by many chefs in France and Italy. They are very expensive.

A chemical compound extracted from shiitake mushrooms has been approved as an anticancer drug in Japan after it was proven to repress cancer cells in laboratory studies.

Chef's Secrets

To keep mushrooms white and firm when sauteing them, add a teaspoon of lemon juice to each quarter pound of butter.

If you are not sure of the safety of a mushroom, don't eat it regardless of the following test. However, the experts use the method of sprinkling salt on the spongy part, or the gills. If they turn yellow, they are poisonous, if they turn black they are safe.

Store mushrooms unwashed and covered with a damp paper towel, then place inside a brown paper bag.

OKRA

The pods should be green and tender. Do not buy if the pods look dry or shriveled because they will lack flavor and be tough. Okra spoils quickly and should be refrigerated as soon as possible. Available May through October.

Okra has a flavor between eggplant and asparagus.

Never wash okra until your ready to use it or you will remove a protective coating that keeps the pods from becoming slimy.

ONIONS

Should be hard and dry. Avoid onions with wet necks, this indicates decay. Also, avoid onions that have sprouted. Onions can be stored at either room temperature or refrigerated.

To shed fewer tears when slicing onions, cut the root off last, refrigerate before slicing and peel them under cold water.

When cutting onions, place a piece of bread on the tip of the knife to absorb the fumes.

After slicing onions, wash your hands in cold water, then rub them with salt.

Salt or vinegar will remove onion smells from your hands.

If you chew gum while peeling onions you may not cry. Try it!

Varieties of onions include pearl, yellow globe, Spanish, white globe, boiling, large whites, red globe, shallots and large reds.

 Chef's Secrets

If you need only half of an onion, use the top half. The root will stay fresh longer in the refrigerator.

PARSNIPS
A root vegetable with a celerylike nutty flavor. Flavor is best in winter and will have a sweet taste after two weeks storage. Water hemlock is sometimes confused with parsnips since it looks similar but is a poisonous root.

Parsnips are best cooked as they tend to be very fibrous.

PEAS
Pods should be selected that are well-filled without bulging. Do not purchase flabby, spotted or yellow pods. Refrigerate and use within one week.

Chef's Secrets

When you cook fresh peas, add a few washed pods to the water, this will improve the flavor and will give a better green color to the peas.

Better yet, cook the peas in their pods, as they cook the peas will separate from the pods and float to the surface.

When dried peas are placed in water the good ones will sink to the bottom and the bad ones will float to the top.

PEPPERS: SWEET, GREEN, RED OR CHILI

Sides of peppers should be firm. Do not purchase dull colors, or ones with soft areas. These usually indicate decay. Refrigerate and use within 3 days. High in vitamins A and C. Available all year.

Varieties include habanera, poblano, chile de arbol. pimento, anaheim, banana, Hungarian wax, cayenne, serrano, mexi-bell, jalapeno, casabel, ancho, cuanelle, cherry and bell.

"EYE CHIHUAHUA"

When cutting hot chili peppers it is best to wear rubber gloves so that your hands will not be burned and you don't rub your eyes. If you get hot pepper juice in your eyes you will never forget the experience.

New Mexico has one of the lowest incidence of heart disease. Researchers say that it is due to the high consumption of chili peppers, which are grown there. Over 55,000 tons are eaten annually in New Mexico. They may also lower blood fat levels and increase the blood coagulation time.

Chili peppers contain an oil that will actually burn your skin. You can get relief by washing the area with white vinegar.

Chilies are probably the oldest known spice having been found in archaeological digs in Mexico that have been dated to 7000 B.C.

"ANCIENT TEAR GAS"
Chili peppers were burned by American Indians when they were fighting off the invading English. The fumes kept the English at bay.

"MAMA MIA!"
Capsaicin gives chili peppers their hot bite, but the seeds and outer and inner walls are not the hottest parts. The inner membrane that holds the seeds is the hottest part of the chili pepper, almost 100 times hotter.

"THAT'S A FACT"
Sweet red peppers contain more vitamin C than an orange.

 Chef's Secrets

When making stuffed peppers, coat the outside of the pepper with vegetable oil and it will retain its color.

Stuffed peppers should be cooked in muffin tins to retain their shape.

RADISHES
Available year round. Choose medium-size that are firm, rounded and should be of good color. Larger radishes tend to be pithy. Check for spongy feeling. Don't buy those with yellow or decayed tops.

Varieties include black, California mammoth whites, daikons, red globe and white icicles

Radish leaves can be added to salads of stir fried vegetables to add a little zest to the flavor. They are not as spicy as radishes.

SALISIFY

Also called "oyster plant." Their appearance is similar to parsley but tastes like oysters. Blossoms on the plant always close at "high noon" and thus was called the "Johnny Go To Bed At Noon" plant.

SPINACH

To retain the nutrient level in spinach, boil it in as little water as possible and for the shortest time. Boiling it in one cup of water instead of two will help the spinach retain almost 50% more of its nutrients.

SPROUTS

Varieties of sprouts are soybean, alfalfa, bean, radish, mung bean, sprouted oats, pea, lentil, red bean, adzuka, clover, daikon and sunflower.

Sprouts are not really that high in nutritional content, but adds zest and livens up salads.

SQUASH

Available all year. Soft-skinned types should be smooth and glossy. Hard-shelled should have firm rinds. Refrigerate all soft-skinned types and use within a few days.

Firm rind variety should be stored at room temperature. Buy squash that are hard and heavy with a dull skin.

Varieties of summer squash include chayote, patty pan, yellow crookneck, yellow straightneck and zucchini.

Varieties of winter squash include acorn, banana, buttercup, butternut, calabaza, delicata, golden nugget, hubbard, spaghetti, sweet dumpling, turban and pumpkin.

Winter squash develops more beta-carotene after being stored than it has immediately after picking.

The smallest are usually the tastiest.

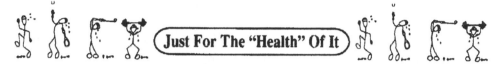

Squash is a good source of beta-carotene, one of the best antioxidants.

Squash is low in calories, fat and sodium and a good source of fiber and potassium.

TOMATOES

Available all year. Should be well formed and free from blemishes. Green tomatoes will eventually turn red, but will not have good flavor. A vine ripened tomato is best. Refrigerate, but do not allow to freeze. The color may be deceiving since sometimes chemicals are used to redden them.

Tomatoes will keep better if stored at room temperature. Also, if stored stem down, they will last longer.

"OR IS IT A FRUIT?"

Americans obtain more of their vitamins from tomatoes than from any other vegetable.

Salsa has replaced ketchup as the top selling condiment in the United States. New products due out in 1995 will be a salsa/ketchup combination.

One ounce of tomato puree has twice the vitamin C and 20% more beta-carotene than one ounce of fresh tomato.

Chef's Secrets

To peel tomatoes easily, place them in boiling water and remove from heat, allow to stand for 1 minute them plunge them into cold water.

Another way to peel a tomato is to place a long fork into it and hold it over a gas burner until the skin blisters. The skin should peel off easily.

Tomatoes will keep longer if you store them stem down.

Tomatoes may be broiled and sprinkled with grated cheese for a different taste treat.

Tomatoes should never be left to ripen in direct sunlight, as they will lose most of their vitamin C.

When slicing tomatoes, it will be easier if you use a bread knife with saw teeth. It won't even tear the skin.

Tomatoes are sometimes picked green and ethylene gassed on their way to the supermarket right in the trucks. This can be accomplished during an overnight run.

There is a big difference in vitamin loss and taste in a gassed tomato and a vine-ripened one.

Americans eat approximately 24 pounds of tomatoes per person, per year.

"BRRRRRRRRRR"
If you are expecting a frost and have tomatoes on the vine, pull them up by the roots and hang them upside down in a cool basement until the fruit ripens.

The federal government can detect only 55% of the 100 approved pesticides.

"THE BUDDY SYSTEM"
Green tomatoes will ripen faster if you store them with apples. Both give of ethylene gas when ripening and the extra shot of gas will make them ripen faster.

"NEWS YOU CAN USE"
Green tomatoes will also ripen faster if stored in a cool place wrapped loosely in newspapers. This method may take a week or two.

TURNIPS
One-half cup of turnips has more fiber than an apple.

WATER CHESTNUTS
Chestnuts are actually the underground swollen tip of a tuber and stores carbohydrates for the plants growth Unless they are kept cool they will sprout. Good source of potassium.

MIX AND MATCH SALAD GUIDE
Use one or more ingredients from each column, for each portion

---

GREENS	2 TABLESPOONS	FLAVOR	PROTEIN
Romaine	Red Cabbage	Anchovies	Cheese
Boston	Red Pepper	Bacon Bits	Boiled Eggs
Escarole	Stuffed Olives	Onion Rings	Tuna
Chicory	Grated Carrots	Sauerkraut	Cooked Beans
Raw Spinach	Tomatoes	Chutney	Peanuts
Cabbage	Pickled Beets	Garlic	Cooked Fish
Endive	Melon Chunks	Pickle	Turkey Salami
Chinese Cabbage	Orange Slices	Raisins	Shrimp

TEXTURE	DRESSING
Carrot Chunks	Vinaigrette
Celery Slices	Creamy French
Croutons	Blue Cheese
Sprouts	Yogurt
Tossed Almonds	Thousand Island
Radish	Green Goddess
Green Pepper	Cottage Cheese
Water Chestnuts	Sour Cream

EDIBLE PLANTS FOR LANDSCAPING

NAME	LANDSCAPE USE	EXPOSURE
Asparagus	Tall, Fine textured	Full sun, perennial
Basil	Herb	Full sun to partial shade
Beans/Legume	Bush or climbing variety	Full sun
Bitter Melon	Very large leafed vine	Full sun
Cabbage	Colorful foliage	Full sun, to partial shade
Chard	Decorative, very large foliage	Full sun to partial shade
Chinese Cabbage	Compact, glossy green foliage	Full sun to partial shade
Chives	Very low-growing herb	Full sun
Cucumber	Bush or as a vine	Full sun
Eggplant	Compact, very ornamental bush	Full sun
Kale	Highly decorative foliage	Full sun to partial shade
Lettuce	Fancy-leaf types	Full sun to partial shade

Mint	Lush herb/repels rodents	Shade or part sun
Nasturtium	Edible flowering vine	Full sun or partial shade
Parsley	Decorative herb	Full sun or partial shade
Peppers	Ornamental bush with red or yellow fruit	Full sun or partial shade
Sage	Colorful accent herb	Full sun
Snow pea	Sprawling bush or vine	Full sun or partial shade
Spinach	Glossy green foliage	Full sun or partial shade
Summer squash/ Zucchini	Large hairy leaves	Full sun or partial shade
Thyme	Low-growing herb	Full sun
Tomato	Rambling vines or small bushes	Full Sun

Chapter 5

Spud Facts

POTATOES

Available all year. Should be smooth and well shaped, and unbruised. Do not buy if they have sprouted or have a green tint to the skin (this indicates high solanine content). Store at room temperature in a dark area and do not refrigerate. Refrigeration may turn a percentage of the starch into sugar. Keep away from heat or cold.

SWEET POTATOES/YAMS

Available all year round. Skin should be uniformly copper or light tan-colored. Do not purchase if they have white areas or are damaged; this probably means decay. Store in cool dry place and do not refrigerate.

Yams are less sweet than sweet potatoes and originated in Asia.

The best sweet potato is called a "boniato" or "Cuban Sweet Potato" and has a very light yellow flesh.

Sweet potatoes have 10 calories per ounce less than yams.

 Chef's Secrets

French fries will be deliciously golden brown, if sprinkled with flour before frying.

Ginger root stored with potatoes will help both of them stay fresher longer.

To bake the perfect potato, rub butter over potatoes before baking to prevent skin from cracking and to improve the taste.

A potato will bake faster if the skin is oiled rather than being wrapped in tin foil.

Russets make the best mashed potatoes.

To make potato salad more quickly, cook the potatoes already diced and peeled.

However, this will reduce the nutrients from exposing the surfaces to air, light, heat and water.

For the greatest gourmet french fries; let cut potatoes stand in cold water an hour before frying. Dry thoroughly before cooking. The trick is to fry them twice. The first time, just fry them for a few minutes and drain off the grease. The second time fry them until golden brown.

To boil potatoes in less time, remove a small strip of skin from one side. After they are done the balance of the skin will come off much easier.

When boiling potatoes, they may get a little mushy and be difficult to drain. Try cooking them in a deep fat fryer basket, then just remove and their drained.

To keep peeled potatoes white, place them in a bowl of cold water, add a few drops of vinegar, and refrigerate.

If you add hot milk to potatoes when you are mashing them it will keep them from becoming heavy and soggy.

Baked potatoes should be pricked with a fork to release the steam as soon as they are finished baking. This will keep them from becoming soggy.

If you add a teaspoon of baking powder to potatoes when mashing, beat them vigorously, it will make them light and creamy.

Old potatoes should have a small amount of sugar added to the water when cooking, to help bring back some of the lost flavor.

To keep potatoes white during cooking, add a teaspoon of white vinegar to the water.

To reharden potatoes, place soft raw potatoes in ice water for half an hour or until they become hard.

"UP, UP AND AWAY, ON A BUFFET"

If you go to a buffet and take a serving of mashed potatoes, you will probably have little or no nutrient value left. After approximately 45 minutes its all gone. Best to get them when they are first put out.

When you see potato salad with a rich yellow flavor, it has probably been doctored with mustard or if your unlucky an artificial yellow food coloring.

Americans eat approximately 54 pounds of potatoes per year, per person.

"DON'T COOK A NAKED POTATO"

Baking a potato with the skin will retain the highest level of nutrients. Boiling without the skin causes a 30% nutrient loss, and when mashed the loss can exceed 75%.

"THAT'S ALL FOLKS"

If you store a boiled potato in the refrigerator for 3-5 days you will have between 0-3% of the nutrient value left. Potatoes only store well for 1-2 days.

"HOT POTATO, COLD POTATO"

Vichyssoise, a cold potato soup was invented when King Louis XV of France was so worried about being poisoned that he had a number of his servants taste his food before he ate it. As they passed the soup around, it got cold by the time it reached him. He liked it so much that way that he had it served cold thereafter.

To shorten the baking time, insert a nail (saves about 15 minutes), or boil them in salted water for about 10 minutes before placing them into a very hot oven.

Green potato skins and sprouts contain a toxin called solamine and may be hazardous to your health.

When you store potatoes, place half an apple in with them and they won't sprout. The apple will absorb the moisture before the potato.

To peel sweet potatoes easily, take them from the boiling water and immerse immediately in very cold water. The skins will almost fall off by themselves.

Bake potatoes in muffin pans so that they will not roll around and be easier to remove from the oven.

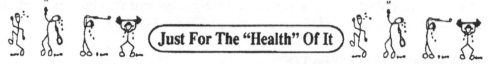

Just For The "Health" Of It

Brown areas on sliced potatoes mean that they have been exposed to air and light and the vitamin C has been destroyed.

The digestive time for a medium potato is approximately 2 hours.

Sweet potatoes contain the same number of calories as white potatoes. However, they contain more vitamin C and three times the beta-carotene as white potatoes.

For the best mashed potatoes ever, try using buttermilk and a small amount of the water the potatoes were boiled in. Make sure that the milk and water are still very warm before adding them to the potatoes.

When peeling potatoes, try using a rubber thimble on a few fingers, the ones you want to keep whole.

"ONE POTATO, TWO POTATO, FAKE POTATO?"

Frozen, flaked and powdered potato product sales have risen 500% in the last 30 years. The less a potato is processed the higher the nutrient content.

If you leave the skins on potatoes when cooking they will retain more of their nutrient value. Then remove the skin before serving.

Yams do not have the same nutritional value as sweet potatoes. They are about 10-20% less overall.

"YAM-A-DABA-DO"

The best way to tell the difference between yams and sweet potatoes is to look at the flesh, which should be orange in a sweet potato, not red. Many sweet potatoes are labeled yams by supermarkets.

"DO THE MASHED POTATO"

In the last 30 years Americans are eating 40% less fresh potatoes.

It is best not to eat potato skins in any form. A number of toxins and possible pesticide residues may be left even after they are cooked and washed. There are very few nutrients actually in the skin, most are just under the skin.

"KEEPING US SAFE?"

The EPA has registered 90 different pesticides for use on potatoes. The FDA laboratories can only detect 55% of these. Most of the problem pesticides such as: Chlordane, Aldicarb, Dieldrin and DDT are for the most part in the skin. Removing the skin is the best advice.

THREE CHEERS FOR THE "CHIPPER"

Potato chips were invented at Saratoga Springs, New York in 1853 when Commodore Vanderbilt complained to his steward that he made his french fries too thick, the steward who was a little put out, sliced some potatoes as thin as he could, placed them in boiling grease and served them. Needless to say the Commodore was delighted.

Commercial potato chips are cooked in long vats of oil (75 feet long) with the oil being filtered and rarely changed. Production is about 200 pounds an hour. Since the oil is continually kept at 375°F., the chips should contain a high percentage of trans-acids (a harmful fat).

Fabricated potato chips are made from dehydrated potatoes (Pringles).

Potato or corn chips have 10 times more fat than pretzels or air popped popcorn (not the microwave type).

There are 28 flavors of potato chips on the market.

There is the equivalent of 2 ½ pats of margarine in 1 ounce of potato chips.

Potato chips are 61% fat.

Real Potato Chips

Cut potatoes in half crosswise exposing two flat surfaces. Use a wide potato slicer and cut paper thin slices. Place individual slices on an oiled cookie sheet. Brush the tops of the potatoes with a pure vegetable oil, preferably a corn oil. Bake at 450°F. approximately 10 minutes or until golden brown. Finally, place the chips in a brown paper bag with a small amount of sea salt (1/4 tsp. per potato) and shake. Low-fat and crunchy.

Chapter 6

Vitamin and Mineral Facts

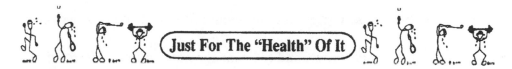

Just For The "Health" Of It

If you wish to avoid a hangover, remember to take your vitamin and mineral tablets during the period you are drinking. Your body tends to get depleted when you overindulge. The following are the supplements needed to metabolize alcohol: Vitamins B1, B2, niacin, pantothenic acid and biotin. Minerals; iron, zinc, copper, manganese, magnesium and potassium.

Both meats and sugar tend to cause a loss of calcium in the urine.

Remember to take a chewable vitamin C to counteract the effects of nitrites in bacon, lunch meats and hot dogs.

Mushrooms contain hydrazines, a substance that can affect vitamin B6 absorption.

Chocolate contains oxalates and theobromine which effects calcium metabolism and how the body utilizes protein.

Vitamins B and C are destroyed by boiling.
Many vitamins are acidic and are changed into a salt by contact with baking soda.

Chlorine reduces the effectiveness of vitamin C.

One years supply of folic acid (a B vitamin) would fit into 1/6th of a teaspoon.

Raw fish, shellfish, brussel sprouts and red cabbage contain thiaminase which may destroy the vitamin B's. Cooking, however, will inactivate them.

The FDA has taken isolated amino acids off the list of substances, generally regarded as safe (GRAS) saying that they may cause an imbalance of other amino acids and effect their absorption.

Tea and red wine contain tannins which interfere with the utilization of iron, thiamine and B12.

MINERAL INFORMATION, JUST THE FACTS

Iodine
Stimulates the thyroid
A deficiency may cause obesity, sluggish metabolism
needed to utilize fat

Zinc
A constituent of insulin
A constituent of male reproductive fluid
Combines with phosphorus to aid in respiration
Improves vitamin action
Helps food become absorbed through intestinal tract
Essential to nucleic acid metabolism
Used up fast in patients with major burns
Deficiency may be a factor in hardening of arteries

Magnesium
Acts as a starter for some chemical reactions
Sleep promoting material
Keeps you cool and calm
Relaxes your nerves

Manganese
Helps food in the digestive process
Aids in nerve health
Found to be deficient in alcoholism
Works with B vitamins to provide energy

Sodium
Helps maintain a normal water balance
Provides strength to your muscles
Deficiency may cause stomach gas
Helps process amino acids
Assists in the formation of stomach acids
Joins with chlorine to improve blood quality

Molybdenum
Possible role in iron metabolism
Is deficient in dental caries

Chromium
Necessary for normal glucose metabolism
Deficiency may be related to adult diabetes
Deficiency may be caused by excess of white sugar
Often deficient in pregnancies and malnutrition

Copper
Must be present to convert iron into hemoglobin
May prevent general weakness
Deficiencies occur in pregnancies
May prevent impaired respiration

Potassium
Works with sodium to regulate heartbeat
Joins with phosphorus to send oxygen to the brain
Stimulates the kidneys to dispose of body wastes
Deficiency may cause constipation and insomnia

Calcium

Needed for blood clotting
Needed to activate enzymes
Relaxes heart muscle
Prevents osteoporosis
Needed to help transport nerve impulses

Iron

Needed to prevent anemia
Carries oxygen to the brain
Deficiency may be implicated in a poor memory

Cooking not only destroys certain water soluble vitamins, but some of them will bind with other chemicals and then will not be absorbed by the body. Use very little liquid and cook for a short period of time.

A new soft drink that advertises that it contains 25% of your daily vitamin needs, only provides you with the more common vitamins that you could get in the most mediocre diet.

Coffee interferes with iron absorption and tends to leach magnesium out of the body.

Chocolate, cashews, collard greens, beet greens, Swiss chard, spinach, rhubarb and beets contain oxalates which interfere with the ability of the body to absorb calcium.

Vitamin C helps the iron in foods to be absorbed. We normally absorb only 15-30% of the iron in foods.

High doses of vitamin C may not be absorbed at the high level taken. Your body will only metabolize about 200-250mg per hour at the most.

PABA may retard graying hair and has even been known to bring back the original color.

Vitamin E is best absorbed in the intestines in the presence of fat. Best to take with meals containing some fat, even a glass of 2% milk would help.

Americans spend 3.4 billion on nutritional supplements annually.

A report in the Journal of the American Medical Society cited studies that revealed eating excessive amounts of foods high in vitamin A, such as; liver, carrots, etc. may cause headaches and vomiting.

Taking one teaspoon of pure crystalline vitamin C when you awake with 8oz. of water usually results in a bowel movement within 30 minutes.

For white males and black females calcium losses begin at a faster pace than the rest of the population after age 30. For white women, it begins at age 18. Black men seem to be exempt from this problem.

Calcium is best absorbed when taken with meals, since it is absorbed best in an acid environment.

Boron may assist bones to utilize calcium more efficiently. Best sources are prunes, raisins, almonds, peanuts, dates and honey.

Vitamins keep their potency longer if kept in the refrigerator.

Supplements have their highest absorption levels when taken with food.

New studies show that smoking one cigarette can destroy up to 100 milligrams of vitamin C.

Your body will lose vitamin C three times faster if you take aspirin.

Vitamin C helps the body absorb iron.

Calcium and vitamin C should be taken in small doses four times per day for the highest utilization rate.

If you lack vitamin A in your diet, it may lead to a weakened immune system and a loss of vitamin C. Also, adequate vitamin A is necessary to help your body absorb dietary zinc.

A small amount of sugar taken with a calcium supplement will increase the absorption rate.

If you drink soft water you should take a magnesium supplement.

If you are taking more than 500mg. of calcium daily, space out your dosage, it will absorb better and you shouldn't have a constipation problem.

"SOUNDS FISHY, BUT ISN'T"
Sardines are an excellent source of calcium. Three of those little fish supplies approximately 370mg. of calcium, more than 8oz. of milk.

Vitamins A,D,E and K should be taken with food, since they are fat soluble and will be absorbed more efficiently.

Vitamins B and C are water soluble and are absorbed easily in the intestinal tract.

"CHOP, CHOP, SLICE, SLICE, NO,NO"
Cutting or chopping any food high in vitamin C releases an enzyme that can destroy the vitamin. Leave all fruits and vegetables whole or in large pieces until ready to eat when possible.

PMS robs your body of vitamin C. Recommend 250mg. four times per day.

Breast cancer death rates are the highest in areas with the least amount of sunshine. Lack of vitamin D could be the problem.

Beta-carotene is only available from plants, Vitamin A comes from animal sources. Recommend a beta-carotene supplement every other day for antioxidant protection.

Vitamin Robbers

Vitamin A   - Mineral oil, air pollution, antacids, barbiturates, cholesterol lowering drugs.

Vitamin D   - Anti-convulsive drugs, mineral oil, antacids, sedatives, barbiturates, cortisone

Thiamine B1   - Antibiotics, excess heat/cooking, sugar consumption, alcohol, stress, antacids, coffee, raw shellfish.

Riboflavin B2   - Antibiotics, exposure to light, excess heat, alcohol, oral contraceptives, antacids, diuretics.

Niacin   - Antibiotics, sugar consumption, excess heat, alcohol, reduced during illness, diuretics, penicillin.

Pantothenic Acid B5   - Aspirin, methyl bromide.

Pyridoxine   - Aging (after 50), steroid hormones, B6 high blood pressure drugs, excess heat, food processing, antacids, aspirin, cortisone, diuretics, penicillin.

Folic Acid   - Oral contraceptives, stress, anti-
                        convulsants, vitamin C deficiency,
                        barbiturates, diuretics, antibiotics,
                        antacids.

Vitamin B12   - Stress, oral contraceptives,
                        menstruation, colchicine.

Biotin   - Excess heat, antibiotics, sulfa
                        drugs, avidin (in raw egg whites).

Choline   - Sugar consumption, alcohol.

Vitamin C   - Smoking, stress, aspirin, carbon
                        monoxide, alcohol, corticosteroids,
                        diuretics, antihistamines.

Inositol   - Antibiotics.

Vitamin E   - Oral contraceptives, food processing,
                        rancid fats and oils, chlorine.

Vitamin K   - Antibiotics, mineral oil, radiation,
                        anticoagulants, alcohol, phenobarb,
                        sulfonamides, tetracyclines.

Vitamin C and aspirin should not be taken together, according to studies done at the University of Southern Illinois. The studies indicate that when combined, heavy doses produce excessive stomach irritation, which may lead to ulcers.

Studies by the USDA Human Nutrition Research Center suggests that vitamin C may prevent cataracts.

Processing Of Foods

Exposure To Heat:

Fried Foods - The longer the food is fried and the higher the temperature, the more vitamin and mineral potency is lost. Frying temperatures usually reach 375°F. Corn and safflower oils are best, due to their higher smoke points of 450° to 500°F.

Canned Foods - Nutrient losses occur from blanching and sterilization, which utilizes temperatures of 240°F. or higher for 25-40 minutes.

Frozen Foods - Many are cooked before they are frozen. Higher quality foods are usually sold as fresh. Lower quality foods are used in frozen foods due to their poor appearance.

Dehydrated Foods - Very dependent on the quality of the initial product. Some methods of commercial dehydration may use temperatures of 300°F.

Dairy Products - Many vitamins lose their potency or maybe totally destroyed by the pasteurization process. The homogenization process breaks down the normal-size fat particles, thus allowing the formation of the enzyme "Xanthene Oxidase." A Canadian study has shown that this enzyme may enter the bloodstream and destroy a vital body chemical that ordinarily provides protection for the coronary arteries.

NOTE:
Various nutrients have different degrees of stability under the conditions of processing and preparation. Vitamin A is easily destroyed by heat and light. Vitamin C is not only affected by heat, but also by contact with a variety of metals, such as bronze, brass, copper, cold rolled steel or black iron, found in some types of food processing equipment.

Studies conducted on the canning of foods found that peas and beans lose 75% of certain B vitamins, and tomatoes lose 80% of their naturally occurring zinc.

Exposure To Cold:

Frozen Foods - Freezing may have only minimal effects on vitamin and mineral potency, depending on the methods used and how soon they were frozen in relation to the time they were picked. Remember, the highest quality of foods are sold to restaurants or are sold fresh.

Fresh Fruits And Vegetables - Sometimes harvested before they are ripe, then allowed to ripen on their way to market, either naturally or with a bit of ethylene gas. This may cause a reduction of some of the trace minerals.

NOTE: There are four methods of commercially freezing foods:

(1)   *Air Blast Freezing* - Products are frozen by high velocity cold air. This method is the most widely used on all kinds of products.

(2)   *Plate Freezing* - The product is placed in contact with a cold metal surface.

(3)   *Cryogenic Freezing* - Freezing at very low temperatures (below 100°F.) in direct contact with liquid nitrogen or carbon dioxide. Use for freezing meat patties and other meat products.

(4) *Freon Immersion Freezing* - Utilizes freon to freeze the product instantaneously, thus allowing the product to retain its total weight. Presently, being used to freeze hard-boiled eggs, scrambled egg patties and shrimp. Some foods may retain more nutrients when they are frozen shortly after harvesting. A Stanford University study showed that frozen spinach had 212% more vitamin C than fresh. Frozen brussel sprouts had 27% more vitamin C than fresh.

Quality Of Food Processed:

Fruits And Vegetables - May be affected by genetic differences, climatic conditions, maturity at harvest, or soil variances.

Meat And Poultry - The lowest quality is used for canned goods, frozen foods and TV dinners.

Enrichment And Fortification:

Refining/Replacing Nutrients - Bread and milk are the two most abused products in this area.

Fortification - Vitamin D is added to milk, almost all breakfast cereals are fortified and vitamin C is added to hundreds of products.

NOTE: During processing more vitamin E is lost than any other vitamin. Wheat flour (except the 100% varieties) lose up to 90% of its vitamin E value. Rice cereal products may lose up to 70% of their vitamin E.

Nutrient Depleted Soil:

Soil Problems

Fertilizers - Farmers normally only replace the minerals that are crucial to crop growth, such as phosphorus, potassium and nitrates.

Trace Minerals - The selenium content in soils may vary by a factor of 200 in the United States. A kilogram of wheat may contain from 50mcg-800mcg of selenium depending on where it is grown.

Chromium and zinc are also critically deficient in the soil. This problem is presently under extensive study by the USDA.

NOTE:

Studies performed at Rutgers University by Dr. Firman E. Bear show that some carrots tested for nutrient potency were almost completely without nutrients. This reduction in nutrient potency occurred in carrots from different farms all over the United States.

Dr. William Albrecht at the University of Missouri has shown that over a 10 year period the protein content of grains in the Midwest has declined 11%.

The use of nitrogenous fertilizers is causing copper deficiencies and the overuse of potash fertilizers is creating magnesium deficiencies.

Smoking Effects On Vitamins:

Vitamin C - Studies have shown that smokers require approximately 40% more vitamin C intake than non-smokers to achieve adequate blood levels. Every cigarette reduces bodily stores of vitamin C by about 30mg., which means a pack of cigarettes require at least a 600mg. increase in your vitamin C intake.

Vitamin B12 - Cigarette smoking reduces the blood levels of vitamin B12.

Storage of Foods:

Canned And Packaged Products - Supermarket foods may have an extended stay on the shelves as well as long warehouse times resulting in reduced potencies of vitamins and minerals.

Fruits And Vegetables - Usually are harvested before they are fully ripened then allowed to ripen in the markets. Fruits and vegetables are regularly cut into smaller sizes which expose their surfaces to the effects of light and air (oxidation) for long periods of time, thus reducing their nutrient potency.

Rotation Of Foods - Canned, frozen and packaged products in the home are rarely dated and rotated properly. Dehydrated foods as well, lose a percentage of nutrient potency over time and should be rotated.

Restaurants - Purchase in large quantities, possibly resulting in long storage times, especially if the restaurant is not too busy. Fast food chains avoid this problem due to faster food turnover.

NOTE:

Excess storage times may result in the purchase of foods thought to contain adequate amounts of certain nutrients only to end up with little or none. Oranges from supermarkets have been tested and found to contain no vitamin C content, while a fresh picked one contains approximately 180mg. Vitamin and mineral potency losses may occur before the product receives its expiration code date.

A potato in storage for a period of six months can lose approximately 50% of its vitamin C content. Most food charts will deduct 25% of the nutrient value of foods to allow for the effects of storage, packaging, transportation, processing, preservation and cooking. In some cases this is not enough.

Poorly Balanced Meals:

Meal Planning - Too few people plan their meals in advance. This results in poor combinations of foods, leading to inadequate vitamin and mineral intake.

Restaurants - The majority of these meals are lacking in fruits and vegetables.

Air Pollution:

Smog - All major cities in the United States have some form of chemical air pollution. This pollution affect your lung capacity to deliver oxygen efficiently to the cells of the body. The anti-oxidants (vitamins C, A, E, selenium and beta-carotene) may prove to be effective in combating some of the effects of smog.

Smoke - Smoke from cigars, cigarettes and pipes all have a detrimental effect on the oxygen carrying capacity of the red blood cell. Smoke contains carbon monoxide may adhere to the site on the red blood cell that should be carrying oxygen.

Stress:

The Nervous System - The health of nerves and especially their protective sheath depend on an adequate supply of vitamin B.

Stress Tolerance - When under stress bodily needs for vitamin C may increase 100 times.

Dieting:

Endless Programs - Due to the multitude of diet programs available today, it is impossible to relate the nutritional inadequacies found in many of the programs. These programs do not take into consideration the individual life style differences in persons using their methods or products. Supplementation should be recommended in most programs.

Chapter 7

Egg Knowledge

Boil cracked eggs in aluminum foil twisted on the ends.

When making Easter eggs remove an egg that has cracked from boiling water and pour a generous amount of salt over the crack. This will seal the crack and contain the egg white.

There are three grades for eggs: U.S. Grade AA, U.S. Grade A and U.S. Grade B.

When using eggs and solid shortening, break the egg into the measuring cup before measuring the shortening, the shortening will come out easier.

"EGG-SCUSE ME"
In recent studies, egg yolks have less cholesterol than previously thought, and have been revised from 250mg to 200 mg per average yolk.

"BE SOMEWHAT GENTLE"
Egg whites should be beaten in a bowl with a small rounded bottom to reduce the work area and increase the volume.

Weight Of Eggs Per Dozen:	*Calories:*
Jumbo..........................30 ounces	1 Large Egg.....80 calories
Extra Large.................27 ounces	1 Egg White....20 calories
Large..........................24 ounces	1 Egg Yolk......60 calories
Medium......................21 ounces	
Small..........................18 ounces	
Pewee........................15 ounces	

Refrigerator shelf life of an egg is approximately 10-14 days.

To store deviled eggs, place the halves together with the filling and wrap tightly with tin foil, then curl the ends.

Egg will clean off utensils better with cold water then using hot water.

Keep unbroken eggs in a covered bowl because the shells are porous and will absorb odors as well as lose moisture.

Never buy eggs in styrofoam containers, always buy them in paper cartons so that they will be recyclable.

Whole eggs cannot be frozen, the shells will crack as the liquid expands.

Yolks last longer when covered with water.

Egg whites should be kept in a tightly sealed container.

To remove eggs that are stuck to cartons, try wetting the carton.

To insure lasting freshness of eggs, rotate and mark them. If you place a small pencil mark on old eggs you will be certain to identify them and use them before recently purchased eggs.

FRESH   3-4 DAYS OLD

ABOUT 10 DAYS OLD   VERY OLD - SHOULD NOT USE

To tell how old an egg is place the egg in a pan of cold water if it lies on its side, it's fresh; if it tilts on an angle, it's approximately 3-4 days old; if the egg stands upright, it's probably about 10 days old; if the egg floats to the top, it is old and should not be used.

"TOUGH GUY"
Hard cooked eggs should never be frozen because it changes the taste and texture of the egg.

Add salt to water when hard-cooking eggs, it makes them easier to peel.

"PEEK-A-BOO"
To easily separate egg yolks from whites, poke a small hole in the end of an egg and drain the white through the hole. After you've drained the egg white, just crack the egg open for the yolk.

To tell if an egg is hard boiled or raw, place the egg on it's side and spin it evenly on a level surface. If it wobbles it's raw.

To insure longer lasting freshness, rub oil, butter, or pure glycerin over the whole egg shell.

Never use aluminum bowls or cookware when beating egg whites, eggs tend to darken. Use glass, enamel or stainless-steel.

Dishes with caked on egg should be washed first in cold water which will release the egg protein better than hot water.

"NEW PRODUCT"
An excellent new product called "Just Whites" is a powdered egg white only product which reduces the fat in eggs and can be used in cakes, muffins, meringue and souffles.

"GETTING OLD FAST"
Eggs will age more during one day at room temperature than they will in one week under refrigeration. Eggs will only last 2-3 days without refrigeration.

Always thaw frozen eggs in the refrigerator.

Egg whites become firm at 145 degrees F., yolks at 155 degrees F.

Egg whites contain more than ½ the protein in an egg.

The twisted strands of egg white (chalazae) cords that hold the yolk in place are more prominent the fresher the egg.

The yolk color depends on the chicken's food source.

The yolk contains 3/4 of the eggs calories.

Never buy eggs that are shiney, they are probably old and of poor quality.

"QUACK, QUACK, QUACK"
Duck eggs develop harmful bacteria when they age. This can only be destroyed by boiling the eggs for 10-12 minutes.

For a good plant fertilizer, dry eggshells in the oven then pulverize them in a blender to make bonemeal.

 Chef's Secrets

When you poach eggs, try adding a little vinegar and salt to the water. This will set the eggs and keep them in shape.

When making scrambled eggs, use a small amount of water instead of milk. Milk makes the eggs watery and doesn't blend well. Water makes eggs fluffy.

When freezing eggs, you should always break the yolks. Whites can be frozen alone, yokes can be frozen alone or you can freeze them together. Yolks do not freeze well unless broken. This is also handy when you need just whites for angel food cake.

Remove eggs from the refrigerator at least ½ hour before beating. You will get more volume.

If you are going to whip eggs, they should be approximately three days old and at room temperature for the best results.

Always use fresh eggs for baking projects, the end results will always be better.

When poaching eggs, add a small amount of butter to the tin before placing the eggs in. It will prevent them from sticking and the yolks from breaking. Pan is easier to clean too!

To beat egg whites quicker and fluffier, add a small amount of salt, let them stand until they are room temperature, then beat.

When beating egg whites add a teaspoon of cold water and you will almost double the quantity.

Omelets won't collapse if you add a pinch of cornstarch and a pinch of confectioners sugar to the yolks before folding in the whites.

If you add one teaspoon of vinegar to water when boiling eggs they may not crack.

To guarantee a white film over the eggs when cooking, place a few drops of water in the pan just before the eggs are done and cover the pan.

When you fry eggs try dropping a small amount of flour into the pan to prevent splattering.

If you come up one egg short when baking a cake, substitute two tablespoons of mayonnaise. This will only work for one egg.

Add food coloring to the water before boiling eggs, then you can tell the hard-boiled ones from the raw ones.

To keep the yolks centered, stir the water while cooking hard-boiled eggs. Great for deviled eggs.

An easy way to separate eggs is to place a small funnel over a small measuring cup. Break the eggs into the funnel.

Eggs should always be cooked at low temperature to guarantee a tender white and smooth yolk.

Remove all traces of egg yolk with a Q-tip or edge of a paper towel, before trying to beat egg whites. The slightest trace of yolk will effect the results. Also, make sure your beater blades do not have any vegetable oil on them.

"A LITTLE DIP WILL DO YA"
If you are making a number of omelets or batches of scrambled eggs, try wiping the pan with a piece of paper towel dipped in table salt after three batches. Your results will be much better with less food sticking to the pan.

To make a better omelet or scrambled egg dish, try adding a small amount of water instead of milk when you are beating the eggs. Milk products tend to harden the yolk, while water tends to slow down the coagulation of the yolk.

"NOT SLIPPERY WHEN WET"
When handling eggs or removing them from the carton, try wetting your hands first and they won't slip away.

To remove an egg shell, crack the egg and roll it around in your hands with gentle pressure. You then insert a wet spoon between the shell and the egg white and rotate the egg.

You can substitute 2 egg yolks for 1 whole egg when making custards, cream pie fillings and salad dressings.

You can substitute 2 egg yolks plus 1 teaspoon of water for 1 whole egg in yeast dough or cookies.

Eggs yolks will keep better if you cover them with cold water and keep refrigerated.

Hard-boiled eggs will slice easier if you dip the knife in water before cutting.

There is no difference between white eggs and brown eggs in either nutritional quality or taste.

Measuring Eggs:

```
1 Large Egg (2 oz.)................................1/4 cup
1 Medium Egg (1 3/4oz.)......................1/5 cup
1 Small Egg (1 1/2oz.)..........................1/6 cup
```

The best egg shells should be dull not shiny or bright.

Egg sales have dropped 25% since 1984.

In a very fresh egg, the yolk will hardly be visible through the white.

The average hen produces about 200 eggs per year. The laying begins about 5 months after they are hatched.

Dried egg solids have 90% of the water removed.

"EGG KNOWLEDGE"

All egg cartons that are marked "A" or "AA" are not officially graded. Egg cartons must have the USDA grade shield to have been officially graded.

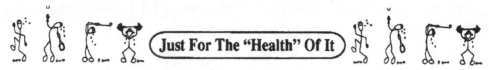

Just For The "Health" Of It

To reduce calories, fat and cholesterol in recipes, use more egg whites and fewer yolks. You won't know the difference.

If an egg has a crack of any kind it is best not to use it.

While eggs contain cholesterol, they also contain lecithin which may provide enough good cholesterol (HDL's) to counteract the bad cholesterol (LDL's).

The FDA regulations now say that eggs must be refrigerated at all times during shipping and when they are stacked in stores.

Because of recent Salmonella outbreaks on the East Coast, the internal temperature of eggs must be kept below 45 degrees Fahrenheit. Never buy eggs unless they are under refrigeration and ideally at a humidity level of 75%.

If eggs are dirty, do not wash before storing. You will remove a protective coating and they won't store as long.

A soft-boiled egg is safe to eat as long as its cooked for 3 ½ minutes. This should raise the temperature of the egg to approximately 140 degrees and will pasteurize it.

Some eggs have been found to contain "microcracks" that may allow harmful bacteria to enter. Cooking will kill these bacteria.

Basted eggs should be cooked for four minutes covered to be safe from bacteria.

The total digestive time for an egg is 4 hours.

The difference in the quality of eggs can be determined by the amount of spread when they are broken. U.S. Grade AA eggs will have a small spread, be thick, very white and have a firm high yolk. U.S. Grade A eggs will have more spread with a less thick white. U.S. Grade B eggs will have a wide spread, little thick white and probably a flat enlarged looking yolk. U.S. Grade C eggs have an even wider spread with a thin watery white.

HEALTH HINT:

After you make hard-boiled eggs, never place them in cool water after they are peeled. Eggs have a thin protective membrane that if removed or damaged and placed in water or a sealed container may allow for bacterial growth to begin.

To cool boiled eggs allow them to remain at room temperature and then refrigerate in an open bowl.

"TURNING GREEN?"
Don't overcook eggs or the yolk may turn a greenish color as a result of the leaching out of an iron compound. Happens more frequently in older eggs and is harmless.

Chapter 8

Cold and Freezing Facts

Do not buy frozen foods unless they are frozen solid and do not contain ice crystals which may be the result of thawing and refreezing..

Keep a frozen food inventory, foods tend to get lost in a large freezer.

Almost 97% of Americans eat ice cream regularly, however, the switch to low-fat yogurt is gaining momentum.

The average American consumes 15 quarts of ice cream annually.

To avoid "freezer burn" and ice crystals forming on foods, wrap the foods with plastic wrap or freezer paper and cover it with tin foil. If your storing foods for an extended period of time also place the packaged food in a sealed baggie.

A high quality ice cream has a butterfat content of 15%.

Frozen sandwiches will thaw by lunchtime, butter the bread and it won't absorb the filling.

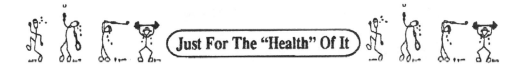

Just For The "Health" Of It

Frozen foods are more nutritious than canned foods due to the method of processing.

Make your own frozen TV dinners from leftovers. They will be much higher in nutritional value than most store bought ones.

Date all frozen foods using a piece of tape or permanent marker pen.

"TO FREEZE OR REFREEZE, THAT IS THE QUESTION"

Refreezing foods will lower their quality. When foods are frozen the cellular fluid expands into crystals and causes a break in the cell membrane, disrupting other structures, thus changing the texture of the food. This may alter the taste of the food but does not affect the food safety factor regarding spoilage. Meats are an exception as well as dairy products since bacterial growth starts when they warmup and refreezing may just place the bacteria in a state of animation until the food is thawed out.

Remember the longer you freeze, the better the chances are to lose a percentage of the food quality.

Seal all freezer wrapped foods as well as possible so that freezer burn will not occur, double wrapping will help.

A good trick when you go away on vacation is to place a baggie with a few ice cubes in the freezer. If a power failure occurs while you are gone and the food thaws and then refreezes, you will know about it when you get home.

Baker's yeast will freeze for years without going bad.

If you freeze wild rice it will last for 3-4 months but only a week in the refrigerator.

A corned beef roast can be kept for up to one week in the refrigerator and up to two weeks if frozen.

Always remove meat from store packages and re-wrap using special freezer paper or aluminum foil if you are planning to freeze meats for more than 2-3 weeks.

Chops, cutlets and hamburgers should be freezer wrapped individually. This will assure maximum freshness and convenience.

Brown sugar won't harden if stored in the freezer.

Save the wrappings from sticks of butter or margarine. Keep them in the refrigerator in a plastic bag for future use in greasing baking utensils.

Unsalted butter can be stored in the freezer indefinitely if it is wrapped and sealed airtight. Salted butter can be stored for a shorter period of time in its original container with no wrapping.

Leftover whipped cream; drop dollops of whipped cream on a cookie sheet, then freeze before storing in plastic bags.

Freeze eggs whole or separated. Egg whites may get tough when frozen in a potato or macaroni salad.

Freeze fish in clean milk cartons full of water. When thawing the fish, use the water for fertilizer on household plants.

Flour can be frozen.

Honey can be frozen in ice cube trays. If the honey becomes granulated, simply place the cubes in a jar and place in very hot water.

If ice cream thaws it should not be re-frozen.

Fruits and vegetables should be frozen at their peak of flavor.

The freezer in your refrigerator is not the same as a food freezer. It is best used for storing foods for short periods only. Foods should be frozen as quickly as possible and temperatures should be 0 degrees Fahrenheit or below.

Jelly, salad dressing and mayonnaise do not freeze well on bread products.

When freezing casseroles, cook for a shorter period of time than normal, then cool quickly to stop cooking action. Make sure it is packed as solidly as possible, the fewer air spaces the better.

To prolong the freezer storage time for roasted meats, cover them with gravy.

Meat loaf may be frozen cooked or uncooked.

Freezer Temperature Changes And Their Effects On Foods:

Freezer Temperature	Quality Changes After
30°	5 Days
25°	10 Days
20°	3 Weeks
15°	6 Weeks
10°	4 Months
5°	6 Months
0°	1 Year

Potatoes will become mushy when frozen in stews or casseroles. Their cells are high in water content and break easily when frozen.

Any bakery item with a cream filling should not be frozen. They will become soggy.

Custard or meringue pies do not freeze well. The custard tends to separate and the meringue will become tough.

Mashed potatoes freeze well.

Waffles and pancakes may be frozen, then thawed and cooked in the toaster.

Freezer Storage Times At Zero Degrees Fahrenheit

MEATS

Food	Months
Beef, Lamb	6 - 12
Chops, Cutlets, Beef Hamburger	3 - 5
Ground Pork	1 - 3
Sausage	1 - 2

Bacon (unsliced)	3 - 5
Bacon (sliced)	< 1
Fish	3 - 6
Ham	3 - 4
Liver	3 - 4
Poultry	4 - 6
Giblets	3
Duck, Goose	5 - 6
Rabbit	9 - 12
Shrimp or shellfish (cooked)	2 - 3
Turkey	6 - 8
Hot Dogs	2 - 3
Luncheon Meats (ready to eat)	0

DAIRY PRODUCTS

Milk	< 2 weeks
Ice Cream	2 - 4 weeks
Cream (40%)	3 - 4
Eggs (not in shell)	7 - 10
Margarine	2 - 4
Butter	2 - 4
Cheddar Cheese	5 - 6
Frozen Milk Desserts (commercial)	1

FRUITS

Apples (sliced)	10 - 12
Apricots	10 - 12
Berries	11 - 12
Cherries (sour)	12

Chapter 9

Let's Not Chew The Fat

JUST THE NITTY GRITTY

Polyunsaturated Fats: This type remains liquid at room temperature. sunflower, safflower and corn are examples and tend to lower cholesterol levels in some studies.

Monounsaturated Fats: These are still liquid at room temperature but thicken when refrigerated. Examples are found in avocados, olive oil, rapeseed, and many nuts. Recent studies are showing that they may tend to lower cholesterol levels, especially olive oil and Canola oil.

Saturated Fats: These are either solid or semi-solid at room temperature. Examples are butter, hard margarine, lard and shortening. Exceptions to the rule are coconut and palm oils, which have very high saturated fat levels. They tend to raise the cholesterol levels in the body.

To make a creamy salad dressing, try pouring olive oil very slowly into a running blender containing the other ingredients.

An empty detergent or ketchup bottle will make it easier to add cooking oil to pans.

Olive oil needs no refrigeration and will keep longer than any other type of oil.

To remove the fat from drippings, just pour them into a tall narrow glass, leave it for 10 minutes, then remove the layer of fat.

The best quality oil is "Extra Virgin Oil." It is made from the finest plump olives, has the best flavor and is the least processed. Next is "Virgin Oil" then "Pure Olive Oil" which is a blend of both Extra Virgin and Virgin Oils.

Extra virgin olive oil contains less than 1% acidity, virgin olive oil contains 1 ½-3% acidity. The less acidity, the better the quality of the oil. Many oils must have neutralizing agents added to them to reduce their level of acidity.

Oil and vinegar will mix well together in solution if you add the contents of 1-2 lecithin capsules.

Chef's Secrets

To eliminate the fat from soups, refrigerate the soup until the fat hardens on the top, then just remove.

If your recipe requires that you cream shortening with a sugary substance, try adding a few drops of water to the mixture to make it easier.

From preventing a cooking wine from going sour, try adding a tablespoon of vegetable oil to the bottle.

"THE FAT SPONGE"
When you are broiling meats, place a few pieces of dried bread in the broiler pan to soak up the dripping fat. This will eliminate the smoking fat and also reduces the risk of the fat catching fire.

When creaming butter, cut it up in small pieces to give the mixer a better chance to do the job right.

To test whether hot oil is still usable, drop a piece of white bread into the pan. If the bread develops dark specs, the oil is deteriorating.

You could also wrap the ice cubes in a piece of cheesecloth or paper towel and just skim it over the top.

Another good way to remove fat is to use lettuce leaves. Place a few in the pot, the fat will cling to them, then just remove them. This is a very efficient method.

Never allow oil to heat to the smoke point, as it may ignite. It will also make food taste bitter and may irritate your eyes. The oils with the highest smoke points are Canola, safflower and corn oil.

The best butter is U.S. Grade AA which is made from fresh sweet cream. U.S. Grade A is close to AA but has a lower flavor rating. U.S. Grade B is usually made from sour cream. The milk-fat content of butter must be at least 80%.

A Fat Packed Meal

Total Calories		Calories From Fat
252	Hamburger	165
95	Bun	17
110	Cheese Slice	80
125	Special Sauce	100
115	Potato Chips	75

Olive oil is one of the best fats to use in salads or for low temperature cooking, for example in a Wok. It has a low smoke point and when used for higher temperature cooking, add a teaspoon of canola oil to it to raise the smoke point. This trick is also good to use with butter when your using it for cooking. Some studies have shown olive oil to lower cholesterol levels.

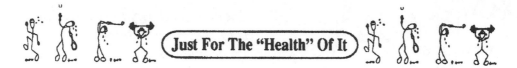

Just For The "Health" Of It

Most margarines contain over 90% fat. Diet margarines usually contain 80% fat, 16% water, 2% salt and 2% non-fat milk solids, and don't forget the colorings and additives. Margarines are naturally white. A liquid diet margarine, however, may contain as low as 40% fat.

Margarine has been found to contain a substance called trans-acids. If you use margarine, use the softest diet you can buy (more air and water) or my recommendation is whipped unsalted butter. Used in moderation the cholesterol content is not that high in 5-7 pats per week.

Do not save cooking oils or bacon drippings. The more these fats are re-cooked the higher the percentage of trans-acids. There are two forms of fats, cis and trans. When you first use an oil, the majority of the fat is of the good (cis) variety, but as it is heated a percentage changes to a potentially harmful substance, called a trans-acid.

"REMEMBER WHEN"
When grandmother fried foods she used to place a peeled potato into the oil to clean out the debris, swish it around remove it and throw it away. The oil was then placed into the freezer for use at a later date. After one using the oil was almost solid trans-fatty acids and the worst product we could put into our bodies.

Lard comes from the abdomen of pigs. Used in chewing gum bases, shaving creams, soaps and cosmetics. Future testing may implicate it in shortened life-spans and a factor in osteoporosis.

Most pork and trout contain approximately 40% fat calories.

Some of the highest fat crackers are Ritz, Town House and Goldfish which contains approximately 6 grams of fat per ounce.

Mayonnaise must contain at least 65% oil by weight. If it contains less, its called salad dressing.

"CAN'T WIN"
Most fat-free mayonnaise contains more sodium than the "real" mayonnaise.

A tablespoon of mayonnaise contains only about 5-10mg. of cholesterol. Very little egg yolk is really used in the product.

"PIG IN A BLANKET"
Pancakes wrapped around sausages on a stick delivers 60% of its calories from fat.

Leaf lard comes from the area of the kidneys in pigs. It is a higher quality than other types of lard.

Pates are bordered with pork fats from the flank of the pig.

The harder the margarine, the higher the percentage of saturated fat it contains. Saturated fat is still guilty of helping the body produce more cholesterol than you need.

From 1963 to 1985, the incidence of skin cancer has doubled to over 300,000 cases per year. Dietary fats are being implicated as one of the key factors.

Refined corn oil is a chemical extraction, a triglyceride with no relationship to the nutrients in a "real" ear of corn. The vitamins that would normally assist with the assimilation of the corn oil such as vitamin E, are absent.

Polyunsaturated fatty acids can cause premature wrinkling of the skin and can possibly be a factor in premature aging as well.

"AIN'T SCIENCE WONDERFUL"

If the list of ingredients lists an oil as "hydrogenated," the product is probably high in saturated fats. Hydrogenation is the process of adding water to the fat, the oil picks up the hydrogen atoms and it makes the fat more saturated and harder.

Always purchase oils in dark-colored or tin containers to avoid any rancidity problem.

Diets high in total fat have been related to cancer of the colon, the prostate and the breast.

High fat diets may reduce the efficiency of the immune system.

Young chickens and turkeys have less fat.

Every ounce of fat contains 250% more calories than an ounce of carbohydrate or protein.

Use buttermilk for baking, pancakes and especially mashed potatoes. Buttermilk is low-fat.

Fats should be included in all dietary plans, even those for weight control. Your body requires the "essential fatty acids."

A person can survive very nicely on only 5% fat in their diet, the right fats, of course.

Approximately 10 grams of fat is cleared from the stomach per hour. Two scrambled eggs, bread and butter, coffee and milk = 50 grams of fat. Assimilation time is 5-6 hours.

"AND AWAY IT GOES"

A high fat intake can cause calcium and vitamin C losses through the urine.

Butter will go farther and have fewer calories per serving if you beat it well. This increases the volume by adding air.

75% of the calories in bacon come from fat, the same amount that comes from cheddar cheese.

"OINK, OINK"
Americans spend $3 billion a year on bacon.

Most non-dairy creamers are made from coconut oil, which is very high in saturated fats. Mocha Mix is your best bet.

Rapeseed oil (Canola) for years has been grown as a forage crop for animals in the United States. Originally it was banned in the U.S. when imports from Canada showed high levels of erucic acid. However, new varieties have shown to contain lower acid levels and is now being produced and sold in large quantities. It is higher in monounsaturated fat and has a high smoke point, making it the preferred oil for frying.

Current studies show that if your body is higher in "brown fat" rather than "white fat," your fat is of the more active type and be able to control your weight better. These studies are now being conducted at Harvard Medical School.

Fats from beef should be from very lean cuts with all visible fat removed. Lean veal and lamb are permissible. Poultry should have all fat and skin removed, no duck or goose. Fish should be baked or broiled.

Most fats should be consumed either at breakfast or lunch, few, if any, for dinner. High fat meals during the evening hours may cause the digestive system to overwork while you are sleeping, causing restless sleep patterns.

Most butters and margarines contain about the same amount of saturated fats.

Doughnuts and cakes add a high amount of saturated fat to your diet. It is best to make these yourself and put lower fat ingredients in them.

"YOLKS AWAY"
To reduce fat when preparing omelets, discard every other yolk this will reduce the fat and cholesterol levels and you will never know the difference.

More soy oil is sold in the U.S. than any other kind of oil.

Cottonseed oil is 25% saturated fat and not the best to use.

Soy oil changes in flavor, the longer it is stored, due to the changes in the linolenic acid it contains.

64% of the calories in caviar are from fat.

Butter will absorb refrigerator odors and should be stored covered.

Butter stores in the refrigerator for only two weeks. If longer time is needed, freeze it.

One pound of butter = 2 cups.

If a recipe calls for butter, you may be able to replace it with a solid shortening, measure for measure. The water in the butter will balance off the air in the shortening.

Eight ounces of potato chips is the equivalent of eating 12-20 teaspoons of fat.

Try using water instead of fat in recipes. Fat does make dressings, etc. feel smooth to the taste, but if you thicken water with flour, cornstarch or potato starch it will save you calories.

Oils should be stored in opaque containers and placed in a dark, cool location to reduce the risk of rancidity.

"WHY CAROB?"
When carob is made into candy, fat is added for texture which brings the fat content closer to real chocolate. In fact, cocoa butter use in real chocolate is 60% saturated fat while the fat in carob candy is 85% saturated in most cases.

Using non-stick cookware and spraying with a vegetable spray will help lower fat intake.

Never eat a salad dressing or mayonnaise-based salad unless you are sure it has been refrigerated until just before you are ready to eat it. This causes thousands of cases of food poisoning yearly.

An 8oz. bag of potato chips contains approximately 6 tablespoons of fat.

The oils associated with fish are more beneficial than those associated with meats. Fish contain a high percentage of omega 3 fatty acids.

Any margarine containing coconut or palm oil will be very high in saturated fat. New labeling now calls them "tropical oils."

New fat substitutes are appearing in our foods, be aware that these are still synthetically produced and not a "natural" food. They should not be viewed as a panacea to replace the fats in our diet.

1. **Olestra** - *Procter & Gamble.* "This product has been approved by the FDA and is now available." No-cal fat substitute. Chemical name; *sucrose polyester.* It is a combination of sugar and soybean or other oil. The molecule is so large and dense that our enzymes that normally breakdown fat don't recognize it and it just passes through the body. The product will be sold in the following forms: 35% of a cooking oil or shortening, 75% of oils used in deep fat frying in restaurants and 75% of oils used in salted snacks.

2. Simplesse - As of January 1995 this fat substitute is being used in over 24 products. Originally it was made of egg whites and skim milk but is now being made from whey, a milk protein, and is a good quality product. Contains a few calories. Looks like mayonnaise and can be made as thick or thin as desired. Products seen on the market using Simplesse are for the most part salad dressings and frozen desserts.

3. Oatrim - (Trim Choice) made from oat flour is a carbohydrate now being used as a fat substitute. It was developed in 1993 by the USDA. It may also be called "hydrated oat flour." It adds a creamy fat-like texture to foods and is good for baking. Contains only 1 calorie per gram compared to fat at 9 calories per gram.

The best butter is made from U.S. Grade AA sweet cream.

One ounce of sunflower seeds contains 160 calories and is not a "diet" snack food.

A burrito topped with sour cream and guacamole may be as high as 1,000 calories and 59% fat.

Recent studies have shown that stearic acid one of the saturated fats has little effect on raising cholesterol levels. We are finding out more about which specific fats will raise cholesterol and which foods to avoid.

"AS THE COOKIE CRUMBLES"
Reduced fat oreo cookies contains 47 calories and 1.67 grams of fat. The original cookie has 53 calories and 2.33 grams of fat. Not a big savings.

"LET'S PULL THE WOOL OVER"
The new reduced-fat peanut butter has the same number of calories per serving as regular peanut butter, approximately 190 per serving, sweeteners were added in place of the fat.

When oils are refrigerated and become cloudy, it is due to the buildup of harmless crystals. Manufacturers will sometimes pre-chill the oils and remove the crystals in a process known as "winterizing." These oils will remain clear when refrigerated.

Salad and cooking oil use:

1909 - 1.5 pounds per person
1972 - 18 pounds per person
1990 - 29 pounds per person
1994 - 32 pounds per person

Margarine use:

1950 - 6 pounds per person
1972 - 11 pounds per person
1990 - 16 pounds per person
1994 - 18 pounds per person

Lard has large crystals and butter small ones. This has a lot to do with the texture of the fat and is controlled during the processing. Crystal sizes can be altered by agitating the oil when it is cooling.

Studies have shown that dieters miss fat more than sweets.

Persons who consume a high fat diet are more prone to colon cancer, prostate cancer and breast cancer. Studies in the future may show that there is also a detrimental effect on the immune system.

The average American diet is about 44% fat. Dietary guidelines suggest no more than 30% of total calories. My recommendation is no more than 25% or less. Your intake should lean more toward the polyunsaturates and monounsaturates with a maximum amount of fat from saturated fat at 10% or less of the 25%

Recent studies show that the percentage of fats vary in different foods that we associate with high fat content. The following are the results:

Potato Chips	40%
Cheese Puffs	39%
Corn Chips	37%
Tortilla Chips	24%
Doughnuts	22%
Fried Chicken	18%
French Fries	14%
Fried Fish	10%

Rating the oils by percentage of saturated fats from best to worst:

Canola........safflower.......sunflower.......corn......olive.......soybean.......peanut....... margarine........ palm oil........butter..........coconut oil.......

There are 312 fats and oils that can be used for frying.

"WHERE'S THE FAT?".....HERE'S THE FAT"

Most of us never realize how much fat we really do eat. The following information will help you become more aware of the higher fat foods. We rarely think of fat in "teaspoons," but you may find it easier to comprehend when presented in this form.

MEATS/FISH

Hot Dog/All Beef	1 medium	2 ½ teaspoons
Bologna	1 slice	2 teaspoons
Big Mac	1	7-9 teaspoons
Turkey Pot Pie	12 oz	6 teaspoons
Sirloin TV Dinner	1 medium	7 teaspoons
Ham TV Dinner	1 medium	3 teaspoons
Chicken TV Dinner	1 medium	7 teaspoons
Lean Beef	3 oz	2 teaspoons
Medium-Fat Beef	3 oz	4 ½ teaspoons
Chicken Breast/No Skin	4 oz	1 teaspoon
Chicken Breast/Skin	4 oz	2 ½ teaspoons
Fried Oysters	1 serving	3 ½ teaspoons
Trout/Raw	3 ½ oz	3 teaspoons
Bacon	1 strip	1 1/4 teaspoons
Canadian Bacon	1 strip	1 teaspoon
Hamburger	1/4 pound	3 ½ teaspoons
Frog Legs	2 large	2 ½ teaspoons
Ham/Lean	2 slices	1 1/4 teaspoons
Pork Chop	3 ½ oz	6 ½ teaspoons
Veal Cutlet	3 ½ oz	4 teaspoons
Duck/Roasted	3 ½ oz	7 teaspoons
Goose	3 ½ oz	5 ½ teaspoons
Rabbit	3 ½ oz	1 ½ teaspoons
Squab	3 ½ oz	5 ½ teaspoons
Turkey	3 ½ oz	2 teaspoons
Lobster Newburg	3 ½ oz	2 ½ teaspoons
Salmon/Canned	3 ½ oz	3 ½ teaspoons

"EDUCATION STILL LACKING"

Americans consumed 53 pounds of fats and oils per person in 1970. In 1994 we consumed 65 pounds, this is not the direction we should be going.

Chapter 10

Cheese Facts

Cheese making is fast becoming the latest "yuppie" fad. For information call the Tillamook Cheese Hot Line at 1 (800)542-7290.

To keep cheese moist, wrap it in a soft cloth wrung out of vinegar and keep in an earthen jar with the cover slightly raised.

When too much fat is removed from cheese, it may have a rubbery texture. The fat in cheese gives it the smooth texture we prefer. Cheeses that are the exceptions, like ricotta, camembert and brie have a higher water content, and a low fat content.

Most cheese substitutes are produced from soybean vegetable fat.

The higher the water content of cheeses, such as cottage cheese, the faster they tend to go bad. Cottage cheese lasts for only three weeks after it is produced. Remember to store it upside down and mix the liquid (whey) back in.

Cheddar cheese is so low in moisture that it can last for years. However, it will get a stronger taste as it ages. Low-fat cheeses do not have a long shelf life due to their increased water content. Your just paying for more water.

Grate small bits of cheeses that are leftover to get variety. Makes a great topping for salads and casseroles.

100 grams of cheese = 25 grams of protein.

The average woman needs 46 grams of protein per day, the average man 56 grams.

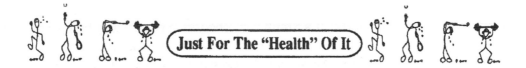

Just For The "Health" Of It

It takes 8 pounds of milk to make one pound of cheese. One ounce (average slice) of cheese = as much fat and protein as one cup of milk. Also, it is a concentrated source of cholesterol and saturated fat.

The cheese industry has developed numerous methods of changing a good quality product into a chemical smorgasbord. While most cheeses are naturally white (not yellow), the industry has resorted to a variety of artificial chemicals to make cheeses "more appealing" to us visually.

The following is just a partial list of these chemicals that are used to give cheese their sharp taste, to color them, to make them smell more appealing or to thicken them. They include: malic acid, tartaric acid, phosphoric acid, alginic acid, aluminum potassium phosphate, diacetyl, sodium carboxymethyl cellulose, benzyl peroxide and certain yellow dyes.

While all these chemicals have been approved by the appropriate federal agencies, we are told that in small quantities, they are harmless. However, if they are so harmless why are most of them still under further investigation?

These same chemicals that are used to alter cheeses are used for making cement, bleaching clothes, producing cosmetics and even rust-proofing metals.

 Cheese is an excellent food but you should be more aware of the kinds of cheeses to choose from. Try to purchase cheeses made from "part-skim milk," "low-fat milk" "non-fat milk" and are labeled "natural." Also, try to find one that says that it contains "no preservatives or additives."

An ounce of cream cheese may contain as much as 110 calories. True, it does have fewer calories than butter for a comparable weight, but we use more

Try to choose from low-sodium and reduced-fat cheeses. New varieties seem to be appearing weekly.

A recent dental study showed that a number of cheeses will actually help to prevent cavities. These include; Romano, Muenster, Gouda, Swiss, Edam, Monterey Jack, Tilsit, Port du Salut, processed American cheese singles and aged Cheddar.

Moldy cheese may contain a harmful toxin (aflatoxin), especially gorgonzola, blue cheese and roquefort.

If a cheese is "natural" the name of the cheese will be preceded by the word "natural" or will not have anything preceding the name of the cheese.

One cup of grated cheese is made from 1/4 pound of cheese.

The wax coating on cheeses will protect it. If there is an exposed edge try covering it with butter to keep the cheese moist and fresh.

 Chef's Secrets

Cottage cheese will remain fresher for a longer period of time if you store it upside down in the refrigerator. When this book was being researched we noticed that many chefs keep a number of different products upside down if they will move in the container. Slows the effects of oxidation.

To keep cheese longer without it forming mold, place a piece of paper towel that has been dampened with white vinegar in the bottom of a plastic container that has a good seal before adding the cheese.

Another way to prevent mold from forming on cheese is to store the cheese in a sealed container with two lumps of sugar.

Soft cheeses can be grated using a metal colander and a potato masher.

Dishes with cheese should be cooked slower to avoid curdling and stringiness.

A dull knife works better to cut cheese. Warm the knife and the cheese will cut like butter.

Yellow cheese: 71% of the calories are fat, 39% is saturated fat.

Dried out cheese (without mold) should be saved and grated, then used for cooking.

The U.S. is the leading producer of cheese in the world. Wisconsin is the leading state.

There are approximately 800 varieties of cheese in the world. The U.S. produces 200 of them.

Ripening Classifications

Unripened   These are consumed shortly after manufacture. One of the most common is cottage cheese, a high moisture soft cheese. Unripened low-moisture cheeses are Gjetost and Mysost.

Soft   Curing will progress from the outside or rind of the cheese, toward the center. Specific molds or cultures of bacteria which grow on the surface of the cheese assist in the specific characteristic flavors, body and texture. These cheeses contain a higher amount of moisture than semi-soft cheeses.

Semi-Soft   These cheeses ripen from the inside as well as from the surface. Curing will continue as long as the temperature is favorable. These are higher in moisture than firm-cheeses.

Firm   Ripen, utilizing a bacterial culture
                 throughout the whole cheese. Ripening occurs
                 as long as the temperature is favorable.
                 Lower in moisture than the softer varieties
                 and usually require a longer curing time.

Very Hard   Cured with the aid of a bacterial
                 culture with enzymes. Slow cured and
                 very low-moisture and contains a higher
                 salt content.

Blue-Vein   Curing is with the aid of mold bacteria and a
                 specific mold culture that will grow
                 throughout the inside of the cheese and produces
                 the familiar appearance and unique flavor.

Most Popular Cheeses

Blue (Bleu)   - Noted for its white and blue-streaked
                     markings, blue cheese has a soft and
                     often crumbly texture. Available in
                     various shapes. 1 ounce = 40 calories.

Brick   - A softer, yellow cheese available in
                     slightly soft-medium firm texture.
                     Commonly available in sliced, and brick
                     forms.

Brie   - Has an outer edible white coating, and
                     a mild-strong creamy inside. Originally
                     from France, brie is available in
                     wedge and round shapes.

Camembert -Reputed to be the favorite cheese of Napoleon, Camembert has a soft, yellow inside. It's outer coating is also edible and is usually a grayish-white color. This cheese takes from 4-8 weeks to ripen.

Cheddar -Normal color is white to medium-yellow. Mild to very sharp taste. Firm smooth texture. Comes in numerous shapes and originated in England. 1 ounce = 105 calories. Artificial color is usually added to make it more yellow.

Cheshire -A semi-firm, mild creamy cheese, loosely textured and crumbly. The flavor of red and white are similar. The red is colored with natural vegetable dye from the seeds of the annatto tree and is the most expensive. They ripen within a few weeks. Ideal for Welch rarebit.

Colby -A white to medium-yellow-orange cheese. Has a mild to mellow flavor and has a soft texture similar to cheddar. It is available in cylindrical, pie-shaped wedges. Originated in the U.S.

Coldpack -Fresh and aged cheeses with whey Cheese Food solids added. Mild flavor and is very spreadable. Numerous flavorings are added.

Cottage Cheese -Made from cow's skimmed milk, plain cured or plain cured with cream. Soft texture. Originated in the U.S. If you see "curd by acidification" on the label, don't buy it. Look for a more natural one.

Cream Cheese   -Made with cream or concentrated milk.
Very soft and spreadable. Never buy
a cream cheese if it contains the chemical
propylene glycol alginate.   Does not provide a
good source of protein.

Edam   -Creamy yellow or medium yellow-orange
cheese with a surface coating of red wax.
Has a mellow nut-like flavor. Semi-soft
to firm texture with small irregular
shaped round holes. Milkfat content is
lower than Gouda. Usually available in a
cannonball shape. Imported cheeses will
usually be free of additives, domestic
varieties are not. Originated in the
Netherlands.

Feta   -A curd cheese which is set in a very
concentrated salt solution. Made from
either goat's or sheep's milk. A sharp,
salty cheese and usually found chemical-
free.

**Farmers
Cheese**   -Similar to cottage cheese and pot
cheese but is pressed into a block form.
Usually free of preservatives if bought
in bulk from a Deli.

Gjetost   -Golden brown colored cheese with sweet
caramel flavor. Made from whey or goat's
milk. Has a firm buttery consistency.
Available in cubes or rectangular pieces.
Originated in Norway.

Gorgonzola   - Has a creamy white inside, mottled or streaked with blue-green ribbons of mold and a clay-colored surface. Has a tangy, peppery flavor and a semi-soft crumbly texture. Similar to Blue cheese. If made from goat's milk, it will be best.

Gouda   -A creamy yellow or medium yellow-orange cheese that usually has a red wax coating and a nutlike flavor. Semi-soft to firm texture. Higher fat content than Edam cheese. Contains small irregular shaped or round holes. Comes in a bell shape with flat top and bottom.

Gruyere   -A variation of Swiss cheese, but usually without the use of bleached milk making it higher in vitamin content. If mold inhibitors are added, the information will be on the label.

Limburger   -Has a creamy white interior and a reddish yellow surface. It is a highly pungent cheese with a very strong flavor. Ripens in 4-8 weeks and has a soft, smooth texture. Originated in Belgium.

Mozzarella   -A creamy white cheese made from whole or partly skimmed milk with a firm texture. Available in small round, shredded or in slices. Preservatives may be added in "low moisture" varieties. Originated in Italy.

Muenster   -Has a creamy white inside and a yellow
tan surface. Mild to mellow flavor with
a semi-soft texture. Contains more
moisture than brick cheese. Available in
wedges, blocks and circular cakes.
Originated in Germany.

Mysost   -A light brown cheese with a sweet caramel
flavor with a buttery consistency.
Available in cubical, cylindrical and pie
shaped wedges. Originated in Norway.

Neufchatel   -A white cheese with a mild acidic flavor.
Has a smooth texture similar to cream
cheese but lower in milkfat. Originated
in France.

Parmesan   -Creamy white cheese with a hard granular
texture and sharp piquant taste. It has
less of a moisture content and a lower
milkfat level than Romano. May be made
from partially skimmed milk and may be
bleached. Best to buy ungrated and grate
yourself for a much better flavor.
Originated in Italy.

Pasteurized
Processed
Cheese   -A blend of fresh and aged cheese which
has a constant flavor after it has been
processed. They melt easily and are used
for cheeseburgers, etc.

Pasteurized
Processed
Cheese Food   -A blend of cheeses to which milk or whey
have been added. Has a lower cheese and
fat content. Soft texture and a milder
flavor than regular processed cheeses
due to a higher moisture content.
1 ounce = 90 calories.

Port du Salut   -A creamy yellow cheese with a mellow to robust flavor. Has a buttery texture with small holes. Comes in wedges or wheels. Originated in France.

Pot Cheese   -This is a similar cheese to cottage cheese, but is drier and never creamed. It is usually made without salt and additives.

Provolone   -Has a light creamy interior with a light brown or golden yellow surface. The flavor is mellow and has a smooth texture. May have coloring added and is usually salted or smoked. It may also be produced from bleached milk which will reduce the vitamin potencies. Originated in Italy.

Ricotta   -A normally white cheese with a somewhat sweet, nutlike flavor. Usually made from cow's milk, whole or partially skimmed with or without whey and resembles cottage cheese.

Romano   -A yellow-white cheese with a greenish-black surface and a sharp flavor. It has a hard granular texture and is available in wedges or grated. Similar to Parmesan but made with whole milk giving it a higher fat content. May contain a number of preservatives. The best is made from sheep's milk. Originated in Italy.

Roquefort -Has a white creamy interior and may be marbled or streaked with bluish veins of mold. Usually made of sheep's milk and has a peppery flavor with a semi-soft crumbly texture. It is available in wedges and is usually free of additives. Originated in France.

Stilton -Has a creamy white inside with streaks of blue-green mold. Made with cow's milk and milder than Gorgonzola or Roquefort. The texture is semi-soft and is more crumbly than Blue cheese. Available in wedges and oblongs. Originated in England.

Swiss -A light yellow cheese that has a sweet nut-like flavor and a smooth texture with a variety of different size holes. It has a good firm texture and is available in rectangular forms and slices. Originated in Switzerland. May use bleached milk to give it the yellow color. This will reduce the vitamin content. 1 ounce = 105 calories.

Tilsit -Has ivory to yellow semi-soft interior. Made from raw milk and ripened for about five months. 30-50% fat. Originated in Germany.

Chapter 11

Meat Facts

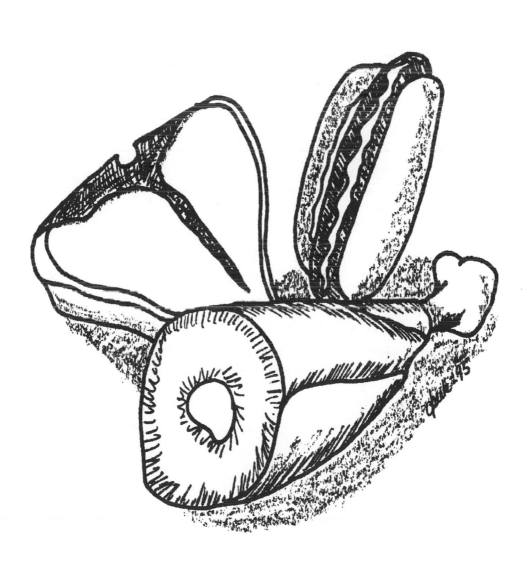

"DON'T BE THE EARLY BIRD WHO GETS THE WORM"

Only 1 in 1000 pigs are now found to contain the trichinosis parasite. However, I would still cook pork to an internal temperature of 160 degrees F. The parasite is killed at 137 degrees.

"EFFICIENCY EXPERT INFO"

Pigs are not an efficient source of protein. They require almost 8 pounds of grain and soy to produce 1 pound of meat. Cows require about 7 pounds and chickens less than 3 pounds.

"REAL BUMMER"

There are 1.3 billion head of cattle worldwide, which consume a third of the world's grain.

A BURGER BY ANY OTHER NAME

Argentina
Burgers are boiled and served with a fried egg on top of a piece of pumpernickel bread.

Germany
The ground beef is mixed with pieces of wet bread, onions, mustard and of course an egg has to be added.

Switzerland
Burgers are served American style but are always eaten with a knife and fork. Very civilized!

Korea
Add a unique touch of their own, kimchee, a mixture of pickled cabbage and very hot peppers.

Sweden
Burgers are called "pannbiff" which is beef mixed in a brown sauce with fried onions and of all things lingonberry preserves. Try it, you might like it!

A 4oz. serving of meat reduces to 3oz. after cooking, so plan accordingly.

Sweetbreads are a calf's thymus gland which helps the animal fight disease and disappears six months after they are born. Three ounces contain 21 grams of fat.

The latest 1994 statistics show that Americans love their beef. 91% eat beef regularly and the beef industry spends $42 million each year on advertising.

Americans consume approximately 11 ounces of meat per day, that calculates to approximately 250 pounds of beef annually, more than any other country in the world. The Japanese only eat 2 ounces of meat daily or approximately 46 pounds of beef annually.

Searing meat will not "lock in juices." It will, however, provide a crusty brown covering which is tasty.

Father's Day is the biggest beef eating day of the year, with over 80 million pounds consumed.

"WANTED, COW MASSEUR"
The Japanese are producing the world's most expensive beef. Kobe beef cattle are fed a diet of soybeans and beer and even given a daily massage. Kobe beef has 2-3 times the fat of prime U.S. beef.

Fall is the best time to find lower beef prices.

Meat grinders and cutting boards should be washed thoroughly after each use. Bacteria grows very quickly and may contaminate the next food.

"DON'T FENCE ME IN"
If you are troubled by meats turning grey when cooking, try cooking a smaller quantity the next time in the same size pot. Excess steam generated by overcrowding is the problem.

"RUDOLPHS IN TROUBLE"
Reindeer meat should be avoided if imported from Finland due to radiation contamination as a result of the 1986 Chernobyl nuclear disaster.

When buying meat, figure the cost per pound, a boneless cut usually cost less per serving.

To make a fatty roast look better, try refrigerating it after its cooked or until the fat solidifies, then remove the fat, baste and cook until re-heated.

Hamburgers will cook faster if you make a few punctures in them before cooking. This allows the heat to circulate more evenly.

Meat may sliced more thinly if it is partially frozen.

Tomatoes added to roasts will help tenderize them naturally. Tomatoes contain an acid that works well to break-down meats.

"FORE"
To eliminate bacon curling , try soaking the bacon in cold water for 2 minutes before frying. Dry well with paper towel. If they still curl, sprinkle with flour. If they still insist on curling poke some holes in them with your golf shoes or ?.

Meats should be stored in the refrigerator for no more than three days in the original wrapper.

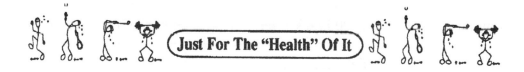

Just For The "Health" Of It

"NOT A GOOD CURE"
In order to cure ham, a solution of brine salts, sugar and of course a good dose of nitrites are injected into the ham. If the total weight goes up 8%, the label may read "Ham, with Natural Juices". If it goes up over 8% it will read "Water Added".

Choose bacon with the most meat. The higher nitrite levels are found in the fat.

Bacon should be cooked on paper towels in a microwave oven to reduce the nitrosamine levels.

If you can find it use nitrite-free bacon. Most imitation bacon products still contain nitrites.

The fat content in some turkey bacon products may be close to equaling the real thing, read your labels carefully.

Never re-freeze meats. That includes luncheon meats and hot dogs. The salt content favors the development of rancidity.

Always completely cook meats, never leave them partially uncooked until another day.

The E. coli bacteria that may cause illness or even death normally resides only on the surface of meats, steaks or roasts grilled on both sides normally will kill any bacteria. Hamburger is another story since when it is ground the outside becomes the inside and a higher temperature is needed to cook the inside of the meat thoroughly.

Very Frank Furter Information

1937 Frankfurter	1990 Frankfurter	Grams Of Protein(3 1/2oz)
Fat..........19%	Fat.........28%	Frankfurter (2).......10
Protein......20%	Protein.....12%	Poultry...............26
No technology to	Technology was	Fish..................25
keep extra fat	developed which	Lean beef, pork, veal.24
and extra water	keeps added fat	Canned tuna...........17
from separating	and water from	
from ground meat.	separating from	
	ground meat.	

Most hot dogs contain large amounts of "edible offal" which may include animal skins, snouts, ears, esophagi, bone and etc., etc.

The best quality hot dog are Kosher, which contain only pure muscle meat. However, even though they don't contain edible offal they still have nitrites.

Bologna may contain up to 30% fat and 10% water.

Pork sausage and breakfast sausage may contain up to 50% fat.

If hot dogs are labeled "All Meat" or "All Beef" they must contain at least 85% meat or beef. The "All Meat" variety can contain a blend of beef, pork, chicken or turkey and of course, edible offal.

Smoked meats should be refrigerated.

Lean veal can have as little as one-tenth the fat as lean beef. Cholesterol content is the same.

Ground meats (hamburger and hot dogs) are prone to a process called "self-oxidation." The more surface of the meat you expose to oxygen, the faster the meat will deteriorate.

"HAVE A GOOD BREAKDOWN"

Meat that has been cooked, (the more well done the better) the more easily broken down and digested to a partial molecular breakdown. This only takes place the longer the meat is cooked, unless it is marinated or tenderized in a papaya-based product.

If meats are cooked only to medium-well (170°F.) it will increase the B1 availability by 15% over well done beef (185°F.).

Small cuts of beef will spoil faster and should not be kept in the refrigerator without freezing for more than 2-3 days. Liver, sweetbreads, cubed meats or marinated meats should be used within a day or frozen.

Amino acids, the building blocks of protein are best absorbed and utilized if they come from beef, approximately 90% absorption rate. Legumes are next with a rate of 80% with grains and vegetables at about 60-88%.

Remember when beef or hamburger is labeled "75% lean" it is still 25% fat content, which is a lot of fat. Since fat has twice as many calories as lean beef, a hamburger patty may be as high as 70% fat.

Beware of the words "lean" and "extra lean" on ground beef. When a steak is labeled "lean" it cannot have more than 10% fat, "extra lean" no more than 5% fat. However, ground beef has different standards and when labeled "lean" or "extra lean" can have as much as 22% fat.

Veal has less fat than any meat and usually comes from young milk-fed calves. It is more costly but has less hormones and is very tender.

Never eat raw meat of any type. Cooking destroys many toxins.

Three ounces of hamburger will supply you with twice the fat as lean beef (top sirloin).

Hormones are fed to almost all beef and fowl that are purchased from a supermarket. They are used to speed up the animal growth. Thus requiring less time from birth to marketable size. This means less food needed to raise them; it also means we are subjected to consuming meats that may contain hormones, the effect of which, on humans, are still under study.

One pound of charcoal barbecued steak contains as much carcinogens (cancer forming agent) as the smoke in 15 cigarettes. The dripping fat on the charcoal causes a chemical substance called a benzopyrene to be released and is found in the black coating on the meat. Wrap the meat in foil for protection.

The best hamburger is made by choosing the leanest piece of round steak you can find, having the butcher cut off all visible fat and grind it through the grinder twice. Grinding twice will break the fat into smaller globules, allowing more to be lost in the cooking process.

"IN THE DOG HOUSE"
Hot dogs contain less protein in 3 ½ ounces than any other meat source. It also contains high quantities of edible offal and a good dose of nitrites.

Hot dogs may contain up to 56% water and up to 3% powdered bone, if listed on the ingredient list.

45% of all-meat hot dogs may consist of water, fat and additives.

Corn syrup is found in most hot dogs.

Pork sausage and breakfast sausage may contain up to 50% fat.

Lower grades of beef, such as standard and commercial are lower in fat, perfectly safe and just as nutritious as the more expensive choice and prime cuts. Their protein to fat ratio is much higher, due to the lower fat content. However, unless your buying hamburger, tenderization will probably be needed.

If meat is prepared several hours before cooking, it should be refrigerated and wrapped loosely, allowing air to circulate around it.

Meat consumed in large quantities can inhibit the absorption of the mineral manganese.

It takes 100 grams of beef to equal 20 grams of protein.

Hamburger will be found in a variety of grades and contains the highest percentage of saturated fat of any meat. Hamburger will be found graded "Lean," "Extra Lean," and even "Extra, Extra Lean." All of these will still have more fat than the ground round steak.

Bacon substitutes such as Sizzlean still contain sodium nitrite.

If you must eat luncheon meats, try to choose ones that are made from chicken or turkey and have the lowest percentage of fat content. Remember, they still contain nitrites.

Rotisserie-cooked meats and poultry will contain less fat than those that are fried or cooked in their own juices.

Ready-to-cook meat products will usually have more fat than the same meats in the meat cases. The market or manufacturer can get away with leaving more fat on the meat.

Ground pork products should be kept frozen for no longer than 2 months.

Meat tenderizers are usually made from extracts of papaya, pineapple or lemon.

Place leftover stews into individual baking dishes or small casserole dishes, cover with pie crust or dumpling mix and bake.

Herbs That Are Best Suited For Certain Meats

Beef..........Basil, thyme, sweet marjoram, summer
savory rosemary.

Veal.........Summer savory, rosemary, thyme, basil, tarragon.

Lamb.........Mint, summer savory, sweet marjoram,
dill, rosemary.

Pork.........Sweet marjoram, thyme, sage, chives,
basil.

Poultry.......Thyme, sage, tarragon, sweet marjoram,
chevil, summer savory.

Fish.........Chevil, fennel, sage, parsley, dill,
sweet marjoram, basil, chives.

"FIXER UPPER"
If you scorch meat, soak it in a towel in hot water and wring out as best as possible. Cover the meat and let it stand for five minutes before scraping off burned area with a knife.

 Chef's Secrets

To prevent the fat from splattering when frying sausage, try flouring them lightly.

Hamburger fried in catsup gives it a barbecue flavor and adds sugar.

If you place a small piece of ice inside your meatballs before browning, they will be moist.

"SAVE WEAR AND TEAR ON YOUR GOLF SHOES"
Flat beer and hard cider are excellent for tenderizing beef. Their fermentation qualities do the trick.

When making hamburger patties, chill them first and they will be easier to form.

To bread meats, shake them in a brown bag with flour and seasonings.

Always cut meats across the grain when possible, they will be easier to eat and have a better appearance.

To bring out the flavor in a ham loaf, add a small amount of rosemary.

To remove a ham rind easily, slit the rind lengthwise before it is placed in the pan. As it bakes, the rind will pull away and can be removed.

When cooking pork buttes, rub the meaty side with table salt an hour before cooking to draw any water in the pork to the surface. This will help tenderize and flavor the pork.

To avoid your meatloaf from cracking, try rubbing a small amount of cold water on the top and sides before placing it in the oven.

When frying meat, try sprinkling paprika over it and it will turn golden brown.

Place dry onion soup mix in the bottom of your roaster pan, when you remove the roast, add 1 can of mushroom soup and you will have a good brown gravy.

Another way to bread meats is to dip them into slightly beaten eggs with a little milk added, then into seasoned bread crumbs. Then place into the refrigerator for 40 minutes to allow the breading to adhere before cooking.

Liver will be more tender if soaked in milk or tomato juice and placed in the refrigerator for 1-2 hours before cooking.

When tenderizing your meat, try spreading a small amount of flour on the surface to help retain the juices.

To stop sausages from splitting open when they are fried, try making a few small punctures in the skins when they are cooking.

If you want cooked meat to remain tender, leave it in its own cooking juices when it is stored.

If venison is soaked in ginger ale overnight it will eliminate the gamey flavor.

Placing meats in white vinegar and water for 5 minutes will make it more tender.

To reduce the shrinkage in sausages, they should be boiled for 3-5 minutes before frying.

For a too-salty ham, partially bake it and drain all the juices. Pour a small bottle of ginger ale over it and let it bake until done.

To keep fat from splattering when frying bacon, sprinkle a small amount of salt in the frying pan.

"THE BOTTOM LINE"
When you figure the cost per meal of a meat portion, consider the weight of the fat and bone. It may account for as much as 30% of the cost.

When preparing meatloaf, place a slice or two of Sizzelean under the uncooked loaf, to keep it from sticking to the bottom of the pan.

Make meatloaf in muffin tins for individual servings that will be ready in only 15-20 minutes in a pre-heated 375 degree oven.

"TENDER BUNS"
When cooking hot dogs, try using the top of a double boiler to warm your buns.

To separate bacon slices, place the package in the microwave for a few seconds.

For a real treat, try mixing seasoned stuffing mix with hamburgers.

When re-heating meats, try placing the pieces in a casserole dish with lettuce leaves in between the slices. The slices will be tender and moist.

"STALKING THE PREY"
To keep lamb chops, pork chops or even poultry from sticking to the bottom of a pan, try placing a few stalks of celery in the bottom to act as a rack to hold them. This will also add flavor and moisture while they are cooking.

"HOW DRY I AM"
If the hamburger is too dry, due to a reduced fat content, try adding one stiffly beaten egg white for each pound of hamburger or adding one large grated onion for each 1 ½ pounds, or you could make the patties with a tablespoon of cottage cheese in the center. Instant potato flakes will also work well.

We get one pound of beef for every 16 pounds of grain.

In an average week, Americans eat 350 million hot dogs. This equates to a hot dog 60 feet thick and the length of a soccer field.

===

Government Meat Grading

U.S.D.A. Prime - Most tender cut, highest fat content.
U.S.D.A. Choice - Very tender cut, most common sold.
U.S.D.A. Good - Less fat, needs tenderizing.
U.S.D.A. Commercial - From older animals, tougher.
U.S.D.A. Utility, Cutter and Canner - Lowest grades.

Hamburger is the most popular meat purchased in the U.S. It contains more saturated fat per ounce than any other saleable meat.

===

"YUK, YUK"
Even though hamburger is sold as 100% pure beef, legally it can still contain "edible offal" which consists of beef lungs, hearts, lips, bone, ears, snouts and esophagi.

"DON'T GET BURNED"
A beef brisket is done when the fat starts to roll off, but will be overcooked if you can pull the fat off with your fingers.

The Skinniest Six Cuts Of Meat

Eye Of The Round
143 Calories
4.2gr. of Fat
1.5gr. Sat. Fat
59mg. Chol.

Top Round
153 Calories
4.2gr. of Fat
1.4gr. Sat Fat
72mg. Chol

Round Tip
157 Calories
5.9gr. of Fat
2.1gr. Sat. Fat
69mg. Chol

Top Sirloin
165 Calories
6.1gr. of Fat
2.4gr. Sat. Fat
76mg. Chol.

Top Loin
176 Calories
8.0gr. of Fat
3.1gr. Sat. Fat
65mg. Chol.

Tenderloin
179 Calories
8.5gr. of Fat
3.2gr. Sat. Fat
72mg. Chol

Americans average 75 pounds of beef, 44 pounds of pork and 40 pounds of chicken per year. This amounts to ½ pound of meat every day.

Gelatin comes from cattle skin and bones which are an excellent source of protein, but is missing two essential amino acids.

Beef should not be seasoned with any type of salt until it is 3/4 cooked. This will help retain the flavor and make it juicier.

When cooking (boiling) tough beef, add a small amount of vinegar to help tenderize it.

"A TENDER LITTLE MORSEL"
The most tender chuck steak is the first cut, which may also be called the blade cut. If you can see a small piece of white cartilage near the top of the steak, you have found the first cut.

"MORE TENDER LITTLE MORSELS"
The eye of the round steak is normally cut into two pieces. Best to buy the roast that has the same diameter ends. This will be the first cut and the most tender.

Always buy round steak in uneven "oyster-cut" shapes. These will be the first cuts and will be nearer the sirloin.

When buying lamb and you are only purchasing half a leg, make sure that it weighs at least 4 pounds. Any smaller and it will have a higher amount of bone and less meat.

To prevent sausages from shrinking, roll them in flour before frying.

An excellent substitute for bread crumbs is quick-rolled oats as a coating for meat loaf.

Place a few grapes in the pan when cooking venison for a special flavor treat.

15 billion pounds of beef were sold through retail outlets in 1990 compared to 19 billion pounds in 1976. Over the same period chicken sales increased from 43 pounds per person to 63 pounds per person.

To make beef easier to slice before cooking, freeze it for 45 minutes first.

SECRETS OF THE INNER COW

The 8 main cuts of beef are; shank, flank, brisket, chuck, round, rib, plate and loin.

The secondary name is the retail cut, such as sirloin, porterhouse, top round, etc. and explains the way the cow was cut up.

The tenderness of beef depends on how it was cut up.

The toughest cuts of beef are pot roasts and are cut from the cow's neck. These are also the least expensive.

Chuck Cuts
These usually need to be cooked for long periods of time in a liquid for tenderizing.

Rib Cuts
These include rib steaks, rib roasts or back ribs and should be cooked slowly in an oven or grilled for approximately 20-30 minutes per pound. Best to use a marinade or sauce.

Loin Cuts
These come from behind the ribs and are the most tender cuts, such as tenderloin roasts and the better steaks, such as porterhouse.

Round Cuts
These are top round, eye of the round, bottom round, etc. and should be braised and roasted similar to pot roasts.

Flank and Plate Cuts
These include flank steaks and skirt steaks. They are long and thin cuts and are best for stir-frying.

Brisket Cuts

Located in the area behind the cow's front leg or from the leg itself and are usually tough and need extensive cooking in a liquid for a considerable time.

For best results when cooking a roast, rotate it 1/4 turn every 20-25 minutes.

Wild game will be lower in fat and cholesterol. Best are venison, wild boar (not a party animal), pheasant, buffalo and elk. Prices are very high on some of these meats.

There are 1.6 million beef producers. They are for the most part on the "honor system" regarding hormonizing cattle to increase growth.

The USDA normally monitors only one to two percent of all beef carcasses for illegal drug residues, or in about 1.5 pounds out of the 74 pounds each person consumed in 1990. By the time a problem is found it is too late to recall the beef anyway, its been sold. The biggest problem is in the retired (older) cattle that are to be used in hamburger, soups, pot pies and of course our favorite TV dinners.

Thaw meats as quickly as possible, preferably under refrigeration, then cook immediately.

The approximate percentage of calories from fat in beef:

    USDA Prime...................50%
    USDA Choice.................39%
    USDA Select/Good.........30%

The best lamb comes from New Zealand (spring lamb). Since it against the law to use hormones and tenderizers, the meat is safer than most countries.

There are five grades of lamb, Prime, Choice, Good, Utility and Cull. Prime never makes it to the markets and is only sold to restaurants. Choice and Good are usually available.

Fresh beef is cherry-red in color. The darker the beef the older the animal. Fat should be white not yellow.

Beef is the most readily available meat, but is usually the most tainted.

To cook ground meat for specialty dishes, try crumbling the meat into a microwave-safe colander and place it over a small bowl. The fat will drain out into the bowl.
A cow is more valuable for its milk, cheese, butter, yogurt, etc. than it is for its beef.

When cooking any type of meat always use a meat thermometer.

Thaw all meats in the refrigerator for maximum safety.

 Chef's Secrets

To keep your meatballs from falling apart when cooking, try placing them into the refrigerator for 20 minutes before cooking.

"WATCH FOR THESE"
Special words are used by supermarkets to make you believe you are getting better grades; "Premium," "Quality," "Select Cut," "Market Choice," "Prime Cut," etc.

High meat intake may cause excessive calcium losses through the urine.

Ratings of Non-Vegetable Proteins:

1. Fish
2. Turkey
3. Chicken
4. Bacon
5. Luncheon Meats
6. Deer
7. Lamb
8. Goat
9. Beef

Leftover cooked meat can be kept 4-5 days in the refrigerator.

Annual consumption of red meat in the United States has dropped from 132 pounds per person annually in 1970 to 112 pounds in 1994.

Chapter 12

Fowl Facts

The NAS (National Academy of Sciences) released a study in 1992 showing that toxic contamination of poultry poses a potential health risk . Most of the toxic chemicals and pathogens are largely undetected using the present poultry inspection procedures.

USDA food inspectors have increased their inspections of chicken slaughtering plants by over 50% in the last 10 years. We still have a long way to go, they have reduced the number of inspectors almost 30% in the last 10 years.

Americans consume over 6 billion chickens per year, of which possibly 2 billion are contaminated.

Chicken farming is a $14 billion dollar industry.

Studies by the National Academy of Science showed that 48% of food poisonings is caused by contaminated chicken. This affects approximately one in 50 persons in the U.S. annually.

THE SAFEST POULTRY IS KOSHER POULTRY:

Fact - During processing, defeathering takes place in cold water only, never in hot or warm water. Non-Kosher chickens and turkeys are always processed in water heated between 125° and 132° which is when bacterial growth is at its highest level. The hot water opens the pores and allows entry of every bit of undesirable matter that is floating in the hot bloody water of the communal bath.

Fact - Kosher poultry is soaked and submerged for 30 minutes in very cold water, then hand salted inside and out and allowed to hang for one hour to remove any remaining blood.

Fact - After salting the birds, they are rinsed 3 separate times to remove all the salt.

Fact - The taste is clean and most people who eat chicken on a regular basis will immediately tell the difference.

Fact - Many Kosher processed chickens never make it to the marketplace even when passed by government inspectors. The quality control differs from most other processors.

Compare nutrition labels when purchasing ground turkey. You may find that some brands have almost as much fat as lean beef.

A 3 pound chicken will yield about 2 1/2-3 cups of cut-up chicken.

A 5 ounce can of boned chicken will yield about 1/2 cup of cut-up chicken.

In a recent 1995 study 8 out of 10 people called the "stuff" inside a turkey "stuffing" and 20% called it "dressing." The 20% were all over age 65.

A lower to moderate cooking temperature will produce a juicier chicken, since more fat and moisture are retained.

To tenderize chicken and give it a unique flavor, try basting it with a small amount of white wine as it cooks.

Freeze leftover chicken broth in ice cube trays, then keep the cubes in a plastic bag in the freezer. When a recipe calls for chicken bouillon cubes, thaw out in the defrost cycle in the microwave.

Whether chicken is fresh or defrosted never leave in the refrigerator for more than 2 days. Same for hamburger.

To save dollars, purchase whole chickens and cut them up. Freeze the sections that you want together.

Ground poultry in supermarkets usually contain dark meat, skin and a high amount of fat.

Ground poultry should be labeled 98% fat free by weight.

A "Wellness Burger" still contains 30% fat by calories.

To thaw frozen chicken, place it in a pan of cold water with at least 1/4 cup of salt added. You will notice the improved flavor and have a cleaner chicken.

The average American ate 20 pounds of turkey in 1991 and 25 pounds in 1994. In 1930 it was only 2 pounds.

When stuffing your holiday turkey, try placing a piece of cheesecloth inside the cavity before adding the stuffing. When you remove the cloth, all the stuffing will come out at one time. Markets are now selling a "stuffing sac," one sac costs more than enough cheesecloth purchased in bulk to do 10 birds.

Turkey is eaten at dinner time over 50% of the time.

Turkey is usually a better buy than chicken, less bone and waste in proportion to its size.

When you buy large chickens they are older birds and will usually be tougher. Try slow cooking to make them more tender.

Dental floss makes an excellent truss for a fowl.

Turkeys should be left out of the oven 20-30 minutes covered with tin foil before carving. Hot birds are too difficult to cut properly. If you must, then use an electric knife or a very sharp bread knife.

Never buy a chicken on a Monday. It is likely you'll get one that wasn't purchased over the weekend.

Defrost a chicken by soaking in cold water, this will draw out any blood residues and will leave the breast very white.

Chef's Secrets

After flouring a chicken, chill for one hour. The coating will adhere better during frying.

If you add a few slices of lemon to stewing chickens they will be more tender.

Try baking your "fried" chicken. Bread as you normally would then baste with orange juice to keep it moist and enhance your normal seasonings.

If you rub the skin of a turkey or other fowl with white vermouth it will make the skin a glossy brown color.

Have you ever wondered how the restaurants serve a very tender, moist chicken breast all the time? They submerge the breast in buttermilk for 3-4 hours under refrigeration before cooking.

If you must baste a chicken, never use butter. Just place a few bacon strips across the breast, works great, but also adds fat. Turkey bacon might be a good substitute.

Chickens should bear a shield shaped grade mark carrying the designation "U.S. Grade A", "U.S. Grade B", or "U.S. Grade C".

If the U.S. Grade stamp does not appear on the chicken, it is probably labeled by the supermarket as "Premium" or "Superior" and is in all actuality U.S. Grade B or C.

U.S. Grade A chickens are sold as fresh in supermarkets. U.S. Grades B & C are used for frozen dinners and canned products since they are more blemished.

One large chicken slaughtering plant may use up to 100 million gallons of water daily. This is equal to a city of 25,000 people.

Don't buy birds that are injected with a basting solution. You are just paying for extra fat.

A 3 pound chicken is raised on 6 pounds of feed, using hormones, of course.

Broilers and fryers come to market 7-10 weeks after they hatch.

A 3 pound chicken will provide approximately 1 pound 5 ounces of edible meat. It may be more expensive to buy a whole chicken than the parts.

If turkey salad is made, wait until fowl is fully cooked before adding any type of salad dressing.

Cook all poultry to a center temperature of 185°F.

A yellow chicken doesn't necessarily mean a healthier more nutritious chicken when compared to a pale one. Yellow skin results in the amount of yellow corn found in chicken feed. Some suppliers of feed also add substances which contain yellow pigment. Marigold petals are known to give chickens a healthy sheen.

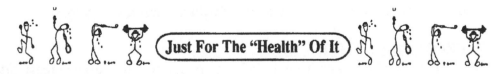

Just For The "Health" Of It

The USDA reports that chickens today are getting fatter. In fact, today's poultry is bred to reach market weight in 6-8 weeks. This is half the time it previously took! This, however, has resulted in a disproportionate increase in body fat.

Dark meat turkey has a higher fat level, 4 grams of fat or more per 3 1/2 oz.

The poultry skin and the fat just under the skin have the highest percentage of total fat and cholesterol.

Remove all chicken-fat globules that are visible inside the chicken.

Americans are now eating 61 pounds of poultry annually compared to only 34 pounds in 1970.

Never stuff a turkey or other fowl with warm stuffing and leave overnight, even if refrigerated, always keep the stuffing separate and stuff before cooking.

Never leave gravy, stuffing or cooked fowl at room temperature for more than 30-45 minutes before refrigerating.

A 3 1/2 oz. serving of white meat turkey without the skin contains only 115 calories and one gram of fat which is approximately 10% less than white meat chicken.

Turkeys reach maturity in 14 to 22 weeks. They are more tender than chickens and have proportionally more breast meat.

"A FOWL SITUATION"
Most chickens in the U.S. are raised in giant coop farms holding more than 10,000 birds. Each bird is housed in a box and will have feed available with a light on so that they can eat 24 hours a day.

If you eat chicken in a foreign country you will probably notice the difference in the flavor. Most foreign countries do not allow fowls to be raised under the conditions that the U.S. fowls are raised under.

When stuffing a turkey, try sealing the opening with a small raw potato.

"VIEW FROM THE OTHER SIDE"
To keep white meat on a turkey from drying out, try cooking the turkey breast-side down, then turn it right-side up for the last hour. Juices will not buildup in this period of time and the bird will be easy to turn, especially if you use a "V" rack.

"GETTING BUFFALOED"

An order of chicken wings (buffalo wings) may supply as much as 30 grams of fat, more than half the fat you should be consuming in an 1800 calorie daily intake.

Chicken will keep longer if re-wrapped in wax paper instead of the plastic wrap used by the markets

A CHICKEN "YOLK" OR TWO

If the odor of a fresh chicken is offensive, try giving the bird a massage with the juice of 1/2 lemon and 1/4 teaspoon of salt. The bird will enjoy this and it will totally remove the odor.

Use poultry shears to de-bone a fowl, its better than hacking it to pieces.

A significant number of the poultry labeled "fresh" has been frozen and defrosted. This may affect the quality of the product.

After working with raw poultry, wash your hands, the utensils used and the surface before placing any other food on it. Poultry can be contaminated with a number of bacteria.

One of the easiest ways to singe a fowl is to saturate a wad of cotton with rubbing alcohol. Place it on the end of a short wire, and light it. This will never leave any black marks.

A quick way to stuff small poultry is to use salad tongs to insert the stuffing.

One of the biggest chicken farmers in the United States ships out approximately 23 million chickens weekly.

38 million chickens are processed in the United States in one day according to the National Broiler Council.

"GET A GRIP ON"
Use white cotton gloves to remove fat from inside chickens and turkeys, however, if you use your hands they are more easily washed for reuse.

Americans averaged 66 pounds of chicken annually in 1992.

A free-range chicken has approximately 11 - 24% fat compare to a standard supermarket bird at 15 - 18%.

Breast meat on migratory fowls is dark. The reason its white on the supermarket birds is that they don't fly and exercise.

"NEWS YOU CAN NEVER USE"
There are 426 chickens per person in Arkansas.

4.9 billion pounds of chicken are sold each year, deep fried by fast food outlets.

Almost 1/3 of the nations meat consumption is chicken.

95% of chickens sold in the U.S. are broilers or fryers, different name, same chicken.

In 1989 chicken farmers purchased almost $300 million worth of animal antibiotics.

"A REAL FOWL FACT"
Americans consume over 6 billion chickens per year, of which possibly 2 billion are contaminated.

Poultry Hotline - 1 (800)535-4555

Chapter 13

Fathoms of Fish

Try not to eat the skin or fat on fish. Most contaminants will be found in these areas.

If you marinate fish always do it in the refrigerator, never at room temperture, fish deteriorate very quickly at room temperture.

"BE SAFE NOT SORRY"
A "packed under federal inspection" (PUFI) label on the package means that the seafood has been processed and packaged in the presence of a federal inspector.

"SEAFOOD SAUNA"
To steam fish, place the fish in a microwave-safe (plain, no colored design) paper towel. Moisten under water and microwave for about 5 minutes.

"SKIP THE DETERGENT"
At the Montreal Expo '67 Eskimo women demonstrated how they cooked salmon in a dishwasher.

Fish should be labeled "Grade A."

"A WORD TO THE WISE"
If you see a seafood product with "USG Inspected" on the label it is not an authorized designation.

"A-10"
Petrale Sole is considered to be the highest quality fish for eating in the Pacific Ocean.

"EASY DOES IT"
Always cook fish at a low to moderate temperature to retain the moisture and preserve the tenderness. Never more than 350°F.

"AND AWAY SHE GOES"
If you doubt the freshness of a fish. place it in cold water, if it floats (or swims away) it has recently been caught.

"FISH SHAKE?"
Thaw frozen fish in milk. The milk draws out the frozen taste and provides a fresh caught flavor.

"NEW BAR DRINK"
If you soak oysters in club soda for about five minutes, they are usually more easily removed from the shells.

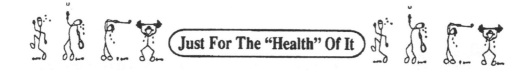

Just For The "Health" Of It

"PESKY LITTLE CRITTERS"
You should refrain from tasting meat, poultry or fish until the cooking has been completed. Parasites may not be dead and infestations have been known to occur from partially cooked fish especially.

Consumption of seafood in the United States has only risen from an annual consumption in 1970 of 12 pounds to 15 pounds in 1994. The contamination problem is a cause of concern to many.

Depending on the species 11-27% of the total fat in fish and shellfish is saturated. This can be compared to 37% in pork and 48% in most beef.

"THE FISHING LINE"
If you're going to the Caribbean, Florida or Hawaii and plan on eating tropical fish, it would be best to call the fish safety hotline to help you avoid "ciguatera" poisoning. They will tell you the current fish with problems.

FISH HOTLINE 1 (305)361-4619

Eating raw shellfish may cause viral and bacterial diseases. Most problems have been caused by shellfish caught in sewage polluted waters on the East Coast.

A regular course of fish 3-4 times per week will help keep you supplied with essential nucleic acids, DNA and RNA.

Due to contamination of fish in general, pregnant woman should not eat fish of any type more than twice per week.

A single 3 1/2 ounce serving of sardines is higher in calcium and phosphorus than a glass of milk. Sardines also contain vitamin D to assist the calcium in working properly.

A 100 gram serving of sardines provides up to 53% of your minimum requirement of protein. More than the same weight of T-Bone Steak.

New evidence shows that eating as little as one serving of fish per week can significantly reduce your risk of heart disease.

All shellfish are naturally high in sodium.

Bonita, a substitute for tuna and swordfish from the Pacific Ocean has been found to contain high levels of PCB's.

A high fish diet may aide in reducing the effects from increased salt intake.

"AH SO"
Sushi may contain larva of a parasite roundworm. Fish must be cooked to an internal temperature of 140° F or frozen for three days at -50° F to kill larva. Susceptible fish include; Mackerel, Herring, Squid, Sardines, Bonita, Salmon, Sea Trout and Porgy.

A frequent trip to the sushi bar may leave you short of vitamins thiamine and B1. Raw fish contains a substance that destroys these vitamins.

White Croakers are one of the most popular fish sold in markets on the west coast. They have been found to contain the highest levels of DDT and PCB's of any fish.

The safest fish to eat are halibut, sole, skipjack tuna, commercially raised trout and turbot.

Since most people do not eat large amounts of fish on a daily basis, the levels of contaminants that are consumed are negligible, and therefore you should not give up eating fish.

Mollusks, Clams and Oysters are "filter feeders" and may build up concentrations of any toxins present in water. Hepatitis has increased recently, resulting from shellfish caught in areas contaminated by human sewage. Cook all shellfish for protection against contaminants.

Shellfish live by filtering 15-20 gallons of water a day.

"BUYER BEWARE"
60% of all fish eaten in the United States comes from 116 foreign countries, many of which have poor sanitation conditions. Only 5% are actually inspected by U.S. Food & Drug.

"IT'S A BIRD, IT'S A PLANE, NO IT'S A FISH INSPECTOR"
The United States has approximately 2500 fish processing plants, 70,000 fishing ships and less than 200 inspectors who would have to be faster than a speeding bullet to do even an adequate job.

Fish that feed on the bottom of lakes, such as carp, and high-fat fish such as bluefish and bass have a higher incidence of contamination than others.

Cooking fish removes many of the contaminants which are usually found in the fat.

Clams and oysters are simple to open, if first washed with cold water, then placed into a plastic bag and kept in the freezer for 1/2 hour.

"CLAMMING UP"
Throw away any clams that do not open when steamed or boiled they are dead and probably contaminated.

"RELAXATION TECHNIQUE"

Clams may also be dropped into boiling water and let stand for a few minutes. This will relax their muscle and make them easier to open with a knife or beer can opener.

How To Choose Fresh Fish

Skin - Should be firm and elastic. Skin should be shiny and color not faded. The skin should spring back when a finger pressure is exerted.

Eyes - Bright, clear and somewhat bulging. Stale fish eyes are usually cloudy and sunken.

Scales - Tight to skin, not falling off. Bright and shiny.

Gills - No slime, reddish pink and clean looking. Not grayish.

Odor - Not overly strong. Fish should never smell "fishy." The smell is from a chemical compound called "trimethylamine". It is produced from the deterioration and breakdown of the fish.

How To Choose A Frozen Fish

Odor -   Should have little or no odor. Don't buy if
                         they have strong fish odor.

Skin -   Should be solidly frozen and have no
                         discolorizations.

Wrappings   Moisture-proof with no air spaces between
                         fish and wrapping.

The best seafood is the freshest seafood you can get, no more than 2-3 days out of water.

Total Fat In 3 1/2 Ounces Of Fish/Shellfish:

Bass	2.4 grams lean
Bluefish	6.5 grams lean
Butterfish	8.5 grams fat
Cod	4.6 grams lean
Flounder	3.9 grams lean
Grouper	2.8 grams lean
Haddock	4.9 grams lean
Hake	5.2 grams lean
Halibut	4.3 grams lean
Herring	9.0 grams fat
Mackerel	13.8 grams fat
Mullet	3.0 grams lean
Ocean Perch	2.8 grams lean
Pollack	4.2 grams lean
Pompano	9.5 grams fat
Porgie	10.4 grams fat
Red Snapper	4.5 grams lean
Salmon	8.6 grams fat

Shark	1.9 grams lean and mean
Sole	3.3 grams lean
Striped Bass	8.3 grams fat
Swordfish	2.2 grams lean
Tuna (bluefish)	6.5 grams lean
Crab	1.3 grams lean
Shrimp	1.1 grams lean
Oyster	2.4 grams lean

Supermarkets can offer up to 200 varieties of fish, some may be fresh.

Cooking fish should be more concerned with retaining flavor than tenderness as with meats. Fish is naturally tender.

Market Forms Of Fish

Whole Fish	- Marketed just as it is caught.
Drawn Fish	-Only entrails removed. Still needs cleaning.
Dressed Fish	- Scaled and entrails removed. Ready to cook.
Fish Steaks	- Slices cut crosswise.
Fish Fillets	- Boneless pieces cut from the sides.
Butterfly Fillets	- Two sides cut away from the backbone.
Cured Fish	- Cured by smoking, drying, salting or pickling.
Cold-Smoked	- Cured and partially dried. Won't keep long.
Hot-Smoked	- Partially or wholly cooked. Needs freezing.
Dried Fish	- Air or heat dried and salted. Lasts forever.
Salted Fish	- Dry-salted or brine-cured. Can be pickled.

"DO THE TWIST"
When purchasing live lobsters there should be movement in the legs.

Squid, shark and snails rate among the highest foods Americans hate the most.

The size of shrimp will not affect their quality. They should be tender and firm if cooked properly.

"PEEK-A-BOO"
Mussels, clams and oysters should be alive when purchased. Gaping shells should close when tapped. Discard dead ones.

"FISHERMAN'S FACT"
Minnows will stay alive longer if you add 6-8 drops of iodine to the water they are transported in.

THE "NOSE" KNOWS
If you wash your hands in cold water before handling fish your hands won't smell fishy.

To eliminate the fishy odor from a pan, try placing a small amount of vinegar in the pan before washing.

Cooked crab shells should be bright red in color (not orange) and have little or no odor. They should always be displayed on a bed of ice.

Frozen fish can be skinned easier than fresh ones.

Americans are eating more fish than ever, approximately 18 pounds per person in 1990. 21 pounds per person in 1994.

Aquaculture is fast becoming a major protein food industry in the United States.

The best eating fish and the safest are: Aquaculture raised Trout and Catfish, Halibut, Turbot, Skipjack, Sole and Pollack.

A small amount of grated onion added to the butter when cooking fish will add an excellent bit of flavor.

If you are planning on a fish barbecue, use the high-fat fish, they won't dry out as fast and will be juicer and more tasty.

Most fresh fish and shellfish are never inspected, make sure you are dealing with a quality fish market.

Never keep a shellfish in fresh water, it will kill them very quickly.

Try not to thaw frozen fish completely before cooking or it may make them very dry and mushy.

 Chef's Secrets

To eliminate the canned taste of shrimp, try soaking them for 10-15 minutes in a mixture of 2 tablespoons of vinegar and 1 teaspoon of sherry.

"CALL THE MASSEUR"
Lemon juice rubbed on fish before cooking will enhance the flavor and help maintain a good color.

The flavor of canned shrimp can be greatly improved if you soak the can in ice water for at least 1 hour before opening.

To de-vein shrimp, hold the shrimp under a slow stream of cold water and run the tip of an icepick down the back of the shrimp. This will clean the shrimp and leave it whole.

When frying fish sprinkle the bottom of the pan with a small amount of salt or use unsalted butter and the fish won't stick to the pan. Salted butter doesn't work well.

A small amount of grated onion added to the butter when cooking fish will add an excellent bit of flavor.

"A LITTLE TENDERNESS"
When making clam chowder, add the chopped clams during the last 15 minutes of cooking to avoid them from becoming mushy and tough.

When cooking fish wrapped in tin foil, add a sprig of dill and a lemon slice for a great taste treat.

When cooking shellfish, a heavily salted water will draw the sea salt out.

To make scaling a fish easier, try rubbing vinegar on the scales first.

When baking fish, try wrinkling up the tin foil before wrapping the fish. This will cause the fish to brown better and it won't stick to the foil.

Avoid making tough shrimp by first cooling the shrimp under very cold water for 1-2 minutes, then place them in a deep pot (not over the heat) with a small amount of salt, then cover them with rapidly boiling water, tightly covered. Large shrimp take approximately 5-7 minutes, average size are done in about 4 minutes.

Shark is an excellent eating fish, young ones are best.

The best tuna is labeled "white" and is albacore. Three other types are sold, namely "light", "dark", and "blended". The darker the tuna, the stronger the flavor and usually the oilier. These are mostly Skipjack and Bluefin.

SHELLFISH

Abalone- The edible portion is the foot, which is very tough and needs to be pounded into tenderness. Has been so overfished that they are becoming rare. The price is very high and they are considered the delicacy of shellfish.

Clams - Hard-shell are the most sought after. Soft-shell clams cannot close its shell because its neck sticks out too far. The largest soft-shell is the geoduck, which may weigh up to 3 pounds. Sea clams are usually used for canning or in packaged soups.

If you dig your own clams, you must purge them of sand and debris before eating. Allow the clams to stand 20-25 minutes in clear sea water. The water should be changed at least 3-4 times to be sure they are free of residues.

Crab - Blue crab is from the Atlantic and Gulf areas. Dungeness is caught in the Pacific Ocean. King and snow crab are caught in the north off the coast of Canada and Alaska. Stone crab comes from Florida.

Soft-shell crab comes in 4 sizes; "spiders" which are the bare legal size of 3 1/2 inches across, "hotel prime" at 4-4 1/2 inches, "prime" at 5-5 1/2 inches and "jumbo" at 6-7 inches across.

Crayfish - Small freshwater crustaceans. Louisiana produces about 20 million pounds a year. Similar to shrimp, all the meat is in the tail. Also called "crawdads."

Langostinos - A crustacean, sometimes sold as rock shrimp. Usually sold frozen and used mainly in soups and salads.

Lobster - Two main lobsters are sold in the United States they are: Maine and Spiney. The most prized Maine lobster is excellent tasting and more sought after. The Spiney lobster has most of the meat in the tail and has smaller claws.

The "Newburg" in lobster means that the recipe contains a cream and sherry mixture. Newburg pertains to an old Scottish fishing village.

Mussels - Mussel farming is becoming a popular business. They are raised on ropes, which keep them from the silty bottom, thus making them more cleaner and more salable. When -grown in this manner they are also twice the size of ordinary mussels.

Oyster - Over 90 million pounds are consumed worldwide. About 50% are now aquafarmed. The flavor and texture will vary depending on where they are harvested.

Scallops - A mollusk that dies very quickly when removed from the water. They should not be overcooked or will become tough. They are usually shucked at the time they are caught and placed on ice. There are over 400 varieties of sea scallops.

Shrimp - There are over 250 varieties of shrimp. They are classified as number of shrimp per pound. The jumbo shrimp should average 16 to 25 per pound, large shrimp average 20 to 32 per pound, medium shrimp average 28 to 40 per pound, while tiny ocean shrimp can average over 70 per pound. One pound of raw shrimp will yield 1/2 to 3/4 pound after cooking. Large shrimp are called "prawns."

White shrimp are milder in flavor and more expensive than brown. Brown feed more on algae and have a stronger iodine taste.

If shrimp has a slight ammonia smell, it is deteriorating.

The FDA has taken action against some firms that overbread shrimp to raise the weight and price.

Shrimp may have more cholesterol than any other shellfish but are very low in saturated fat.

"OFF WITH THEIR HEADS"
Shrimp with heads are more perishable than those without their heads.

"TALK ABOUT THINGS IN A SMALL PACKAGE"
A shrimp head contains almost all its organs including most of the digestive system.

The dark colored intestinal tube running down a shrimp's back is OK to eat as long as its cooked. However it may be a little gritty due to the bacteria and other residues of digestion. The bacteria is killed by cooking the shrimp.

Shrimp deteriorates very quickly and should be used the same day you purchase it, or at least no later then the next day. Never refreeze thawed shrimp, most of the shrimp you buy has been frozen. If you wish to keep it longer, buy it frozen solid.

Squid -   Usually not thought of as shellfish. Normally called "calamari." To keep it tender, don't cook it for more than 3 minutes. If stewing it, cook it for at least 15-20 minutes. The whole body and tentacles are edible. Squid has more cholesterol than shrimp.

SALTWATER FISH

Anchovy -   The majority of anchovies gathered in Southern California waters (250 million pounds) are ground up and sold as poultry feed. The average market size is 4-6 inches. Commercially, they are sold rolled or flat and are cured in olive oil and canned.

Chef's Secrets

If anchovies are too salty, try soaking them in tap water for 10-15 minutes, then store in the refrigerator for 30 minutes before using.

Angler - This category includes the Monkfish, Sea Devil, Bellyfish, Lotte and Goosefish. They are for the most part all low-fat with a firm texture. They can weigh from 2-25 pounds and only the tapered tail section is edible. Tastes similar to a lobster.

Barracuda - A moderate-fat fish that runs from 4-8 pounds. The only variety that is best for eating is the Pacific Barracuda which has an excellent taste. Great Barracudas are known for their toxicity.

Blue Fish - Usually weighs in at 3-6 pounds. Does not freeze well. When using, be sure to remove the dark strip of flesh running down its center. This may give the fish a strong undesirable flavor.

Butterfish - Also, known as Pacific Pompano or Dollar fish. It is a high-fat fish that usually weighs in at 1/4 to 1 pound. These are small fish that are usually cooked whole or smoked. A very fine textured fish.

Cod - The three main types are: Atlantic Cod, Pacific Cod and Scrod. They are a low-fat fish with a firm texture. The Atlantic is the largest variety and the Scrod is the smallest (a young cod). Available in many cuts; fillets, steaks, whole or dressed.

Croaker -   Varieties include; Atlantic Croaker, Redfish,
Spot, Kingfish, Corvina and Black Drum. All are
low-fat except Corvina. Size varies from 1/4
pound for the Spot to 30 pounds for the large
Redfish, a popular chowder fish.

Cusk -   A fish gaining popularity with a taste similar
to cod. Low-fat and excellent for stews and
soups. Weights in at 1 1/2 to 5 pounds. Sold as
fillets or whole.

Eel -   A firm-textured fish that may run up to 3 feet
long and has a tough skin that is removed prior
to cooking. More popular in Europe and Japan.

Flounder -   Also, called Sole. The most popular fish in the
United States. The varieties seem endless and
all are low-fat with a fine texture. Most are
found 1/2 to 3 pounds with some varieties
weighing in at up to 10 pounds. One of the best
eating fishes.

Grouper -   Can weigh in from 3-25 pounds and may be called
"Sea Bass." The skin is tough and should be
removed. It has a firm texture and may be
cooked in almost any manner.

Haddock -   A close relation to the Cod and usually weighs
in at 3-5 pounds. Smoked Haddock is known as
"Finnan Haddie."

Hake -   Usually caught in the Atlantic during summer
and early fall. It is a low-fat, firm textured
fish. Usually weighs in at 1-8 pounds and is
very mild flavored.

Halibut -   A flatfish that usually weighs in from 5-20 pounds. A low-fat very popular fish with a firm texture.

Herring -   A small 1/4 to 1 pound fish with a fine soft texture and is high-fat. Usually used for appetizers and sold pickled or smoked.

Mackerel -   Sold under a number of names, such as: Wahoo, Atlantic Mackerel, Pacific Jack, King Mackerel and Spanish Mackerel. A high-fat fish with a firm texture. A commonly canned fish.

Mahi Mahi -   Also, known as the "Dolphin Fish" or "Dorodo." However, it is no relation to the Dolphin nor does it look like a Dolphin. May weigh up to 40 pounds. Excellent eating fish.

Mullet -   The fat content will vary, but is usually a moderate to high fat fish with a firm texture. Has a mild nut-like flavor.

Ocean - Perch   A low-fat fish with a firm texture. Most is Perch imported from Iceland. Usually weighs in at 1/2 to 2 pounds and available fresh or frozen.

Orange - Roughy   One of the most popular fish sold. Imported from New Zealand and is low-fat with a firm texture. Available in 2-5 pound weights. Very similar to Sole but at a better price.

Pollack -   A close relative to Cod with a firm texture. Fresh usually weighs in at 4-12 pounds. Best when sold as fillets.

Pompano -   Rated as one of the best eating fishes. It has a moderate fat level and a firm texture. One of the more expensive fishes.

Porgy -   A firm textured, low-fat fish that usually   . weighs in at 1/2 to 2 pounds. Primarily caught in New England waters.

Red -
Snapper   Has a very rose-colored skin and red eyes. It is low-fat with a firm texture. Excellent for soups and stews.

Rockfish -   Available in more than 50 varieties. Often sold under the name of Pacific Snapper. They have a firm texture and are low-fat.

Sablefish -   Also, known as Alaskan Cod or Butterfish. A very high-fat fish with a soft texture due to its fat content. Makes an excellent smoking fish and is usually sold as smoked.

Salmon -   (Blueback) Red salmon is the highest in fat, is the most expensive and the highest grade. The lower grades are red or sockeye, chinook or king, and pink salmon is the lowest grade.

Three ounces of salmon contains 120 calories. 1/2 cup of salmon contains more grams of protein than two lamb chops.

"GOOD NEWS FOR BAGELS AND CREAM CHEESE"

Smoked salmon (Lox) is heavily salted unless you purchase the "Nova" variety. Salmon used for smoking is usually raised on aquaculture farms and has never had a reported incidence of parasite contamination.

Salmon used for sushi gives you a 1 in 10 chance of consuming a roundworm from the "anisakis family" of parasites, according to the FDA in samples from 32 restaurants.

If you see a label on canned salmon that says "Norwegian Salmon" be aware that there is no such species.

Sardines - These are actually soft-boned herring. They are descaled before being canned and the scales used to make artificial pearls and cosmetics. The Norwegian bristling sardine is the finest. Maine sardines are almost as good and cost considerably less. They are high-fat and best used for appetizers.

Sea Bass - A moderate fat fish with a firm texture. It has a mild flavor and is a popular seller.

Sea Trout - A moderate fat fish with a fine texture, excellent baked or broiled. Usually caught in the Southeastern United States.

Shad - A high-fat fish with a fine texture. A difficult fish to bone and almost always sold as fillet. The eggs (roe) are considered a delicacy.

Shark - Shark steaks are one of the most vitamin-rich foods in the sea. It is low-fat and has a firm, dense texture, occasionally sold in chunks. Is fast becoming a popular eating fish.

There are 350 species of Shark. In Asia, dried Shark Fins sell for $53 per pound and are used to make Shark soup. In Hong Kong, a bowl of Shark soup sells for $50 per bowl.

Shark cont.   The 60 foot Whale Shark is the world's largest fish. In 1990 over 100 million Sharks were caught.

Skate -   The wings are the only part that is edible. They have a flavor similar to scallops and are low-fat with a firm texture.

Swordfish -   The flavor is not as strong as Shark and is best served as steaks. It is somewhat higher in fat than Shark but has a similar texture.

Tuna -   White Tuna is from Albacore tuna and is the best grade of tuna.
                         Light Tuna comes from the other five species of tuna. It is nutritious and usually tastes just as good.

The average American eats more than 3.7 pounds of tuna per year.

Tuna packed in oil has 50% more calories as water packed tuna.

Recent studies show that mercury contamination in tuna is too low to be concerned about.

Solid pack tuna is tuna that is composed of the loins of the tuna with a few flakes.

Chunk tuna will include pieces that will have a part of the muscle structure attached.

Flake tuna has the muscle structure and a high percentage of the pieces are under 1/2 inch.

Grated tuna is just above a paste.

When tuna is packed in olive oil it is sometimes called "tonno tuna."

Bluefin tuna may weigh up to 1000 pounds.

If you are making tuna salad for sandwiches, it may not matter which tuna you choose. It is more a matter of taste.

If you have noticed that tuna in cans is darker than it used to be, your right, the reason being is that smaller nets are being used so that the porpoises won't be netted. This means that the larger tuna won't be netted either. The smaller tuna has darker meat.

"SOUNDS LIKE A HORSE RACE"
Tuna still ranks as the number one consumed fish in the U.S. in 1994. Shrimp came in second with cod coming in third. Alaska pollack finished fourth due to its popularity in imitation crabmeat.

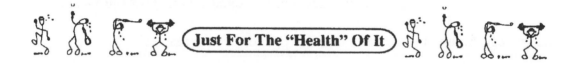

Watch the tuna label for the chemical pyrophosphate, a preservative that you should not eat.

Turbot -   A low-fat fish with a firm texture. Similar to flounder, a flatfish. Usually sold only as fillets.

Whiting -   A relative of Hake. Low-fat with a firm texture. Best broiled or steamed.

FRESHWATER FISH

Buffalo -   A moderate fat fish with a firm texture.
Fish   Usually caught in the Mississippi and the Great Lakes. Weighs in fresh at 2-8 pounds.

Carp -

The first fish to be aquacultured hundreds of years ago in China. A scavenger fish which is only recommended for fishing if aquacultured. Usually a moderate fat fish.

Catfish -

Approximately 70% of all catfish sold are from aquacultured farms. There are over 20 varieties of catfish. They are low-fat with a firm texture. Another scavenger fish which is healthier and only purchased from the farms.

Perch -

A small fish which is usually pan-fried whole. A low-fat, firm textured fish that is excellent eating.

Pike -

Has been fished out of existence. An excellent eating low-fat fish. The most popular being the Walleyed Pike.

Smelt -

A very small fish that is usually pan-fried and eaten whole (head and all). Larger ones are usually cleaned and gutted in the usual manner. They are high-fat with a firm texture.

Sturgeon -

The largest freshwater fish in the world. They can weigh up to 1000 pounds They are high-fat with a very dense texture. Their eggs (roe) is a favorite for caviar.

Trout -

There are three main varieties: Lake Trout, Rainbow Trout and Steelhead. All contain moderate to high levels of fat with a firm texture. One of the best eating fishes with a delicate flavor. All Rainbow Trout are presently from aquacultured farms.

Whitefish -

Ranks as the best freshwater eating fish. It is high-fat with a firm texture and is best when broiled or baked.

Biologic Value Of Protein Foods

When amino acids are broken down, a percentage of the protein is lost in the process. Therefore, the quality and quantity of that protein that will remain useful to the body is called the "biologic value" of that protein. The following is a classification of the more common proteins we consume:

Protein Foods	*Biologic Value %*
Egg Yolk	95
Egg, Whole	94
Milk, Whole	90
Milk, Evaporated	88
Milk, Skim	84
Egg White	83
Pork Tenderloin	79
Corn, Germ	78
Beef Liver	77
Beef Muscle	76
Wheat Germ	75
Rice	75
Soybean Flour	75
Ham	74
Swiss cheese	73
Watermelon Seed	73
Red Salmon	72
Cashew	72
Sweet Potato	72
Coconut	71
Sesame Seed	71
Limburger Cheese	69
Potato	67
Whole Wheat	67
Brewer's Yeast	63
Pumpkin Seed	63
Pecan	60

Corn, Whole	60
Soybeans, Raw	59
Rye	58
Peanut, Roasted	56
Walnut	56
White Flour	52
Almond	51
Peas, Raw	48
Cocoa	37

SEAFOOD HOTLINE 1 (800)332-4010

Chapter 14

Beverage Facts

The average person consumes about 129 gallons of fluid per year. This includes water, milk, colas, beer, wine, etc.

More beer than milk is consumed in the United States. We average 34 gallons of beer per person opposed to 26 gallons of milk.

Americans spend an average of $297 per person on alcoholic beverages annually.

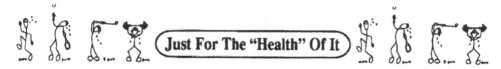

Just For The "Health" Of It

If your nerves are on edge, try a glass of celery juice or tonic.

Food slows down the absorption rate of alcohol and you won't feel the effects as fast.

Alcohol consumption has been linked to breast cancer in recent studies by Harvard University.

The liver must handle 90% of the alcohol, the other 10% is excreted in the urine or expired in air.

"THE DELICATE BALANCE"
The body uses 8 ounces of water to metabolize (break down) just 1 ounce of alcohol. Effects of dehydration may include dry mouth, hangovers, headaches and queasy stomachs.

Fatty foods will slow down the rate at which alcohol is absorbed into the general circulation. Any food will actually slow the rate down to some degree, fatty foods break down slower than the other foods.

Canned juices are usually an enriched product since the heat used in the processing destroys most of the vitamins.

If the fruit juice is labeled "cold-pressed" it is a higher quality product with most of its vitamin content intact.

Scotch has been found to contain small amounts of nitrosamines (a carcinogen) as a result of the way malt barley is dried.

Studies show that 3 beers a day may control your cholesterol levels. It seems to cause an increase in the good cholesterol (HDL), however, so does moderate exercise in the same study. The two together do not work beneficially.

Those who drink one or two alcoholic beverages per day are less likely to die of coronary heart disease than those who abstain. Helps to reduce stress levels.

Some of the hangover problems are caused by cogeners (toxic substances caused by fermentation). Alcoholic beverages with the lowest levels of cogeners are vodka and gin. Some of the worst are bourbon, blended scotch, and brandy.

An ounce and a half of 80 proof whiskey, a 5 ounce glass of wine and a 12 ounce can of beer all have the same amount of alcohol.

Food sensitivities may increase if you consume alcohol at the same time.

Red wine, in recent studies has been associated with stomach cancer. It was not determined in the study, however, whether the problem is from the grapes and the chemical quercetin, or as a result of the processing.

To improve the taste of tomato juice, pour it into a glass bottle and add one green onion and one stalk of celery cut into small pieces.

Hot drinks do not raise body temperture.

Watered down juices go under a variety of names: "orange juice drink", "orange drink", "orange-flavored drink" and "orange juice blend."
Canned beer tends to start deteriorating in approximately 3 months, however, it takes 5 months when bottled.

A "juice-drink" may contain up to 50% juice. An "ade-drink" may contain up to 25% juice and a "drink" can have as little as 10% juice.

Chef's Secrets

When making lemonade, put the lemons through a meat grinder. You will get more juice and it will have a richer flavor.

As a rule of thumb for almost all sauces or soups containing wine, use 1 tablespoon of wine per cup of sauce or soup.

To keep juice cold without watering it down, place a tightly sealed plastic bag of ice into the juice.

A "lite" beer may not refer to the fact that the beer is lower in calories, but may pertain to the color of the beer.

When serving fruit juices, lemonade or punch, try making ice cubes from the drinks. These will keep the drinks from becoming watered down.

ALCOHOL OVERUSE:

Vitamins and Minerals - To be broken down by the body alcohol requires numerous B vitamins and minerals. The following is a list of nutrients that need to be available.

B Vitamins	Minerals
Thiamin	*Iron*
Riboflavin	*Zinc*
Niacin	*Manganese*
Pantothenic	*Phosphorus*
Acid	*Copper*
Biotin	*Magnesium*

NOTE: Alcohol causes excretion of zinc, possibly contributing to prostate problems as a man ages.   It also causes excretion of magnesium, which may lead to extreme nervousness.

Two glasses of white wine per day can supply you with half your daily supply of chromium. Plain grape juice will work just as well.

Wine is composed of water, alcohol, various pigments, esters, some vitamins and minerals, acids and tannins. It does not remain in a constant state and is continually changing.

Traditional Wine/Food Combinations

Meats	- Rose or Cabernet Sauvignon
Seafoods	- Chablis, Chardonney, Pinot Blanc, Sauterne
Pasta	- Chianti
Cheese/Fruit	- Port, Muscatel, Cream Sherry, Tokay
Dessert	- Sweet Sauterne

Fruit juices help to maintain a proper acid-base balance in the stomach.

Ulcers may be irritated by fruit juices.

Bourbon is too sweet to be used in most recipes.

Wines should not be used in tart or heavily seasoned foods.

Wine should be counted as part of the total liquid in any recipe,

To avoid curdling in recipes containing dairy products in which wine is added, try adding the wine before adding the dairy product, then keep the dish warm until served.

Brandy, sherry and whiskey will reduce the "fishiness" of a seafood recipe.

When heating wine, remember that wine will reduce from 1 cup to 1/4 cup in approximately 10 minutes of cooking.

"DON'T WHINE ABOUT YOUR WINE"
If you wish to taste the wine in your recipe, don't add the wine until you are near completion, the alcohol content will be lost to the cooking.

Keep smaller bottles to store leftover wine. The less space between the wine and the cork, the longer it will retain it freshness.

Wine should be used in cooking with the utmost discretion, since it should not dominate the taste. Just use it to improve the flavor of the ingredients.

WHAT WINES TO USE WHERE

SHERRY	Best when used in soups and sauces. The most popular dishes are those with seafood, chicken and in desserts.
WHITE WINE	Usually used in fish and chicken dishes.
RED WINE	Usually used in meat dishes, stews, gravies and sauces. Also, used to marinate meats.
DESSERT WINES	These are the sweet wines and are used in fruit compotes and sweet sauces.
BRANDY	Used in meat and chicken dishes as well as puddings and custards. Very popular in fruit compotes.
RUM	Usually used in desserts containing pineapple or in sweet sauces.

Chapter 15

Grain and Nut Facts

"DO THE TWIST"
Pretzels are the fastest growing snack food in the United States, most products are almost fat-free.

"THE FIRST REAL POPPERS"
The Aztecs were the first to pop corn and use it as a decoration.

"REAL CORNEY"
Every man, woman and child in the United States eat approximately 47 quarts of popcorn each year. After the fat content was released in 1994, consumption decreased approximately 15%.

"A SLIPPERY SUBJECT"
Movie theaters that were offering popcorn popped in both coconut oil and canola, dropped the coconut oil popcorn completely after sales dropped below 10% of all sales.

"GOOD FAT, BAD FAT"
Canola is now used in almost all movie theaters. At least we now get an oil that is high in monounsaturated fat instead of saturated fat.

"BRING YOUR OWN"
Use herbs to replace salt on popcorn. Garlic powder, chili powder, basil and oregano work well.

There is no nutritional difference between regular popcorn and gourmet popcorn. There is only a variation in size.

"BETTCHA CAN'T EAT JUST ONE"
Two quarts of plain popcorn = the calories in 15 potato chips.

"WEAR YOUR GOGGLES"
Corn used for popcorn needs to contain enough moisture to puff up the starches when it is heated. The hull is thick enough to contain steam, yet is easily able to explode.

"CAN'T WIN"
Air poppers make the popcorn pop into larger blossoms, but they are usually tougher and less crisp.

Jasmine rice has an aroma and flavor similar to popcorn or roasted nuts. Makes a great side dish.

"BUTTERY ROULETTE"
Buttered flavored popcorn may be real butter, margarine, butter flavored oil or a soy-based artificial concoction. Ask the theater, they may know!

"TOO POOPED TO POP"
To restore moisture to "old maids" (stubborn kernels that refuse to pop): Fill a one-quart jar three quarters full of unpopped kernels, add one tablespoon of water, cover the jar and shake for 2-3 minutes or until all the water is absorbed. Store the container in a cool place (not the refrigerator) for 2-3 days before popping.

When brown rice is cooked it looks similar to white rice but retains a higher amount of nutrients.

To Crunch Or Not To Crunch

Wheat berries (cracked wheat) is made from toasted grain keeping the bran and germ intact. It is usually prepared by grinding it into coarse, medium or fine granulations for faster cooking. Cracked wheat can replace rice in most recipes but it is a little more crunchier.

To make an exceptional dessert from leftover rice , try folding stiffly beaten whipped cream, then add fresh fruit.

Many hot cereal products are "degerminated" reducing their nutritional quality to make them more palatable. These include Cream Of Wheat and Farina.

"A.K.A.'S"
Cereals are now changing their names so that you won't see the "sugar." Post's Super Sugar Crisp is now Super Golden Crisp and Kellogg's Sugar Frosted Flakes has been changed to Frosted Flakes.

A peanut butter sandwich without jelly will last for 2-3 days without refrigeration.

One of the best cereals on the market is Cherrios. It has an excellent nutrient content and is low in sugar.

"VISA VERSA"
If you run out of chopped nuts, try using a coarse bran, you'll hardly notice the difference. If you run out of coarse bran, use chopped nuts.

To shell nuts more easily, store them in the freezer.

Brown rice is only available in small boxes because the bran portion is higher in fat which may cause the rice to go rancid if not used in a short period of time.

Corn chips in all colors have the same amount of fat and calories, unless they are labeled fat-free or baked.

"TOOK A WHILE TO FIGURE THIS ONE OUT"
Blue corn chips are made from blue corn instead of yellow corn.

Remember one-half cup of rice is only equivalent to 2-3 heaping tablespoons.

Twice as much of our protein was coming from grains and cereals in the early 1900's compared to 1995.

Natural peanut butter will remain fresh longer if you store the bottle upside down in the refrigerator.

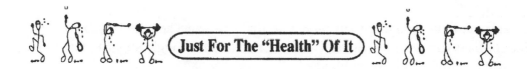

Just For The "Health" Of It

Enriched rice has a few of the vitamins that were lost in the milling process added back. As the rice is washed and cooked it will be lost again, for the most part.

6 tortillas plus 1/4 cup of beans = 14 grams of top quality protein, contains good fiber and is high in vitamins and minerals. Corn tortillas has less fat then flour ones.

"THE PERFECT PROTEIN"
1 ½ cups of beans plus 4 cups of rice = the protein in a 19 ounce steak.

½ cup of peanut butter plus 100% whole wheat bread, made with 3 cups of whole wheat flour and 1/4 cup of skimmed milk = the protein equivalent of a 16 ounce steak.

Wheat flour is not as good as whole wheat flour, and that is not as good as 100% whole wheat flour or whole grain flour.

Wheat bran contains 86% of the niacin, 73% of the pyridoxine, 50% of the pantothenic acid, 42% of the riboflavin, 33% of the thiamin and 20% of the protein. This is what is thrown away when we process bread.

Whole wheat flour is more difficult to digest than white flour. It may also cause gas and intestinal upsets in susceptible persons.

Consumption of grains in 1970 was 135 pounds per person annually. In 1994 it was 189 pounds.

A good test for the nutritive quality of grains: pour a quantity of the grain into a pot of water, if the majority of the grain sinks to the bottom, they still contain most of their nutrients.

The higher the percentage of sugar in cereals the less room for nutrients. Some cereals can have as much as 56% sugar.

Spaghetti products that are advertised as "lite" are lower in calories due to their ability to absorb more water.

Nuts, beans, whole grain, corn and peanut butter should be thrown out if there is the slightest signs of mold or unusual odor. They may contain dangerous aflatoxins.

Triticale is a man-made hybrid grain. It is a cross between rye and wheat and has a higher protein biologic value than even soy beans which contains all the essential amino acids.

GRAINY INFORMATION:

Couscous
Finely cracked wheat granules with a soft buttery flavor. makes an excellent bed for salad dishes or stews.

Bulgur
Granules of crushed wheat with a nutty flavor. Best used in a broth, bean dishes or mixed with rice for an unusual pilaf.

Roasted Buckwheat Groats
Also known as kasha. They are not really grains, but resemble grains and have a brown pyramid shape. Best used in broths and stir-fried eggs.

Barley
Grains look like smooth small pearls. Excellent source of soluble fiber and in some studies has been shown to lower cholesterol. Best used in salads or with tuna.

Amaranth
Resembles golden poppy seeds. When cooked it has a consistency of a crunchy porridge. Has a corn-like flavor and best used as a breakfast cereal.

Quinoa (keen-wa)
A mild-flavored grain that will substitute for rice. Has a bitter coating and should be rinsed under cold running water several times before cooking.

Millet
A popular grain used for numerous vegetarian dishes or in tomato sauce.

If you eat pasta without a protein dish you may feel sluggish 1-2 hours later. This is related to a blood sugar level changes in some individuals.

Oriental noodle soups and many of your popular soups usually contain MSG.

Oats have the highest fat content of any grain.

Corn is one of the least nutritionally complete grains.

Long grain rice contains more protein, but has fewer minerals than most standard rice.

"FLUFFIER BEATS MUSHIER"
Converted rice is actually parboiled rice, rice which has been soaked, steamed and dried in such a way as to make it fluffier instead of mushier.

Granola bars when they first arrived on the scene contained 50-60% sweeteners and fat. The present bar averages 70-80% sweeteners and fat and only have a slight edge over a candy bar.

"CAN'T CHOOSE YOUR RELATIVES"
Eating poppy seeds may cause you to have a positive urine test for drugs. Poppy seeds are a relative of morphine and codeine.

"NATURAL HIGH?"
Sunflower seeds produce a similar action on the body as smoking a cigarette. It causes the body to produce adrenalin, which will go to the brain, resulting in a pleasant feeling. The seeds must, however, be raw, not roasted.

Millet is one of the highest nutritional quality grains.

Amaranth, originally an Aztec grain, unlike other grains is not deficient in the amino acid lysine. When this grain is eaten with rice, wheat or barley it can provide a complete protein containing all amino acids.

There are 70,000 seeds in 1 pound of amaranth.

Amaranth can be popped like popcorn.

"HIC"
The majority of barley grown in the United States is used to produce alcoholic beverages. The malt is made by soaking whole barley seeds until they convert to sugar.

"STRANGE FAMILY TREE"
Buckwheat is not related to the wheat or grain family, but is actually a fruit and a relative of rhubarb.

Minute and instant rice have the lowest nutritional content of any rice.

"UP, UP AND AWAY"
Quinona (keen-wa) is a grainlike product, related to Swiss chard and spinach. Often referred to as a "supergrain" because of its high levels of iron.

"DOWN THE DRAIN"
Never rinse packaged domestic rice before cooking, it's not necessary and may wash away some of the nutrients that were added as an enrichment. The cooking removes enough anyway.

"USE YOUR PASTA-MAKER"
Pasta products can be considered a low-fat food, homemade is best.

Avoid any pasta product that lists "disodium phosphate" on the label. It is a chemical softening agent that helps the pasta cook faster.

"NATURAL RELAXER"
Serotonin, a chemical produced by the body that helps you relax, can be increased by a complex carbohydrate (pasta) meal.

"USE IT, OR LOSE IT"
Whole wheat flour should be used within 2 months of purchase to avoid rancidity. Refrigeration, however, will delay the rancidity for up to 4 months.

Pasta products are easily digested due to their low fiber content. This makes them an ideal food for young children, infants and the elderly.

Most pasta is made with very little or no salt. Good for low sodium diet.

Uncooked pasta has a protein content of approximately 12%. 3.4 grams per 3/4 cup serving.

Triticale is made from wheat and rye and is more nutritious than wheat. One of the highest nutrient flours. Highly recommended.

"A LITTLE OF THIS AND A LITTLE OF THAT"
Be aware that your favorite brand of grain cereal may contain so many additives that it may not be as healthy a product as you are made to believe.

The best quality pasta is made from amber durum wheat which comes from Russia.

"DEFINITELY, NOT SQUARE"
90% of all durum wheat grown in the U.S. is grown in Northeastern North Dakota. This area is known as the "durum triangle."

When durum wheat is cooked it is always tender and does not become mushy or pasty.

If you use durum wheat pasta it is not necessary to rinse it before using.

"AN ALL AROUND WINNER"
Chestnuts are the only nut that contains vitamin C and has a low fat and calorie content.

Before cooking chestnuts, cut an "X" on the pointed end. This will keep them from exploding when roasting and also will make them easier to peel.

Dry-roasted nuts and regular roasted nuts have about the same number of calories.

A Nut By Any Other Name

Roasted Nuts
Usually fried in oil, and not always a good oil. many are roasted in coconut oil which is high in saturated fat.

Dry-Roasted
Not cooked in oil, but still contain a high fat content and is usually high in salt, sweeteners and preservatives may be added.

Raw Nuts
Usually sold in vacuum packed cans to retain the freshness. May go bad and become rancid rather quickly. Try and keep them refrigerated, this will slow down the process and they will last longer.

Defatted (lite) Peanuts
Some of the oils have been removed through processing, but this doesn't change their fat content appreciably.

"BONE FOOD"
One ounce of almonds have as much calcium as 1/4 cup of milk.

"NUT, NOT RELATED TO THE NUT FAMILY TREE"
Peanuts are really not in the nut family, but are legumes, a type of bean.

"MODERN-AGE NUT CRACKER"

Black walnuts are very difficult to crack open. One of the best ways if you have a trash compactor or have a friend who has one, is to place a wood platform on the bottom raising it up a few inches, make sure you have a clean bag and crush away.

 Chef's Secrets

To remove the burnt taste from rice, try placing a piece of very fresh white bread on top of the rice, then cover the pot. It should only take a few minutes for the burnt taste to disappear.

Never add salt to rice until fully cooked, it will toughen the rice.
When making lasagna, use a small amount of olive oil in the water to prevent the sections from sticking together.

"I WONDER WHERE THE YELLOW WENT"

To keep rice white while cooking, add a few drops of lemon juice to the water.

A few minutes before your rice is done, place a double paper towel just under the lid and finish cooking. The rice will come out more fluffy and dry.

"RICE SCIENCE 101"

To obtain the right amount of water to cook rice without measuring, place a quantity of rice in a pot, shake the pot to smooth out and settle the rice, then place your index finger lightly on top of the rice - don't make a dent - add water until your first knuckle is covered (about 1" above the surface of the rice).

If you are chopping nuts in a blender, add a small amount of sugar and they won't clump together.

One cup uncooked pasta = Two cups cooked pasta.

PASTA SAUCES:

Genovese -   A thick meat sauce, flavored with garlic,
                  tomato and herbs.

Marinara -   A zesty tomato sauce flavored with garlic,
                  and herbs.

Neopolitan -   A blend of tomato sauce, herbs, garlic,
                    mushrooms and bell pepper.

Alfredo -   Made with fresh cream, garlic and
                 parmesan cheese.

Alla Panna -   Combines fresh cream, garlic, marsala
                    wine, parmesan cheese, mushrooms and
                    smoked ham.

Formaggi -   Made with fresh cream, garlic, parmesan,
                  romano and Swiss cheeses.

Pesto -   Made from extra virgin olive oil, fresh
               basil, garlic, pine nuts and fresh cream.

Clam Sauce - Made with clam broth, tomatoes, crushed
                  red pepper. Red is spicy, green is mild.

"MAKING A RAINBOW"

Pasta made from durum flour and whole eggs is naturally a golden-yellow color. When spinach is added, you will get green, blending tomato paste into the dough and will result in a salmon-toned pasta.

Kasha (buckwheat groats) is the fruit of the buckwheat plant. Prepare the same as rice. Very healthy.

PASTA SHAPES:

Cresti-di-gali	- Looks like a roosters comb.
Cannelloni	- Hollow tubes up to 2 inches long.
Ditalini	- Small thimble shapes.
Farfalle	- Shaped like a bowtie. The word means butterfly in Italian.
Funghini	- These pasta are related to the mushroom family and used in soups and stews.
Fusilli bucati	- Corkscrew-shaped pasta.
Lumache	- Pasta shaped like a snails shell.
Macaroni	- Curved pasta, comes in many sizes with a hollow center.
Occhi-di-lupo	- Very large tubes of pasta sometimes referred to as "wolf's eyes."
Orcchiette	- Pasta shaped like ears.
Pulcini	- Used mainly in soups and called "little chickens."
Ravioli	- Small squares of pasta stuffed with different ingredients.

Riccini	- Pasta shaped like ringlet curls.
Ruoti	- Round pasta with spokes, looks like a wagon wheel.
Tortellini	- Pasta that is supposed to resemble the Roman Goddess Venus' navel.
Vermicelli	- Italian word for worms, which they resemble. Also known as spaghetti.
Ziti	- Very short tubular shaped pasta.

Arkansas is the largest rice producer in the United States.

Pasta should be cooked firm and slightly chewy. Excess cooking decreases the nutrient content.

"PASTY PASTA"
Pasta will not get sticky if you place it in a warm colander then into a warm dish. The cold colander causes the starch to get sticky.

There are over 300 types of pasta.

When cooking pasta, cover the pot after you place the pasta into the boiling water. The water should be kept boiling and not cool down to any great degree for the best results.

Pasta consumption in the United States in 1994 was approximately 20 pounds per person and going up every year.

"THE PASTA WINNERS"
Italians, however, consume an average of 60 pounds of pasta annually.

Any pasta that is packaged in clear plastic containers are subject to nutrient loss from the lights in the market. Purchase pasta in boxes whenever possible.

Noodles must contain 5-6% egg solids by law.

Do not purchase any grains that are not whole. If you see numerous broken pieces, don't buy the grains.

Cooked wild rice will only keep in the refrigerator for 1 week.

Bulgar wheat is not a good quality nutritious whole wheat product unless their granules still have their dark brown coating.

Bulgar should be steamed, then dried and cracked into three different granulations. The coarsest is used for pilaf; the medium is used for cereals; and the finest for tabbouleh.

Bulgar requires less cooking time than cracked wheat.

Tabbouleh is a Middle Eastern dish made from cracked wheat or bulgar, lemon juice,, olive oil, parsley, dill or mint, plum tomatoes, scallions, minced garlic, salt, pepper and other cold vegetables if desired.

Use your frying basket or a large metal strainer when cooking pasta. This will save you the trouble of draining.

After opening pasta, save the unused portion in a glass jar.

Rice was first cultivated in Thailand in 3500 B.C.

Asia produces over 90% of the world's rice.

Rice is the staple grain of over 60% of the people of the world.

Brown rice is rice with only the husk removed.

Converted rice has been parboiled to remove the surface starch.

Unopened packages of rice should be stored at a cool room temperature.

To tenderize brown rice, allow rice to soak for an hour or two before cooking.

To cook rice, bring to a boil, cover and simmer on low heat 35 minutes, turn off heat and let stand covered for 10 minutes.

To make an exceptional dessert from leftover rice, try folding in stiffly beaten whipped cream, then add fresh fruit.

Always wash rice before using, this cleans out the hulls and other debris.

Whole grain products should be stored in solid tightly covered containers.

Glass dishes will bake bread faster than metal pans.

Macadamia nuts have more fat and calories than any other nut.

Before measuring a whole grain flour, sift it with a coarse sifter. Avoid the squeeze handle types. Sifting will make a difference of up to two tablespoons per cup.

Chapter 16

Bread and Muffin Facts

"DON'T CHILL IT, BOX IT"

Storing bread is best in a breadbox at room temperature, it will stay fresh for days if wrapped. Bread goes stale up to 6 times faster at room temperature.

Bread labeled "cracked wheat," "sprouted wheat" or "wheat bread" usually contain white flour.

"HEAVVVY"

Never expect whole wheat bread to raise as high as white bread or be as airy, there is more volume to it.

"CALL THE WARDEN"

If your using a bread mixer, try spraying a liquid oil on the dough hook to keep the dough from climbing up and escaping.

Bread holds water well and will last for weeks in the freezer.

"BAGELLA CRAZE"

Bagel sales have increased 169% in 1994 and now ranks as one of the most popular breakfast foods.

When thawing a frozen bread, it should be consumed shortly after, otherwise it will dry out.

If you make french toast and pancakes ahead of time and freeze them you can pop them into the toaster anytime you want.

Rye bread usually contains white flour. Make sure the label says "whole-rye flour."

 Chef's Secrets

Whole wheat bread will rise faster if you add 1 tablespoon of lemon juice to the dough when you are mixing it.

After you boil potatoes, try using the water in your bread recipe and the bread will stay fresher longer at room temperature. The water will have a high starch content.

If you run out of yeast and need it to make biscuits, try using a teaspoon of baking soda and an equal amount of vitamin C. The results will be the same, since a similar chemical reaction occurs.

"DON'T SETTLE FOR LESS"
When making pancakes or waffles, be sure and mix the batter between batches to avoid settling. You will be surprised at the difference in the quality of the dish.

100% whole wheat bread will be more moist if you add as little flour as possible to the dough. Whole grain tends to absorb water more slowly than standard refined flour and becomes dry as the dough rises.

"IT'S A KILLER"
Add yeast to water, never water to yeast. Be gentle to the little yeasties.

"WHAT A LITTLE SWEETNESS WILL DO"
Remember, yeast is a living organism, there are approximately 3000 billion cells in one pound. Their food supple is sugar and they produce alcohol and carbon dioxide (the riser we want). Enzymes in the wheat starch produce the sugar for the reaction to begin.

"SUSPENDED ANIMATION"
Dry yeast will last longer if refrigerated.

When reheating biscuits, place them in a well dampened paper bag, seal up tightly and heat in oven on low temperature reading.

"MAY NEED SEAT BELTS"
Always bake biscuits on pans without sides, the heat circulates more evenly.

Biscuits will brown to a rich golden color if you add a teaspoon of granulated sugar to the dry ingredients.

To reduce rising time approximately 1 hour, try adding 1 extra packet or cube of yeast. This will not change the taste.

Use the ice cube divider to cut biscuits into small squares.

"TIRE PUMP MAY WORK"
The secret to light dumplings is to puncture them when they are finished cooking, allowing the air to circulate within.

"BE GENTLE"
Remember that salt and cold retard yeast growth, sweetness and warmth (up to a point) increases it. Oven temperatures will kill it.

To place moisture into a stale loaf of bread, wrap it in a damp cloth or towel for about 1-2 minutes then place it in a preheated 350°F. oven for about 20 minutes.

"A COLD SHOWER"
To replace moisture into French or Italian bread or hard rolls, sprinkle the crust with cold water and place into a 350°F. oven for about 10 minutes.

To remove rolls or muffins more easily, try placing the pan directly from the oven on a wet towel for 20-30 seconds.

For a hard to knead doughs, try oiling your hands before working it.

To avoid fresh baked bread from getting moldy, try wrapping the bread in waxed paper and storing in the refrigerator.

Kneading dough is easier if you place the dough in a plastic bag.

"RIP VAN WINKLE"
If you store yeast or a flour product containing yeast in the refrigerator make sure you allow it to warm to room temperature before using it to wake up the yeast. Cold inactivates yeast.

"ANCIENT YEAST TRAPPERS"
Sourdough bread is produced from a living bacterial culture called a "starter." The starter consists of water and flour which ferment and as it does traps wild yeasts from the air giving it its distinctive "sour" taste.

"SAUNA?"

Place a pan of water in the oven when baking breads to keep the crusts from becoming too hard. The moisture and steam works great.

Try placing a piece of tin foil under your towel in the bread basket when serving rolls. It will keep them warm longer.

"CIRCULATE"

Freshly baked breads should be cooled on a rack so that air can circulate around it as it cools. Keeps the bread from becoming soggy.

"LEVITATION"

Use a heating pad on medium to help your dough rise perfectly. Place the dough in a pan then place it on the pad.

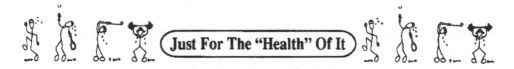

Just For The "Health" Of It

Bread sticks may contain up to 42% fat.

Pita bread pockets usually contain no sugar or added fat.

A quality brown bread should contain 100% whole wheat flour or whole grain flour.

Pita bread has almost no fat and contains only 75 calories per ounce.

A 7 inch pita pocket weighs only 2 ounces and has 120-150 calories.

Avoid any baked product made with most shortenings, hydrogenated oils or lard. It will be high in saturated fat.

Moldy bread should be disposed of. Throw out the whole bread even if only one piece has the mold. Mold sends feelers out that are invisible to the naked eye.

Quick breads are leavened with the use of baking powder or baking soda in place of yeast. No rising time is needed. The baking powder or soda react with water and acid in the dough at the oven temperatures and forms carbon dioxide which causes the rise.

"JOLLY POOR SHOW"
English muffins have no nutritional advantage over white bread.

Bagels have a low-fat content and have more protein than 2 slices of white bread. However they are getting so large that they are no longer considered a low-calorie food.

Toasting bread reduces the protein efficiency ratio from 0.90 out of a possible 2.5, to approximately 0.32.

If you must buy white bread, make sure it says "enriched," many do not!

To increase the protein value of bread, remove 1-2 tablespoons of whole wheat flour and replace it with an equal amount of soy flour.

Enriched white flour - The milling and bleaching process destroys 86% of the niacin, 73% of the vitamin B6, 33% of the thiamin, 50% of the pantothenic acid, 42% of the vitamin B2 and 19% of the protein.

To make cutouts from bread slices, try freezing the bread first. This will give your cutouts clean, sharp edges.

Pumpernickel is usually made from white or rye flour and colored with caramel.

To cut pizza easily, just use a scissors.

Bagels are made from a high protein flour and little or no shortening.

Bread pans should never be scoured to a shiny glean. Bread bakes better in a dull pan.

To keep bread fresh when freezing, tuck a paper towel into the bag with the bread or rolls. The paper towel will absorb the moisture that usually makes breads mushy when thawed.

Buy the thinnest sliced white bread you can. It will reduce the calories about 50%.

Your best white breads are Italian, French or sour dough, if they say "enriched."

White bread should be made from "unbleached flour" instead of "white flour" or just "flour" on the list of ingredients.

Chapter 17

A Cup of Joe, A Spot of Tea

Tea was originated in China and then was introduced to Japan.

Iced tea and coffee can be greatly improved if the ice cubes are made of coffee or tea instead of water.

You can avoid cloudiness in iced tea by letting freshly brewed tea cool to room temperature before refrigerating it. If the tea does become cloudy, pour a little boiling water into it until it becomes clear.

For a new taste in tea, add a small bit of dried orange peel to the teapot.

The Island of Ceylon is the world's leading producer of tea.

"HOW MANY LEAVES CAN A PICKER PLUCK?"
An experienced picker can pluck about 40 pounds of tea leaves a day.

Classifications of Tea

Black Tea - Turns black due to oxidation. This is the best quality tea. Includes; Assam, Ceylon, Darjeeling, English Breakfast, Keemun, Lapsang and Souchong.

Green Tea - Oxidation is omitted. The natural color is green. Two main types; Basket Fired and Gunpowder.

Oolong Tea - Semi-processed, makes the leaves partly green and brown. Two types; Formosa Oolong and Jasmine.

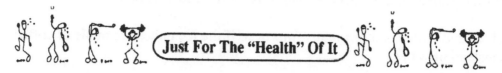

Just For The "Health" Of It

Salada and Bigelow English Teatime are two of the highest caffeine content teas. They average about 60mg. of caffeine per 8oz. cup.

When drinking tea, never use polystyrene cups with lemon. The combination of the hot tea and the lemon will corrode the cup away releasing carcinogens into your drink. It will actually eat right through the cup.

Tannin, found in tea and red wine may interfere with the body's use of iron, thiamin and vitamin B12.

At present there is no risk factor related to drinking tea and heart disease.

"TEA TIME"
Black teas are the most popular in the U.S. We Import 130 million pounds per year. The yearly consumption is 35 billion servings.

"TEA TRIVIA"
Iced tea was first created at the 1904 Louisiana Purchase Exposition in St Louis, MO.

One pound of tea will brew approximately 200 cups (200 teabags).

The U.S. imports approximately 72% of its tea from India.

Toxic Teas

Buckthorn	May cause diarrhea.
Burdock	Blocks nerve impulses to organs.
Comfrey	Can cause liver problems.
Foxglove	May cause heart arrythmias.
Groundsel	May cause liver problems.
Hops	Can destroy red blood cells.
Jimsonweed	Blurred vision problems, hallucinations.
Kava-Kava	May cause deafness, lack of coordination.
Lobelia	May cause liver problems.
Mandrake	May block nerve impulses to organs.
Meliot	Can cause tendency to hemorrhage.
Nutmeg	Can cause hallucinations.
Oleander	Can cause heart stoppage.
Pokeweed	May cause breathing difficulties.
Sassafras	May cause liver cancer.
Senna	May cause diarrhea.
Thorn Apple	Blocks nerve impulses.
Tonka Bean	Causes tendency to hemorrhage.
Woodruff	Causes tendency to hemorrhage.

Decaffeinated Coffee

1973 - Trichloroethylene used - Found in 1975 to cause liver cancer in mice.

1975 - Methylene Chloride - Found in 1981 to cause cancer in lab animals. FDA said that the tests were not conclusive. Residues are low in coffee and may not be harmful in humans.

1981 -   Ethyl Acetate - A number of coffee
companies switch to ethyl acetate which is
also found in bananas and pineapple. In
concentrated form, its vapors have been
known to cause damage to lungs, heart and
livers in lab test animals. It is also
used as a cleaner and solvent for leather
and plastics. Still in use.

1984 -   Water Process - Was developed by Swiss and
Belgium companies. A harmless method, but
may cause some loss of flavor. Now being
used by a number of U.S. companies.

Coffee manufacturers do not have to disclose their method of decaffeination.

Brazil has experienced two major frosts in 1994 that destroyed over 1 billion
pounds of coffee, approximately 10% of the world's coffee supply, raising prices
worldwide.

Consumption of decaf coffee is up 13% and general coffee consumption is down
23% according to the NPD group, inc.

The United States consumes about 1/3 of all coffee worldwide, approximately 400
million cups per day.

The only coffee grown in the United States is Kona, which is grown on the island of
Hawaii. The coffee is grown in volcanic soil and has the richest coffee flavor in the
world.

"BUMMER"
If you give up coffee and are drinking two cups a day or more you will probably
have withdrawal symptoms, such as headaches, nausea and possibly depression.

"BROWN FILTERS ARE BEST"
The safest way to prepare coffee is to boil it in water instead of filtering it. This is
the way it is prepared in the Scandinavian countries.

Fresh roasted coffee beans are usually packed in non-airtight bags to allow the carbon monoxide formed during the roasting process to escape. If the carbon monoxide doesn't escape, the coffee may have a poor taste.

The "Swiss Water" decaffeinated process is the best. Check the label. Other "water processed" methods are not as good.

"CHUG-A-LUG"

The freshness of a cup of coffee only survives 10-30 minutes in a coffee warmer.

Coffee will taste better if you start with a quality cold water, not hot tap water.

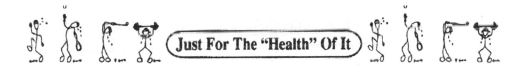

There is a 60% greater risk of heart disease if you consume 2-5 regular cups of coffee per day, and 120% greater risk for over 6 cups per day.

Purchase only "unbleached" brown coffee filters. The chemical digoxin is used to bleach filters white and may leave a residue.

Dripped coffee has almost twice the caffeine as instants.

Beverages that contain caffeine may cause your skin to become dehydrated and promotes premature aging.

The polyphenols in coffee and the tannins in tea may reduce the amount of iron available for the body to use. One cup of coffee consumed with a hamburger reduces the amount of iron absorbed by approximately 40%, tea by 90%.

Caffeine takes approximately 30 minutes to affect your brain and lasts for 2-6 hours.

Two cups of coffee will cause an increase in hydrochloric acid in the stomach for at least an hour.

Coffee reduces the healing time of stomach ulcers.

One cup of coffee or one cigarette will cause a rise in blood pressure.

Studies also show that caffeine may be related to fibrocystic breast disease.

"A REAL BUMMER"
Caffeine may affect zinc absorption which may adversely affect the prostate gland and possibly reduce sexual urges in some people.

Withdrawal symptoms will appear if caffeine is discontinued. These usually start with headaches but only last for 3-5 days. The cells become dependent on the drug.

If you consume more than 300mg. of caffeine a day it will overstimulate the Central Nervous System and may cause insomnia, nervousness, diarrhea and increase your heart rate.

Coffee drinkers have a higher incidence of heart disease.

Caffeine causes chemical changes in cells that cause excess triglycerides to be released into the blood stream.

Caffeine reduces the body's ability to handle stress.

In pregnant woman caffeine will enter the fetal circulation in the same concentrations as it enters the mother's with a possible relation to birth defects.

A dash of salt added to coffee that has been overcooked or reheated will freshen the taste.

Coffee trees originally came from Africa.

The first people known to actually drink the beverage known as "coffee" were the Arabs who would not allow the beans to be exported. They were finally smuggled to Holland in 1660 and then to Brazil in 1727.

Opened coffee cans should be stored in the refrigerator upside down. The coffee will retain its' freshness and flavor longer.

Leftover coffee and tea can be frozen in ice cube trays then used to cool hot coffee or tea or in other beverages.

"COOL IT"
For a fast cup of coffee, have a cup of fresh coffee in a sealed container in the refrigerator. Coffee will warm up and have an excellent taste.

Hills Brothers Coffee was the first commercial company to sell vacuum packed coffee in 1900.

Coffee trees require 70 inches of rainfall per year.

Ground coffee oxidizes very fast and coffee is best purchased in vacuum cans.

Americans consume 4,848 cups per second, 24 hours a day.

A coffee tree produces approximately one to twelve pounds of coffee cherries" from a six-year old tree.

"BELIEVE IT OR NOT"
Approximately 2000 coffee cherries are required to produce one pound of coffee, the crop of one tree.

The U.S. is the largest consumer of coffee. About three billion pounds are used annually.

When reheating coffee, never boil it, as this will cause an undesirable flavor.

Espresso Beverages

Espresso-   A dark roasted coffee, prepared by a rapid infusion of very hot water through the coffee grounds. The coffee is served in petit cups. Sometimes served with a twist of lemon. The strength of the coffee is controlled by the darkness of the beans after roasting, how dense they are packed and the amount of water that is forced through them.

Cappuccino-   A combination of one shot of espresso, hot steamed milk, topped with a frothy head of milk, and to top it off a shake of cinnamon or cocoa. It will vary depending on the strength of the espresso.

Caffe Mocha-   One shot of espresso, topped with the froth from hot chocolate.

Caffe Latte-   One shot of espresso with a goodly amount of steamed milk. Some are served with a slightly higher amount of milk than espresso. Latte's are usually topped with a large amount of foam, while others have no foam at all.

Macchiato-	One shot of espresso with a dollop of foam on top. Served in a petit cup.
Latte-	Served in a large glass containing mostly steamed milk with a small amount of espresso on top. The espresso should remain on top but colors the milk a coffee color.
Cafe Au Lait-	A mixture of strong coffee (not espresso) and steamed milk. Usually served in bowls.
Caffe Borgia-	A frothy caffe mocha with orange and lemon peels.
Cafe L'Amore-	A petit cup of espresso with a topping of gelato.

Caffeine In Foods

Coffee	**Per 8 oz. Serving**
Perc	190 - 270 mg
Drip	178 - 200 mg.
Instant	90 - 112 mg.
Decaf	3 - 7 mg.
Instant Decaf	3 mg.

Tea   Per 8 oz. Serving

Black 5 Minute Brew...32 - 78 mg.
Iced...34 - 65 mg.
Oolong 5 Minute Brew.....................................45 mg.
Instant...20 - 34 mg.
Decaf... 8 - 16 mg.

Chocolate

Cocoa (8 oz.)... 6 - 8 mg.
Milk Chocolate (1 oz.)....................................... 5 - 6 mg.
Semi-Sweet Chocolate (1 oz.)...........................20 - 35 mg.

Soft Drinks   Per 12 oz. Serving

Jolt Cola...68 mg.
Diet Dr. Pepper..65 mg.
Mountain Dew..49 mg.
Coke...45 mg.
Diet Coke...44 mg.
Dr. Pepper..44 mg.
Pepsi..35 mg.
Diet Pepsi..34 mg.
RC Cola..34 mg.
Mr. Pibb...33 mg.
7 Up... 0 mg.

Drugs	**Per Tablet**
Vivarin	200 mg.
NoDoz	100 mg.
Excedrin	65 mg.
Vanquish	38 mg.
Anacin	35 mg.
Darvon	33 mg.
Empirin	32 mg.
Midol	32 mg.
Soma	31 mg.
Aspirin	0 mg.
Tylenol	0 mg.

Chapter 18

Cake, Pie and Cookie Facts

Pies and tarts are the most popular desserts with people whose dinner check is under $15.

"PIE PAINTING"
Try brushing the bottom crust of fruit pies with egg whites to prevent the fruit juices from soaking in.

"MAKE IT GOOD AND TOASTIE"
Make sure your oven has been pre-heated for 15-20 minutes before placing a cake in.

Always bake on a middle shelf in the oven, the heat will circulate more evenly.

"HOW DRY I AM"
To keep a cake from drying out, attach slices of bread with toothpicks to any exposed cut edges of cakes.

To ice a many layered cake, try attaching all the layers with a few pieces of dry spaghetti.

If your icing becomes too thick, try adding a few drops of lemon juice and mix well.

 Chef's Secrets

To make a delicate cake, use half unbleached white flour and half whole wheat flour.

A teaspoon of vinegar added to pie dough will guarantee a flaky crust.

"SPLAT"
If you want to prevent a cake from falling after you place the batter in the pan, raise the pan and drop it suddenly to the counter to release the air bubbles.

"HARD BODY"
To keep a pie crust from becoming soft and soggy during baking, try warming the pan before placing in the undercrust.

If you want an extra flaky pie crust, try substituting ice-cold sour cream or whipping cream for water. Works great but adds fat and cholesterol.

"CAKE SCENTS"
Try placing a rose germanium leaf on the bottom of the cake pan for a pleasant scent to a white or yellow cake.

"DON'T USE A SECOND STRINGER"
Never use low-fat margarine for baking. Cakes will collapse and cookies may flatten and lose their form. Low-fat margarine contains a higher air and water content which is released during cooking or baking and alters the consistency of the product. Do not substitute margarine for butter in any recipe.

All recipes call for large grade A eggs unless specified otherwise.

"ABBRA-KA-DABBRA"
If you want to add some pzazz to your lemon tarts or pies, try rubbing a sugar cube over the surface of a lemon, the sugar cube will extract oils from the lemon that will be released during the cooking process. Works for oranges too.

Butter cakes should have an adequate amount of air bubbles in them which is produced by creaming the sugar and fat.

Chiffon cakes use oil in place of butter which will produce a more tender crumb.

All fats used for cakes should be at room temperature for the best results. If not they will not blend well with all the ingredients.

"DON'T USE THE SUBS"
Sweeteners contribute to a cake's tender qualities, but remember that you cannot substitute granulated sugars for powdered sugars. Granulated for baking, powdered for frostings and glazes.

"ONLY GREASE YOUR BOTTOM"

If a recipe requires you to grease or flour the pan, read all the directions carefully. They may only want the bottom of the pan done, so that the cake is allowed to cling to the sides as it bakes.

"DON'T GIVE BUTTER A BREAKDOWN"

Butter used in recipes should be soft not melted, if you would like a better texture to your cakes. The more butter that is melted, the more it breaks down.

"OUCH, A SCORCHED BOTTOM"

If you're baking a cake in a glass pan, you should lower your oven temperature by about 25 degrees. It will save the bottom of the cake from getting scorched.

To keep soft cookies from becoming hard, try placing a slice of very fresh white bread in the cookie jar.

"THE PEAK OF PERFECTION"

For the highest meringue, the secret is to add some baking powder to room temperature egg whites before beating them. As you beat the eggs, add 2-3 tablespoons of granulated sugar for each egg used, beating continually. Perfect peaks should form and stand upright without keeling over.

"A SORROWFUL SITUATION"

To eliminate weeping meringue, try leaving the meringue in the oven until it cools. Turn the oven off before it's finished.

When baking acidic fruit pies such as cherry or apple it is best to use ceramic or glass pie pans to avoid the pies turning gray from a reaction with the metal.

"THE INCREDIBLE SHRINKING PIE CRUST"

Chill the dough before working it into the pie tin. The cold firms up the fat and will relax the gluten in the flour so that it will hold its shape better. A relaxed crust is a happy crust.

If you need to use the same measuring cup for eggs and oil, make sure you measure the eggs first then the oil. The eggs will coat the cup and all the oil will slide out easily.

Baking powder retains maximum potency for about 1 year.

Always use unsalted butter when greasing a pan. Chances of having a sticking problem, will be greatly reduced.

When making meringue tortes, always leave the torte in the oven until it has fully cooled to avoid cracking.

When measuring flour for a pie crust, always sift the flour first for a more accurate measurement.

To maintain the shape of a souffle, serve immediately after it is steam baked and always on a warm plate to avoid a collapse.

The secret to keep pancakes from sticking to the griddle is to fill a small piece of cheesecloth with salt, then just before pouring the batter, rub the salt-bag over the surface of the hot griddle.

Pie crusts will turn out better if all the ingredients are cold and the dough is not overworked. The dough should also be refrigerated before it is rolled.

Wheat flour will give you crunchier cookies if butter is used as the shortening. If oil is used the cookies will be more tender and softer.

When making pie dough, it is best to use lard instead of butter. The crust will be flakier and lard actually has less saturated fat than butter. A solid shortening may also produce good results.

When reusing a cooking pan for numerous batches, try running the bottom of the pan under cold water, but don't get the cooking surface wet. This will reduce the risk of "burned bottom cookies."

Cookies will also lose their shape when placed on a hot cookie pan. Try to cool the pan or rotate your pans.

To avoid overbaking cookies, just remove them from the oven a few minutes before they are done, the hot pan will continue to bake them.

If you want to perk up meringue peaks, add 1/4 teaspoon of white vinegar for each three egg whites (during beating). Also, if you add 4-5 drops of lemon juice per each cup of cream it will remain firmer longer.

Another method of perking up meringue peaks is to add some baking powder to room temperature egg whites before beating them.

When you bake meringue kisses, line the baking sheet with a brown paper bag.

Fruitcakes will remain moist if you wrap them with a damp towel.

"TO THE HEART OF THE MATTER"
Make a heart-shaped cake. First bake both a round cake and a square cake. Cut the round cake in half, then turn the square cake so that the corners face you in a diamond shape. Place each half of the round cake on the two uppermost sides of the diamond. Now you have a perfect heart-shaped cake for Valentines Day.

If you bake an angel food cake on the bottom of a rack at 325°F. you will make a moister cake.

"CAREFUL OF THE WINGS"
The best way to cut angel food cake is with an electric knife.

If you want to add a crunchy texture to oatmeal cookies, lightly toast the oatmeal before mixing it into the batter. To toast, just sprinkle the flakes in a thin layer on a cookie sheet and heat at 185°F. for 10-15 minutes or until the flakes are brown.

Adding 1/4 teaspoon of almond extract to cherry or peach pies will give them a better flavor.

Sugar cookies will not get stiff or tough if you roll them out in sugar instead of flour.

When making frosting, try using a pinch of baking soda in the powdered sugar and the frosting won't crumble and dry as quickly. The baking soda will help retain liquids for a longer period of time.

To keep the juices inside the crust when baking pies with juicy fillings, try adding a tablespoon of tapioca before baking. Helps thicken the mixture.

Before baking a pie that is juicy, insert a tube of macaroni in the center of the top of the pie and the juices won't bubble out.

If you must cut a cake while it is still hot, use unwaxed dental floss, instead of a knife.

To prevent a soggy crust on pastry shells, try coating the shells with egg white before baking.

Try adding a tablespoon of maple syrup to pancake batter to improve the taste.

For the lightest pancakes ever, just use club soda in place of the usual liquid in the batter.

For a flakier pastry shell or pie crust, add 1 tablespoon of lemon juice to the batter.

"2ND DEGREE?"
If a pie shell blisters, try placing a few slices of white bread on the shell before baking. Then bake and remove the bread just before it is finished.

To eliminate soggy pie shells, spread a thin layer of butter on the pie plate bottom before putting the dough in.

When using a cream filling in a pie, coat the crust with granulated sugar before adding the cream, This will eliminate a soggy crust.

"RISING TO THE OCCASION"

For a real treat when making pumpkin pie, place a layer of marshmallows on the bottom. While the pie is baking they will rise to the top and form a great topping. The air in the marshmallow is expanded by the heat.

When your recipe calls for flour to be sifted, add the leavening and salt when sifting for a better blend.

If cookies are not browning properly, try baking them on a higher shelf.

THE FLOUR DILEMMA

The secret has been revealed, "All-Purpose Flour" is not really for all-purposes. If you have a recipe that calls for "cake flour" use cake flour. A substitute for cake flour is "bleached" all-purpose flour but you will have to change your recipe by adding 1 ½ teaspoons of cornstarch and using a slightly smaller amount of flour for the best results.

All-Purpose Flour
A blend of hard and soft wheat flours.

Bread Flour
Has a high gluten content. Feels gritty to the touch.

Cake Flour
Made of soft wheats and has a more crumblier texture.

Presifted Flours
Completely pulverized. Has a high gluten content. May toughen cakes.

Pastry Flour
A low gluten flour. Used mainly for quick breads.

Enriched Flour
Nutrients added back after refining, but only a fraction replaced.

Browned Flour
A heated all-purpose flour. May add color to your recipes.

Self-Rising Flour
Contains just the right amount of leavening and salt for baking. may lose potency in storage.

Whole Grain Flour
Contains the full bran portion of the wheat and is high in nutrients. Use slightly more in recipes than all-purpose flours.

Bran Flour
Usually mixed with all-purpose flour and may give a somewhat dry effect to the baked product.

Gluten Flour
This flour is made by washing the starch from a high protein wheat flour. It is basically a starch-free flour.

Corn Flour
Usually a very starchy flour used in sauces as a thickener.

Rice Flour
Good for making delicately textured cakes.

Rye Flour
Usually combined with wheat flour to make rye bread. If rye flour is used alone a sour dough levener is needed to provide the elasticity the bread needs.

Potato Flour
A thickener flour used mainly for soups and sauces.

Cottonseed Flour
A high protein flour, used in baked goods to increase the protein content.

An easy formula for a great cake flour is to mix together 2 tablespoons of cornstarch in 1 cup of all-purpose flour.

To reduce the sugar needed for cake and cookies, try using a small amount of vanilla extract to replace each ½ cup of sugar.

To create a better textured cake, add 2 tablespoons of boiling water to the butter and sugar when they are being mixed.

To keep your cookies moist, try adding a teaspoon of jelly to the batter.

If you want a moist cake, try adding 2 tablespoons of corn oil to the mix.

To make thinner pie pastry, before rolling the dough out, coat the board or waxed paper lightly with olive oil and the dough will not crumble when stretched.

Icing will remain where you put it, if you sprinkle the cake first with powdered sugar.

Butter your knife before you cut a pie with a soft filling.

Allow freshly made doughnuts to stand for 15-20 minutes before frying. This will allow air to escape and make the doughnut firmer. By doing this, it will also absorb less grease. Another method of reducing the amount of grease absorbed into a doughnut is to place the doughnut in boiling water, the instant it is removed from the grease. The hot water will keep the excess grease from sticking to the doughnut and release it into the water. Remove after a few seconds and drain well on top of a metal rack.

BEFORE YOUR "COOKIES CRUMBLE"
Store crisp cookies in a cookie can that has a loose cover. If you tightly seal them they may loose their crispness.

Soft Cookies should be stored in a well sealed cookie jar with half an apple or a slice of bread with them to provide moisture. Change the apple or bread regularly.

When using plastic cookie cutters, they should be dipped in warm vegetable oil while you are working. You will get a cleaner, more defined edge on the patterns.

To make your cakes and pancakes moist, try adding a teaspoon or two of honey to the batter.

To keep waxed paper down on the counter when rolling dough, try wetting the counter first.

Use a salt shaker filled with powdered or colored sugar for sprinkling candy or cookies. Make the holes larger if needed.

The best way to cushion cookies for mailing is with popcorn.

Always cut a cake from the center, then you can slide the remains next to each other to keep it fresher.

Cookie dough should be chilled for 15-30 minutes before rolling. This will eliminate the dough from sticking to the rolling pin.

Make chocolate slivers by using a potato peeler on a candy bar.

When baking any pie or dish with a graham cracker crust, dip the pan in warm water for 10 seconds and it will be easier to remove it in one piece.

Angel food cake should be cooled by turning the pan upside down over a tray of ice cubes.

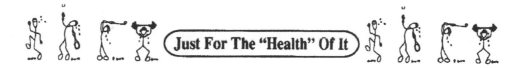

Just For The "Health" Of It

If you increase the amount of egg yolk in a doughnut, it will absorb less grease. Its a toss up whether you increase your fat intake or your cholesterol level.

Never taste the batter when you are baking. It may contain raw eggs and salmonella contamination.

Before you place a cake on a plate, sprinkle the plate with sugar to prevent the bottom of the cake from sticking to the plate.

If you want to revive a stale cake, just dip it quickly in cold low-fat milk and heat it in a 350°F. oven for 15 minutes or until soft.

When mixing batter, spray the beaters with Pam before using them and the batter won't climb up the beaters.

Pastry should be rolled out between two sheets of waxed paper, then remove the top sheet to use the pastry for a pie plate.

HOW TO MAKE A WAFFLE HAPPY

To prevent waffles from sticking to the waffle iron, add a teaspoon of wine to the batter.

To improve the texture of a cake, add a few drops of boiling water to the butter and sugar when creaming.

If your custard pie shrinks away from the crust, you have baked it too long in too hot an oven.

To cut a cake without breaking the icing, wet your knife in boiling water first.

Cream pies are more easily cut if you dip the knife in warm water first.

When a bread or cake browns too quickly, place a small pan of warm water above it in the oven.

Coat dried fruit and nuts with flour being used in a recipe to prevent them from falling to the bottom when baking.

When using a packaged pastry mix for a piecrust, substitute light cream or "lite" sour cream for the liquid in the mix recipe.

Cookies that have become soft can be crisped up by placing them into a low temperature oven for 5 minutes.

When making pancakes, try using a small amount of salt in place of grease on the griddle.

To cook dumplings so that the bottoms don't get soggy, place them on top of the chicken when it is bubbling hot. They will bake faster and be lighter. This will also work for fruit cobblers.

For a great taste try burying a piece of vanilla bean in an airtight jar of granulated sugar for a few days before using the sugar for baking. The gases given off by the bean will flavor the sugar.

Grind up a few black walnuts in a blender then add to pumpkin pie for an improved flavor.

Place at least four toothpicks around the top of a meringue pie and cover with wax paper, if you are going to carry it a distance.

To eliminate a mess, freeze your unfrosted cake before cutting it into decorative party shapes. Your cake will also slice more evenly.

Add a few drops of vinegar to ice water when making pastry. The pastry will come out flakier and lighter.

When storing cake, place half an apple in the container along with the cake. This will help the cake retain freshness.

A "Pie" In The Sky
High Altitude Baking

Over 3,500 feet, increase the temperature 25 ° and add 1 tablespoon more flour to the recipe.

Continue adding 1 tablespoon for every 1,500 feet increase in elevation. ie: 5,000 feet = 2 tablespoons of flour.

When using leavening, if 1 teaspoon is needed at sea level, use 2/3 teaspoon at 3,500 feet and ½ teaspoon at 5,000 feet, then 1/3 teaspoon at 6,500 feet. Use 1/4 teaspoon over 6,500 feet.

Never use warped pans for cookies and cakes, batter may run and will spoil the appearance as well as the product.

Use toothpicks to trace a design on top of an iced cake before adding colored toppings.

Top Selling Cookies

The 4 top selling cookies in the United States in 1994 were:

1.　　Oreo...124 Million Pounds
2.　　Chips Ahoy.................................114 Million Pounds
3.　　Generic Brand Sandwiches..........113 Million Pounds
4.　　Nabisco Newtons......................... 75 Million Pounds

---

"MOVE OVER"
Never overcrowd your oven, heat must circulate freely around all items that are in the oven or they won't bake evenly.

If you are having a problem with your baking soda, powder or cream of tartar they may be too old. Date these products when they are purchased.

"ROCK AND ROLL""
To test the leavening ability of baking powder, place ½ teaspoon in 1/4 cup of hot water. If the powder is usable the water will bubble actively.

Chapter 19

Fast Food Facts

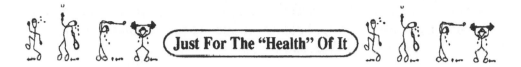

Just For The "Health" Of It

Burger King's Chicken Sandwich contains approximately 42 grams of fat, equivalent to a pint and a half of ice cream.

McDonald's Chicken McNuggets (6) have 21.3 grams of fat, of which 36.5% is saturated fat.

According to the National Restaurant Association, 46 million people are served at fast food restaurants every day in the U.S.

McDonald's french fries contain 11.5 grams of very heavily saturated fat and mostly trans-fatty acids.

Average Fast Food Meal:

	Cal.	Chol.	Sodium	Fat
Hamburger on Bun	550	80mg.	800mg.	57%
Regular Fries	250	10mg.	115mg.	52%
Thick Shake	350	31mg.	210mg.	8%
Apple Pie	260	13mg.	427mg.	21%

"A WORD TO THE WISE"
When in a fast food restaurant try to order wisely. You can cut your fat and salt intake by 10-40% by smart ordering; holding the special sauces, mayonnaise, ketchup, meat pizza toppings, pickles and cheeses.

"NUMERO UNO"
Pizza parlors are the number one fast food outlet in the United States. There are over 44,000 in operation compared to 35,000 burger stands and a total of 140,000 fast food outlets nationwide.

The most popular pizza topping is pepperoni. However, if you order extra cheese you will add more fat that the pepperoni supplies.

"SOUNDS FISHEY"
In Japan the favorite pizza toppings are tuna and scallops.

"FAT CITY"
Carl's Jr. Double Western Bacon Cheeseburger tops all charts with over 1,000 calories and a whopping 63 grams of fat, most of which is saturated. Then add a large order of fries with it.

If you add one packet of ranch dressing to a McDonalds Chef's Salad, it will have more fat than a Big Mac.

When ordering pizza, make sure you ask for "white cheese" only to reduce the total fat.

"DON'T BE A RINGER"
Nine out of ten people consume donuts on a regular basis.

Americans eat 10 billion donuts annually.

The quality of a pizza may depend on the type of flour used to make the crust. It may or may not contain "enriched" flour.

"ROASTED CHICKEN INVASION"

Boston Chicken- ½ chicken with skin contains approximately 650 calories and 40 grams of fat.

Kenny Rogers Roasters- ½ chicken with skin contains approximately 750 calories and 38 grams of fat.

Kentucky Fried- ½ chicken with skin contains approximately 670 calories and 39 grams of fat.

As you can see there isn't much difference. My personal choice, however, is Kenny Rogers. The chicken has a better flavor. Remove the skin to lower the fat content.

Fast food restaurants now have 45% of the dining-out market.

The McLean Burger has 90% fewer calories and 50% less fat than a Quarter Pounder.

"IDAHO'S STATE VEGETABLE"
McDonalds sells 2 million pounds of french fries every day in the United States. They contain approximately ½ million pounds of saturated fat and are high in trans-fatty acids.

200 hamburgers are ordered every second, 24 hours a day.

"NOW, LET'S GET THE PUBLIC TO READ IT AND UNDERSTAND IT"
The FDA has forced fast food restaurants to provide nutritional information to their patrons.

Taco Bell in one year will use the following quantities of food:

> 1.4 Billion Corn & Flour Tortillas
> 119 Million Pounds of Beef
> 83 Million Pounds of Iceberg Lettuce
> 34 Million Pounds of Cheddar Cheese
> 24 Million Pounds of Pinto Beans
> 14 Million Pounds of Fresh Tomatoes

"THE UNINFORMED LEADING THE ADULT"
In over 83% of American families, kids make the decision on which fast food restaurant to go to. The deciding factor seems to be their toy promotion.

Burger king leads the way with the adult population.

Burger King Weight Watchers Fettucini Broiled Chicken is 33% fat by calories.

"AN IMPROVEMENT IN 1994"
McDonald McLean is now 28% fat by calories instead of the old 49%. Leave off the cheese and sauces and it only contains 10 grams of fat.

"LET'S CLOG EM UP EARLY"
Over 1.7 million kids under the age of six eat at a burger restaurant every day. The Vietnam Studies on coronary artery disease showed significant closure of arteries in twenty year olds.

Kentucky Chicken has a new entry into the market "Lite'n Crispy" chicken, which is fried without the skin but is still 52% fat by calories. Contains 17 grams of fat.

Arby's roast beef is not "real roast beef." It is a processed beef with added salt, water and sodium phosphates. However, it is lower in cholesterol and fat than the "real" roast beef.

Arby's spread that is used on their buns is made from a soy product that contains a number of artificial flavors and colors.

There is more sodium in a thick shake than in an order of french fries, due to the additives.

The chocolate coating on soft ice creams is a blend of oils that have a low melting point. It is a high-fat treat.

Chicken coatings contain a higher fat content than most hamburgers.

The pure vegetable oils used by many fast food restaurants for frying may contain high levels of coconut and palm oils. Both are very high in saturated fat content.

A triple cheeseburger contains 983 calories, 576 of those calories come from fat, and contains over 1200mg. of sodium.

When fish is coated and fried it ends up 50% fat in most cases, equal or higher in fat than some burgers.

Baked fish is available at Long John Silver's, a reduction of over 200 calories over fried fish. Even the sodium content is in an acceptable range of 361mg. instead of the usual 1200mg.

A shrimp salad at Jack In The Box has only 115 calories and less than 8% fat, providing you use "lite" dressing.

Arby's now has a roasted chicken sandwich.

Multi-grain buns are showing up everywhere and are an excellent source of fiber.

When fast food restaurants advertise 100% pure beef and you find a large assortment of gristle material in your burger, you might ask them what grade of beef they are using, or what percentage of edible offal they allow in the beef. It's all 100% beef!

A questionable food coloring FD&C Yellow Dye #5 can be found in McDonald's shakes, soft ice cream, Chicken McNuggets, hot cakes and their sundae toppings. MSG can be found in their bacon bits.

Roy Rogers uses MSG as a flavor enhancer in their chicken and roast beef seasonings.

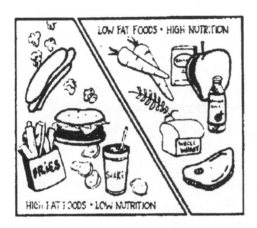

Burger king's chicken sandwich contains 42 grams of fat, equal to a pint and a half of ice cream.

McDonald's has now introduced the "Lite Mac."

Salads and salad bars are now more than ever at fast food restaurants.

Carl's Jr has a BBQ Chicken Sandwich that has been approved by the American Heart Association.

Rating The Fast Foods:

FOOD	BEST RESTAURANT
1. Pizza (vegetarian)	Godfathers
2. Rotisserie Chicken	Kenny Rogers
3. Roast Beef Sandwich	Roy Rogers
4. Hamburger (McLean)	McDonald's
5. Fish Sandwich	None

Since most fast foods contain many additives, large amount of fats and calories galore, you may be interested in writing your favorite one for further information:

Arby's
Ten Piedmont Ctr.
3495 Piedmont Rd. NE
Atlanta, GA 30305

Burger King
P.O. Box 520783
General Mail Facility
Miami, FL 33152

Burger Chef
College Park Pyramids
P.O. Box 927
Indianapolis, IN 46206

Church's Fried Chicken
P.O. Box BH001
San Antonio, TX 78284

Hardee's
1233 N. Church St.
Rocky Mount, NC 27801

Jack In The Box
Foodmaker, Inc.
9330 Balboa Ave
San Diego, CA 92123

Kentucky Fried Chicken
P.O. Box 32070
Louisville, KY 40232

Long John Silver's
P.O. Box 11988
Lexington, KY 40579

McDonald's
McDonald Plaza
Oak Brook, IL 60521

Pizza Hut
P.O. Box 428
Wichita, KS 67201

Roy Rogers
Marriott Corp.
Marriott Dr.
Washington, D.C. 20058

Wendy's
4288 W. Dublin Granville
Dublin, OH 43017

HEALTH HINT:
Milk Shakes "Alias Thick Shake"

The word "milk" in milk shakes use to mean that you were actually purchasing a healthy product that contained "real milk." But, those days are over. Now when you order what you think is a shake, you receive a chemical concoction composed of fat-free milk solids, sweeteners, chemical thickeners, colorings and flavoring agents and a good dose of saturated fat.

These "shakes" are not called milk shakes anymore because they are not even a relative of a "milk shake." New names for these concoctions are: "thick shakes," "super shakes," "vanilla shake," or "chocolate shake." Be aware, however, that some companies are using a small amount of "real milk products" in these shakes so that they can use the word "milk" in their advertisements.

A milk shake is made with "real milk," "real ice cream"and natural syrup or fruit to flavor. These can be made with 1% low-fat milk, a good "natural" low-fat ice cream and "real fruit."

Chapter 20

Food Safety Facts

In a 1994 national survey 44% of the population, results were that the government was only doing a fair job of adequately inspecting fruits and vegetables regarding pesticide and fertilizer residues.

It was determined in a 1994 study that wooden cutting boards may be a source of contamination and cleaning them with hot soapy water doesn't make a significant difference in the bacteria levels. Bleach will do the trick in most instances, make sure you dilute it and rinse thoroughly. Acrylic cutting boards are the best according to the latest studies.

E. coli bacteria may be responsible for 20,000+ cases of food poisoning each year. For your protection cook all meat and poultry to an internal temperature of 160 degrees, wash all fruits and vegetables grown in manure and drink only pasteurized milk and cider.

Many bacteria are found on the surfaces of fruits and vegetables, even melons. Wash all surfaces before slicing any type of food, otherwise the knife may carry the bacteria to the inside.

It takes 4 hours for bacteria on melons to start multiplying. Try to eat it within this period, Refrigeration halts the growth or retards it significantly.

Harmful bacteria do not stop multiplying unless they are refrigerated below 40 degrees. Most refrigerators rarely hold this temperature.

Freezing does not kill bacteria it only stops their growth. The only thing that kills the bacteria is cooking.

Foodborne illness strikes 80 million Americans yearly. Most are mild cases, however, 9,000 are fatal. Most caused from meat and poultry.

Never store wine or spirits in a lead crystal decanter for a long period. They may leach out the lead. Vinegar dressing may also do the same due to its acidic nature.

Reported salmonella food poisoning cases have increased over 40% during the last ten years. A good percentage of these cases have been associated with fast food restaurants.

Boil all kitchen sponges at least once per week to be sure they are contaminant-free.

Never re-heat or save infant formula after a child has drunken from it. Bacteria will still remain alive, should be discarded.

Never slow cook a turkey overnight at 200 degrees. This gives the bacteria too long a period to multiply.

A cooked or raw turkey should never be kept unrefrigerated for more than 45 minutes.

MEAT AND POULTRY SAFETY LINE- 1 (800)535-4555

If the contents of a can or jar have a funny smell, are moldy or have an off color look, don't eat it!

Never eat foods directly from a jar or can, saliva may contaminate the contents.

THE "NOSE" KNOWS
Never smell a moldy food, it may cause an allergic reaction.

Meats should be kept hot. Use a thermometer to keep the temperature of meats, poultry and pork at 140°F.

Always keep eggs under refrigeration.

Refrigerate foods as soon as possible. Bacterial growth starts very quickly at between 45 °F. and 120 °F.

Anyone with an infection or cold should be kept away from the kitchen.

Small areas of mold on solid fruits or vegetables can usually be removed leaving the food still edible. Cut away an extra inch in case the mold has already sent feelers out.

Antibiotics should not be taken with food, it slows its absorption and possibly its potency levels.

Mayonnaise and salad dressing under normal conditions would not have to be refrigerated after opening. The reason it is recommended is that when you are making a salad, you tend to keep dipping the spoon in for more mayonnaise and leave residues of the salad in the jar.

Never eat food if it has been prepared by someone who is smoking at the time of preparation. Saliva from their hands, from continuously touching the cigarette may contaminate the food.

Never cover refrigerator shelves with tin foil. Air should be able to circulate around the foods.

Peanut butter should be stored in the refrigerator after opening to keep the fats from becoming rancid.

Leftovers that have remained in the refrigerator more than 36 hours should be recooked.

Never place cooked foods on the same surface that has fresh food on it.

Thaw frozen foods in the refrigerator, not at room temperature.

Your can opener should be washed after each use. Food left behind may be contaminated after a few days and cause food poisoning. This is one of the most common sources of food poisoning.

Consuming a large quantity of natural licorice may cause hypertension, heart enlargement and sodium retention due to the chemicals glycynhizic acid and menthol. 3 1/2oz. per day over a prolonged period can be harmful.

Always strain soups that may contain pieces of bone through a strainer. Place a coarse strainer inside a fine one for the best results.

To avoid the fat from catching fire when broiling meats, place a few pieces of dried bread in the broiler pan to soak up the dripping fat.

Never stuff a turkey or other fowl with warm stuffing and leave overnight, even if refrigerated.

Do not leave gravy, stuffing or cooked fowl at room temperature for more than 30-45 minutes before refrigerating.

If turkey or chicken salad is made, wait until the meat is fully cooled before adding any type of salad dressing or mayonnaise.

There are 1800 strains of salmonella, most of which will cause food poisoning. Millions of Americans annually suffer from food poisoning episodes. Most problems occur as a result of human error.

A large majority of food poisonings are related to the "pot luck" type of event. These usually are from poor temperature controls of foods containing egg or meat products.

Either keep foods cold or hot and you will reduce the risk of a problem. It is the mid-ranges that cause the most bacteria growth.

If mold is seen in jams and jellies (a small spot), scoop it out with a clean spoon, then scoop out a little more with a another clean spoon. If the balance tastes fermented, throw it out.

Throw out moldy vegetables, especially tomatoes, cucumbers and lettuce.

A good rule of thumb is just to throw out any food item that contains mold. Cheese may be the only exception, but be sure to cut away at least ½ to 1 inch away from the moldy area.

Foods cooked in aluminum pans that are damaged may absorb the metal, if there are any corroded areas marked by pitting and surrounded by white areas and if the pot is used frequently it may result in high risk of impaired kidney function and behavioral anomalies.

When you marinate any meat or poultry, make sure you leave it in the refrigerator while it is marinating.

Never place barbecued meats of any type on the same plate that held the raw meat after it has been cooked. This is one of the most common causes of food poisoning when barbecuing. Also, never continue to use the same utensils that touched the raw meat.

Use a fresh dish towel after you clean up from handling meats or poultry, then throw it in the wash and don't leave it sit out for further use.

A new study completed in 1995 by the federal government Center For Food Safety and Applied Nutrition showed that only one out of four people wash their cutting boards after cutting or preparing raw meats and poultry.

CONSUMER NUTRITION SAFETY HOTLINE
1 (800) 366-1655

Chapter 21

Food, Not For Eating

Hot white vinegar will remove the non-slip decals from the bathtub as well as stickers on dishes.

"BLACK-OUT"
Margarine will remove tar off vinyl surfaces.

"SQUEAKY CLEAN"
A good cleaner that won't leave a film on tile is a mixture of white vinegar and water. Use approximately one quarter cup of vinegar to 1 gallon of warm water.

Peanut butter will remove gum from a person's hair.

"I WONDER WHERE THE YELLOW WENT"
Stale milk or leftover milk makes an excellent cleaner for plant leaves.

Mayonnaise can be used to oil wood.

Salt is handy for sopping up wine spills. Pour the salt on the spill, wait until it dries, then vacuum it up.

After boiling potatoes, use the water to polish silver. Just place the silver in the warm water. Place a washcloth on the bottom of the pot before placing silver in.

A paste of baking soda will remove black heel marks from a vinyl floor.

Top clean stains from aluminum pots, try boiling rhubarb in the pan until the stain disappears.

Meat tenderizer can be used to relieve the pain and itching from insect bites. Dissolve 1/4 to ½ teaspoon in a small amount of water.

Tomato juice will remove ink spots on clothing. Allow to soak for 20 minutes before washing.

Orange juice can be used to clean chrome.

Banana skins will provide an excellent source of plant nutrients if buried just below the surface. Especially good for flowers.

Egg-white sponged on leather will revive its luster.

Half a lemon dipped in salt will clean copper or brass, then rinse in warm water and polish with soft cloth.

Brewer's yeast rubbed on a dog or cat's fur will repel fleas. Giving them a vitamin B supplement approved by your vet will also help.

THE "NOSE" KNOWS
A few drops of vanilla extract placed in a bottle top in the refrigerator, will remove odors.

If your white socks are getting dingy, just boil a pot of water, add 2 slices of lemon or ½ teaspoon of lemon juice and soak for ten minutes. Then wash as you normally would.

Dry mustard will remove onion odors from your hands or cutting board. Rub in then rinse off.

Ink stains can usually be removed by placing a slice of tomato on the stain. It should soak up the stain. Hair spray may also work on an old stain.

Don't buy dustcloths treated to attract dust, just dip a piece of cheesecloth in a solution of 2 cups of water and 1/4 cup of lemon oil, then allow it to dry before using it.

Leftover tea will clean varnished furniture.

After you polish your wood furniture, sprinkle a small amount of cornstarch on and rub until you get a high gloss. The cornstarch will absorb oil and leave a great shine.

Sheer curtains will come out of the washer "wrinkle-free" if you dissolve a package of unflavored gelatin in a cup of boiling water and then add it to the final rinse.

For a brighter shoe shine, place a few drops of lemon juice on your shoes when you are polishing them.

Lemon juice and salt will remove mold and mildew.

Glue on containers can be removed by using vegetable oil.

Diamonds and gold can be cleaned with a solution of vinegar and water. Never place opals, emeralds and pearls in the solution or any other soft stone or costume jewelry.

Costume jewelry can be cleaned with a weak solution of baking soda and water. Then scrub lightly with a toothbrush.

If you burn your tongue, try sprinkling a few grains of sugar on it for instant relief.

To polish brass, use a small amount of Worcestershire sauce, clean off, then polish with olive oil.

Baking soda makes an excellent fire extinguisher. It smothers the flames by cutting off the oxygen supply.

If you have a problem removing a nut and bolt, just pour some carbonated soda on it and let it sit for 15 minutes.

Battery posts can be cleaned with a thick solution of baking soda and water. Allow it to soak for 10-15 minutes before washing it off. Baking soda is a base and will neutralize a weak acid.

To remove unwanted grass from between sidewalk and driveway cracks, try using vinegar or salt.

An inexpensive method of cleaning dentures is to soak them overnight in white vinegar.

Vinegar can be used to clean pipes.

White rings on furniture may be removed using a paste of salad oil and salt. Let the solution stand for a few hours then wipe it off.

Baking soda added to furniture oil may remove stains from woodwork. Adds just the right amount of mild abrasive.

To remove grease stains on your carpet, try placing corn starch on the area, leave overnight, then vacuum up.

Corn starch and water made into a paste may remove grease stains on some wallpapers. Try an area that doesn't show first, to be sure that the wallpaper won't be damaged.

A minor burn can be relieved by rubbing a slice of raw potato on the burn gently.

To stop a bad sunburn from blistering, try using a small amount of white vinegar.

Vanilla extract will relieve the pain of a grease burn.

"SMOKERS BEWARE"
To remove cigarette smoke from a room, try soaking a towel in a solution of vinegar and water, ring out completely, then wave it in a circular motion around the room.

Accidently hitting the smoker also helps.

To tenderize meats when barbecuing, add green papaya to the barbecue sauce. Don't leave the meat in too long or it will become mushy.

Buttermilk can be used to soften dry cheese.

Pecans, walnuts or peanuts can be used to mask scratches on furniture. Use a broken edge of the nut.

"SPOT OFF TEA"
Cold tea is a good cleaning agent for woodwork of any kind.

A slice of bread will often remove makeup smudges from dark clothes. It's not necessary to use the nutritious ones.

Along with your detergent, add a bottle of cola to a load of greasy work clothes. It will help loosen the serious dirt.

Instead of throwing leftover cola down the kitchen drain, dump it down the toilet bowl and watch what happens. After it has soaked for awhile the toilet bowl should be sparkling clean.

Lemon extract will remove black scuff marks from luggage.

Stains from ball-point pens can be removed by sponging the area with milk until it disappears.

"ELIMINATING A CRACK-UP"

A simple way to remove cracks in china cups is to simmer the cup in milk for 30-45 minutes, depending on the size of the crack. If the crack is not too wide, the protein in the milk will seal it.

After grating cheese, clean the grater with a raw potato.

Ball point pen stains can be removed with 70% alcohol or hair spray.

Chapter 22

Packaging and Food Nutrient Facts

IS FRESH FOOD REALLY FRESH?

The freshness and quality depends on many factors such as:

Transportation times
Storage conditions
Methods of packaging
Type of fertilizer used
Time of harvesting
Number of washings in supermarket
Exposure to air and light
Soil nutrient content

Fresh foods are usually the best choice, regardless of these factors. Some supermarket chains have become more aware of pesticide and fertilizer contamination and the percentage of filth on fruits and vegetables and are doing more than ever to correct this problem. One of the best examples of this is the Raley's Supermarket chain in Northern California.

CANNED FOODS:

The majority of canned foods are flavor poor with a "canned taste." Shelf life, however, is excellent and is usually between 2-4 years, depending on the food item.

Many of the vitamins and minerals tend to wash out over time from the liquid, usually resulting in a chemical breakdown of the nutrient. Enzymes are non-existent.

The cost of canned foods are generally twice the cost of dehydrated foods, since the consumer pays for the water weight as well as the food. Up to ½ the weight of a canned product may be water.

Nutritionally the products are generally low in nutrient quality due the intense heat processing they undergo. If you consume most of your fruits and vegetables from canned goods, it is recommended that you take a vitamin/mineral supplement.

FROZEN FOODS:

The flavor varies from excellent to poor depending on the product. If the foods are frozen at the time they are picked, the nutritional quality may be equal to, or even better than fresh, at the time of purchase.

Shelf life and quality is very dependent on the maintenance of proper freezer chest temperature levels.
Also, they should not be relied upon for long term storage or emergency use.

The cost is higher than dehydrated or canned but nutritional quality drops, the longer the freezer time.

DRIED FOODS:

Flavor varied depending on the age. These foods should not be stored for a long period of time, since the moisture content is only 25-30% water.

FREEZE DRIED FOODS:

Excellent flavor, but they yield considerably less servings per can, due to retention of their cellular structure, and have less shrinkage than dehydrated foods.

Shelf life is generally considered to be 4-7 years, if properly packed. Once opened they will spoil within 5-7 days.

The cost is considerably more than dehydrated foods, and has a moisture content of approximately 25-30%.

DEHYDRATED FOODS:

Many are vine-ripened with excellent flavor. In some instances it was found that dehydration actually enhanced the flavor of the foods.

The following is an example of dehydration reduction:

12 pounds of fresh beans = 1 pound of dehydrated
14 pounds of carrots = 1 pound of dehydrated
6 pounds of cheese = 1 pound of dehydrated

Most dehydrated foods are nitrogen vacuum packaged and if unopened may last indefinitely. They would be capable of sustaining life even after many years of storage. However, the nutritive life span is probably only 5-7 years.

For best results, foods should be rotated and used allowing a shelf life of 2-3 years maximum. Once the cans are opened they should be kept covered with a good sealing lid. The nitrogen in the can will leak out if the can is tipped over after opening and the product should then be used up soon after.

Storage locations should be located in a cool place.

Dehydrated foods are processed under a very high vacuum and very low drying temperature, making it possible to remove all but 2-3% of the moisture in the food. These foods also retain their nutritional value since they are not cooked to death in a canning process.

Purchasing and using dehydrated foods may reduce your grocery bill by as much as 40%, if incorporated into the diet properly and frequently.

Generally, as a rule of thumb, dehydrated foods will reconstitute two or three times their weight. This will call for conservative measures when using these foods.

Chapter 23

Soft Drink Facts

The Coca Cola Company purchases more sugar than any other company in the world.

According to an article in the Pennsylvania Medical Journal, a study showed that the increase in carbonic acid use may lead to an increase in nearsightedness.

Due to quantity of refined sugar in soft drinks, they tend to cause a rise in blood sugar levels for a short period of time. The levels then may plummet down causing a severe drop in physical strength and mental alertness.

Excess dietary phosphorus is fast becoming a medical concern. The ideal calcium to phosphorus ratio is approximately 50/50 in adults. The concern is that soft drinks supply an excess amount of phosphorus, upsetting this ratio. This may lead to a calcium deficiency, which should be of special concern to women entering their "osteoporosis years."

The average intake of phosphorus in the U.S. is now about 1500-1600mg per day. The recommended daily allowance is 800mg. The following is the phosphorus content of a few soft drinks:

Soft Drinks	Milligrams of Phosphorus/oz.
Coke	69.9
Pepsi Cola	57.2
Diet Cherry Coke	55.7
Diet Pepsi	49.3
Dr. Pepper	44.7
Tab	44.4
Kool-Aide (lemonade flavor)	31.6
Hires Root Beer	22.4
Hawaiian Punch (lemonade flavor)	16.7
7-Up	3.0
Canada Dry Ginger Ale	3.0
A&W Root Beer	3.0

The "fizz" in soft drinks in most cases is produced by reacting chalk, limestone or bicarbonate of soda with sulfuric acid.

If the drink does not say "natural sources" it probably contains a color or flavoring that is made from "coal tars."

Coca-Cola is consumed 190 million times every 24 hours in more than 80 languages and in over 35 countries.

The soft drink industry is a $40 billion dollar a year business.

Soft-drinks account for one-quarter of all sugar consumed by Americans.

A child who consumes 4 colas per day takes in the equivalent caffeine of two cups of coffee. The carbonic acid and phosphorus content can affect the potency of a number of vitamins.

Colas that contain Nutrasweet may go stale after only 3 months, look for the expiration dates. Drinks may get a bitter taste as the sweetener breaks down.

A study in Florida showed that people who drank a large number of Dr. Pepper or Diet Coke had problems with recurrent kidney stones probably from the phosphoric acid used in the carbonation process. Persons with stone problems should avoid these drinks. Read the list of ingredients, many sodas use the same carbonating agent.

"BOTTOMS UP"
Soda pop is the beverage of choice over milk and juice in children across the United States, mainly due to baby bottles being produced that look like 7-Up. Pepsi and Coke containers.

"SOMETHINGS GONE WRONG"
Americans in 1990 spent three times the dollars on soft drinks than they did on milk, six times more on alcohol.

"LACK OF NUTRITION EDUCATION IN SCHOOLS"

Americans consumed 24 gallons of soft drinks per person in 1970. In 1994 we outdid ourselves and consumed 46 gallons per person.

Diet sodas may still be high in sodium.

Soft drinks may react with certain antacids, leading to constipation, headaches and even vomiting.

We have increased our soft drink consumption 200% over the 1950's.

The efficiency of the certain antibiotics can be reduced by consuming soft drinks.

We consume 500 bottles or cans of soft drinks per person per year.

Millions of American are now being called "colaholics" due to their addiction to the cola beverages.

Withdrawal symptoms usually occur from "caffeine highs" when cola drinks are given up. These include headaches, nervousness, diarrhea and constipation.

Colas have a higher physiological dependence than smoking and alcohol and is harder to give up.

Sugar supplies 99% of the 144 calories in a 12 ounce Coke.

40% of the nation's 1-2 year olds drink an average of 9 ounces of soft drinks per day.

Teenagers now prefer soft-drinks over milk. 10% of these soft-drinks are consumed at breakfast.

Calcium levels are marginal in teenagers due to their soft-drink consumption.

The acid in soft-drinks can erode tooth enamel.

The average adult consumes about 182.5 gallons of liquid annually. The following is the breakdown:

44.5 gallons of soft drinks
44.3 gallons of water
26.3 gallons of coffee
23.8 gallons of beer
20.1 gallons of milk
23.5 gallons of tea, juice, and other
alcoholic drinks

The average level of caffeine in colas is 26.5mg per cola.

Chapter 24

Supermarket Facts

Be sure that all foods that should be under refrigeration are under refrigeration and not stacked up over the cold line. Supermarkets are known to stack whole poultry higher than they should. This causes bacterial growth to begin.

Make sure the store is clean, if not don't shop there!

Are the employees neat and clean looking?

"BRRRRRRRRRRR"
Check the thermometer in the meat cases. They should be between 28° and 38°F. The dairy products should be between 35° and 45°F. Ice cream should be approximately -12°F.

Don't buy frozen foods if there are large ice crystals on the packages, foods may have been thawed and re-frozen.

Processed hams should be under refrigeration, frequently they are not. Canned ones as well.

Never buy a jar if it is sticky, somethings gone wrong somewhere.

"WHAT'S IN A NAME"
Many markets have their own names to make you think that the product is of a higher grade than it really is.

These names are similar to ones used by the USDA in most cases. They include: "Premium", "Quality", "Select Cut", "Market Choice", "Prime Cut", etc.

Shop when the store is not crowded so that you can see the specials.

Most weekend specials start midweek.

Foods on the lowest shelves are usually the least expensive.

Tumble displays are more common than the old pyramid type, since shoppers hate to disturb a neat display.

Buy by the case whenever possible, if the market has a sale.

Check the weights of fruits and vegetables, the heaviest not the biggest is usually the best value.

Don't be afraid to return poor quality products.

The most commonly purchased items are usually found in the center of an aisle.

Highest profit items are found at eye level.

Items found in bins at greatly reduced prices near the checkout register are usually products that have been difficult to sell.

Avoid bruised fruits and vegetables.

Label Terminology:

- All food ingredients must be on the label.
- All additives must be listed.
- Many food products still do not require nutrition information.
- Symbols:

"R" means that the trademark used on the label is registered with the U.S. Patent Office.

"C" indicates that any literary and artistic content on the label is protected by copyright.

"K" indicates that the food is Kosher.

Chapter 25

Restaurant Facts

Restaurants are becoming more willing to serve salad dressings and mayonnaise on the side than ever before. Don't trade with one that doesn't.

Most restaurants will now prepare your food broiled or baked instead of fried when you request them to do so, especially the better restaurants.

If you have a question regarding substitutions, talk to the manager directly and don't deal with the waitress.

Return any meat or poultry that is not fully cooked, this is one of the most common causes of food poisoning, the most common problems are usually in chicken and hamburger.

If you are going to eat a salad or other food from a buffet or salad bar, make sure that they are not browned or dried out before being seated.

Be sure custard, whipped cream and cream-filled desserts are refrigerated. In many of the largest buffets these are just placed out on a tray with the rest of the dessert items.

Are the dishes and silverware clean.

Does the server touch the top of the glasses where you drink from?

Ask for a straw for all beverages served in a glass.

Is the cream for the tea or coffee kept at room temperature instead of being refrigerated.

Are the servers in clean uniforms?

Are the dishes chipped or discolored, restaurants that do not care about the little things are not too careful about cleanliness.

Are the bathrooms clean?

Look at the window sills for insect residues and dirt.

Are the curtains or blinds clean and dust-free?

If the menus are stained with food or have actual food residues, it is best to leave while you have a chance.

The condiment containers should be clean and not caked with the product.

Cream containers should be kept under refrigeration and brought to the table when requested.

Do the employees have their long hair tied back properly.

Chapter 26

Consumer Awareness Facts

If you see a label on an individual food stating that it is "low-cholesterol" it cannot contain more than 20mg. of cholesterol per serving and 2 grams of fat.

The government allows 350 pesticide ingredients to be used on crops. Approximately 70 of these have been classified as possible carcinogens.

If a food is labeled "low-fat" it cannot contain more than 3 grams of fat per individual serving. This may still be high since most companies figure 30% of your calories can come from fat. Still need to calculate and multiply 9 calories per gram times the total amount of fat you are actually eating. I prefer no more than 20% fat in a diet.

The only "low-fat" milks are 1% which is 16% fat after you remove the water, skim and buttermilk.

If the label reads "low in saturated fat" the food cannot have more than 1 gram of fat per serving. Make sure, however, that you count up the total in the full amount your eating, it may be higher than you think.

Filth in food guidelines in foods are controlled by the FDA. The following levels of contamination (insects, etc.) if found in food would be cause for the FDA to take legal action to remove the food from the supermarket. This is just a small example:

Apricots - Canned, average of 2% insect infested or damaged.

Coffee Beans - If 10% by count are insect infested or insect damaged or show evidence of mold.

Citrus Juice - Canned, microscopic mold count average of 10%. Drosophila and other fly eggs: 5 per 250ml. Drosophila larva: 1 per 250ml. If average of 5% by count contain larvae.

Peaches - Canned, Average of 5% wormy or moldy fruit or 4% if a whole larva or equivalent is found in 20% of the cans.

Popcorn - One rodent pellet in one or more sub-samples upon examination of ten 225gm. sub-samples or six 10 ounce consumer-size packages, and 1 rodent hair in other subsamples; or 2 rodent hairs per pound and any rodent hairs in 50% of the sub-samples; or 20 gnawed grains per pound and rodent hairs in 50% of the sub-samples.

Asparagus - Canned. 15% of spears by count infested with 6 attached asparagus beetle eggs or egg sacs.

Broccoli - Frozen, average of 80 aphids or thrips per 100 grams.

Tomato Juice - 10 fly eggs per 3 ½ oz. or 5 fly eggs and 1 larva per 3 ½ oz. or 2 larva per 3 ½ oz.

Raisins -   Average of 40mm. of sand and grit per 3 ½ oz. or 10 insects and 35 fly eggs per 8 oz. of golden bleached raisins.

Wheat -   One rodent pellet per pint. 1% by weight of insect-damaged kernels.

Brussel Sprouts -   Average of 40 aphids per 3 ½ oz.

Flour -   The FDA allows wheat flour to contain approximately 50 insect parts per 2 ounces of flour. These are harmless and won't affect your health.

Sorbital, used as a sweetener in diabetic candies can cause diarrhea.

Pineapple juice may help keep arteries clear with the chemical bromelin.

Label Terminology

Low-Calorie -   Allowed to contain only 40 calories per serving or a maximum of .4 calories per gram.

Reduced Calorie -   Must have at least 1/3 fewer calories than the original product and should include a comparison of both versions.

Diet or Dietetic -   The product may be lower in calories, sodium or sugar.

Lite or Light -   This term can have any meaning the
manufacturer wants to use it for, such
as a relation to taste, texture,
color, or may have a lowered calorie,
fat or sodium content.

No Cholesterol -   Means that the item has no cholesterol
but may still be high in saturated
fats which may assist the body to
produce cholesterol.

Low-Fat -   When pertaining to dairy products,
they must only contain between 0.45
and 2% fat by weight.

Extra Lean -   Usually pertains to meat and poultry.
They must have no more than 5% fat by
weight.

If a food is labeled "extra lean" it may contain more saturated fat than a "low in saturated fat" food.

Lean -   Usually pertains to meat and poultry.
They must have no more than 10% fat by
weight.

Leaner -   Usually pertains to meat and poultry.
Must have at least 25% less fat than
the standard.

Sugar-Free -   Should contain no table sugar, but
or   still may contain some of the
Sugarless   following; honey, corn syrup,
sorbital or fructose. Most of which
are just other forms of sugar and
still high in calories.

Sodium-Free -	Should contain less than 5mg per serving.
Very Low Sodium -	Contains 35mg or less per serving.
Low Sodium -	Contains 140mg or less per serving.
Reduced Sodium -	The normal level of sodium in the product has been reduced by at least 75%.
No Salt Added -	Salt has not been added during the unsalted processing. The food may still have other ingredients that contain sodium.
Imitation -	A food which is a substitute for another food and is usually nutritionally inferior. May still contain the same number of calories and fat.
Organic -	May pertain to almost anything. Usually means a food that is grown without the use of artificial fertilizers.
Natural -	May mean anything, no regulations apply and may be seen on foods that have additives and preservatives.
Enriched -	A degraded, processed product that or Fortified has nutrients added back in.

97% of people who purchased processed foods never read the labels according to a 1988 survey. In 1994 the same survey showed that 84% still don't read the labels. We are making progress but have a long way to go.

RECOMMENDED SHELF LIFE FOR SOME NESTLE PRODUCTS

The Nestle Company was kind enough to release data regarding the shelf life of some of their products and their dating code system. What may surprise you is the length of time that a product is considered safe to sell. There was no mention, however, how much of the nutritional quality was left after 1-2 years in a package.

SHELF LIFE - CONFECTIONS

7 Months:	Baby Ruth- bars, nuggets
10 Months:	Butterfingers, Goobers, Oh Henry
12 Months:	Crunch, 100 Grand, Raisinets, Chunky, After Eight, DeMet's Turtles
15 Months:	Milk Chocolate Bar
18 Months:	Caramel, Licorice, Butter Rum, Chocolate Mint
24 Months:	Sno Caps

SHELF LIFE - BAKING CHOCOLATE

12 Months:	Premier White Morsels
15 Months:	White Baking Bars
18 Months:	Butterscotch Morsels
24 Months:	Semi-sweet and Unsweetened Baking Bars, Choco-Bake, Nestle Cocoa, Milk Chocolate, Mint, Rainbow Morsels

SHELF LIFE - BAKING PRODUCTS

9 Months:	Carnation Lite Skimmed Evaporated Milk
12 Months:	Carnation Low-Fat Evaporated, Non-Fat Dry Milk
15 Months:	Carnation Evaporated Milk
24 Months:	Libby's Solid Pack Pumpkin, Libby's Pumpkin Pie Mix

SHELF LIFE - CULINARY

18 Months: Libby's Dinner, Contadina Pizza Squeeze
24 Months: Contadina Canned Products, Contadina Bread
                  Crumbs, Libby's/Broadcast canned meats,
                  Libby's canned salmon, Libby's tomato sauce

SHELF LIFE - NUTRITIONAL PRODUCTS

9 Months: Sweet Success: Snack Bars, Chocolate Oatmeal
                 Raisin, Chocolate Peanut Butter and Chocolate
                 Raspberry
12 Months: Carnation Breakfast Bars, Carnation Instant
                 Breakfast, Sweet Success: ready-to-drink cans
24 Months: Sweet Success: powder

PRODUCTION CODES

Nestle products display one of two production code formats. This will assist you in determining the age of their products.

1.   *First example: "KA201."*

    The part of this code you will need is the part that tells you the month and the year. The second letter in the code "A" stands for the month. "A" = January, "B" = February and so on, omitting "I." The first number "2" stands for the year. "2" = 1992, "1" = 1991, "0" =1990, "9" = 1989 and so on.

2.   *Second example: "3029WW 1823"*

    The part of the code that you need is the part that tells the year and day of the year. The first number of the code stands for the last digit of the year (in this example, 1993). The next three numbers, 029, stand for the twenty-ninth day (month of January) of 1993. A code of 2259WW1579 would mean that the product was produced on the 259th day (month of September) of 1992.

Chapter 27

Cooking Facts

Microwave ovens that do not have a movable turntable may be guilty of leaving cold spots that result in undercooked areas of the food. This may result in bacteria not being killed in that area.

Measurement Facts:

60 drops = 1 teaspoon   3 teaspoons = 1 tablespoon
2 tablespoons = 1 fl. oz.   8 tablespoons = ½ cup
Juice of 1 orange = 5-6 tsp.   5 large eggs = 1 cup
2 tablespoons butter = 1 oz.

"ANY PAN WON'T DO"
The type of pan you use to cook in may make a difference in the quality of the finished product. Best to bake in a dull finish aluminum pan. A dark pan may cool too quickly and a shinny pan reflects heat to such a degree that you may not get even cooking.

"CURDLING UP"
Always cook recipes that contain eggs, sour cream or cream at a lower setting to avoid curdling.

"GETTING DIRECTIONS RIGHT"
When cooking in a microwave, be sure to place the thicker tougher areas of foods toward the outer edges of the cooking pan.

"PAN ALERT, PAN ALERT"
Non-stick pans, including all of the best brands may be dangerous if you allow them to boil dry. At 400 degrees F. the pans may release toxic fumes after about 20 minutes, enough to make a person sick. This could be even more serious for birds and other small pets.

To avoid damage to your microwave oven, keep a cup of water in it when its not in use. If it is turned on accidently by a child, damage may occur.

If food has a higher water content it will cook better in a microwave.

"KA-BOOM, KA-BOOM"
Never microwave any food in a sealed container, it will probably explode.

"GIVE THE DOG THE BONE"
When microwaving meats with bones, remember the bone attracts more microwave energy than the meat and the meat may not cook evenly.

"USELESS FACT"
Microwave ovens are used most by people age 44 or younger.

It is just as safe to cook foods in a microwave as it is on a range or in an oven.

Never place a whole egg in the shell in the microwave, it might explode and make a mess.

"A FINE MESS YOU GOT INTO"
When cooking an egg that is out of the shell in a microwave, prick the yolk with a fine pin or it may pop and you've got another mess.

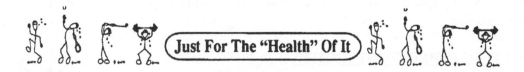

Just For The "Health" Of It

When deep fat frying, use a pure vegetable oil, preferably one with a high smoke point such as corn or safflower. A new oil Canola is also excellent.

Butter, margarine or lard will burn before reaching the temperature desired for frying.

Fat should only be heated to 400°F. Any higher will cause the fat to deteriorate.

Cook all vegetables at the highest power setting in a microwave. The faster they cook the more nutrients will be retained.

Baking soda should never be added to foods that are cooking, since it may destroy certain B vitamins.

Unless you fry or cook an oil, cooking lowers the fat content of any meat.

If fat is too hot, the food is apt to be too brown and dry on the outside and uncooked on the inside.

After you cook in a Wok, wipe the inner surface with vegetable oil to retard any rust forming.

 Chef's Secrets

When foods are cut they should be of uniform sizes to assure that they will cook and be done at the same time.

Foods that are to be fried, should be dried thoroughly before frying to avoid splattering.

If you use glass or Corning Ware dishes in the oven, you can reduce the heat by 25°F.

If you add 1 ½ teaspoons of butter to a cooking pasta or soup it will not boil over.

Always use a shallow pot for cooking a roast, they will allow air to circulate better than deep ones.

Try not to fry too much food at once to avoid a fat overflow. Recommended is only a half-full fryer basket.

To avoid food from sticking together, try lifting the basket out of the fat several times before allowing it to stay in the fat.

All fried foods should be placed on paper towels and allowed to drain for a few minutes before serving.

Cooking Vegetables

Baking Vegetables -   Their skins will preserve most of their nutrient value. When baking, the vegetable must have a high enough water content not to dry out. Root vegetables are the best to bake as well as any potato, winter squash or onion.

Steaming -   Probably the best for all types of vegetables. It retains the nutrients and cooks in a short period of time.

Pressure Cooking -   Will shorten cooking times thus saving the nutrients. The problem here is if you overcook even for a short period of time the vegetables turn to mush. Since vegetables all have a different consistency this is a problem.

Pan Frying -   Using a small amount of oil is another fast method of cooking. A Wok is fine too. Remember, however, that when cooking vegetables in oils, the fat soluble vitamins may end up in the oil. You may want to keep the oil for the sauce.

Waterless Cooking -   Works well for green leafy vegetables using only the water that adheres to their leaves after washing. This usually takes only 3-5 minutes.

Boiling-   Not recommended, due to the high loss of nutrients. If you must use this method, add the vegetables only after the water starts boiling and cook for the shortest period of time possible.

Crock Pot - Should only be used for vegetables if they are precooked then added to the stew, etc. just before you serve the dish.

Microwave - Cooking is fast and will retain the nutrient levels very well. Cooking times will vary depending on the wattage of your unit.

NOTE:

Refrigerate all foods as soon as possible, this will help you retain the potencies of the nutrients. Whole boiled carrots will retain 90% of their vitamin C and most of their minerals, but if you slice it up before cooking you will lose almost all of the vitamin C and niacin content.

HEALTH HINT:

When boiling vegetables there are a few good rules to follow:

(1)   Allow the water to boil for at least 2
        minutes since the water will lose a high
        percentage of its oxygen. It is this high
        oxygen content of the water that causes the
        vitamin C potency to be reduced.

(2)   Cook the vegetables in as large a piece as
        possible, then cut them up after they cook.

(3)   Never place vegetables in cold water and
        then bring it to a boil. If this is done some
        vegetables can lose up to 10-12 times their
        vitamin C content.

When cooking potatoes it is best to pierce the skin with a fork to allow the steam to escape.

Salt should be added after cooking so that it won't draw the liquids out of the foods.

"Cookware - Just The Current 1995 Facts"

Aluminum

50% of all cookware sold in the United States is aluminum. Recent 1994 evidence shows that aluminum cookware does not pose any health risks. Especially increasing the risk of Alzheimers Disease.

Iron

Can supply a small amount of iron to your diet. Acidic foods such as tomatoes and applesauce when cooked for prolonged periods will absorb the most iron. After 25 minutes spaghetti sauce will have about 6mg. of iron per 3 1/2oz. serving.

Stainless Steel

Not the best heat conductor unless they have a copper or aluminum bottom. When acidic foods are cooked in stainless steel it may leach a number of metals into the food, some such as chlorine and iron are useful, but others such as nickel are not as healthful.

Non-Stick Coated

Such as Teflon and Silver Stone, are made of a type of fluorocarbon resin that will not react with foods. If a small portion does flake off and get into the food it would pass harmlessly through your body.

Glass, Copper Pots and Enamalized Cookware

These do not react with foods and are safe to cook in. Copper conducts heat well and is preferred by many chefs. Copper pans should have a liner of tin or stainless steel to be safe.

When cooking a complicated dish that takes a long time to cook, try partially cooking it in the microwave first.

Microwave food packages may now pollute your food. Popcorn and pizza are the two that are under investigation, and may leak hazardous chemicals into the foods.

When cooking custard, place a piece of waxed paper over it while it is still hot to avoid a skin from forming.

Preparation Of Foods:

Washing/Soaking - Many vitamins are water soluble and will be lost through washing, scrubbing or long periods of soaking. Soaking carrots causes the loss of the natural sugar, all the B vitamins, vitamin C and D and all the minerals except calcium.

Dice/Slice/Peel/Shred - The smaller you cut fruits and vegetables, the more surface is exposed to temperature, the air (oxidation) and light. Prepare as close to serving time as possible. Shredding for salads cause a 20% loss of vitamin C and an additional 20% loss if the salad stands for an hour before eating.

NOTE:
The skin of fruits and vegetables contain at least 10% of the nutritional content of that food.

HEALTH HINT:
> The worst pots to use, due to metals leaching into the foods or reactions of acidic or alkaline foods are unlined copper, aluminum or stainless steel pots. Non-stick pots are okay as long as the coating is unbroken.

BARBECUING FOOD FACTS:

Pour enough briquets into a grocery bag for one barbecue and fold it down. When you have a quantity of bags filled, pile one on top of another until you are ready to barbecue. Just light the bag and the charcoal will catch very quickly.

When barbecuing place herbs on the coals to enhance the flavors of meat and poultry. Try using stalks of savory, rosemary or dried basil seed pods.

For a smaller fire, fill egg or milk cartons with briquettes, then light them as needed.

When flare-ups from fat drippings start to burn the meat, place lettuce leaves over the hot coals to eliminate the problem.

Coat your grill with oil before cooking, then clean it shortly after the barbecue.

Window cleaner sprayed on a warm grill will make it easier to clean.

HEALTH HINT:

Charcoal cooking may release a chemical benzopyrene into the foods, a known carcinogen. Also, there may be a relationship between this type of cooking and the effectiveness of some antiasthmatic medications.

Chapter 28

Herb & Spicy Facts

"SALT OF THE EARTH"

The average person consumes about 4500mg of salt per day, about 2 teaspoons. The body only requires about 200mg.

"SCIENCE AT ITS BEST"

Flavoring extracts come in two forms: pure extracts and imitation flavorings. The pure is derived from natural sources and diluted with ethyl alcohol. Imitations are man-made chemicals concocted in a laboratory.

"USE IT, OR LOSE IT"

Spices should never be stored near a microwave exhaust fan or range top. The heat tends to cause a loss of flavor, potency and even color. All spices should be stored in a cool dried location or in the refrigerator.

If your spices seem to have lost their potency, try rubbing them between your fingers for a few seconds to rejuvenate them.

Hot or spicy foods do not irritate your stomach or aggravate ulcers in most people.

Place a toothpick in a garlic clove before placing it into a stew and it will be easy to retrieve.

Sour wines may be used in place of vinegar.

When you are doubling a recipe, don't double the seasonings until you taste the dish.

ALLSPICE:

Has the aroma of a blend of cinnamon, cloves and nutmeg. Grown in Jamaica, Central and South America. Sold both whole and ground. Whole is mainly used in pickling, meats, fish and gravies. Ground is used in baked goods, relishes, puddings and fruit preserves. It can also be found in a number of ready-to-serve foods such as; hot dogs, soups and baked beans.

ANISE:

Used in licorice. Imported from Mexico and Spain. Marketed as anise seed. Also, used in candies, cookies, pickles and as a flavoring for beverages. Gives the liquor anisette its aroma.

BASIL:

Comes from a plant belonging to the mint family, native to India and Iran. Also, known as "sweet basil" and is grown in the United States. Sold in the form of basil leaves. Used in tomato paste and tomato and squash dishes and, of course, turtle soup. Commonly found in ready-to-serve products such as pizza sauce, soups and dressings.

Try adding a small amount of basil to your tuna salad for a great taste.

BAY LEAF:

Oblong green leaves, sold as leaves and used in stews, sauces, soups and pickling. Used in numerous ready-to-serve foods such as soups, French dressing, dill pickles, etc.

CARAWAY SEEDS:

Ripe caraway seeds are usually harvested at night before the dew evaporates. Most seeds come from the Netherlands. Used in rye bread, cabbage, sauerkraut, soft cheese spreads, sweet pickles and French dressing.

CARDAMON SEED:

Spicy, sweet seeds belonging to the ginger family. They are native to India. They are sold whole or ground. Widely used in Scandinavian dishes. Used in pickling, as a demitasse flavoring, grape jellies, marmalade and frankfurters. These seeds are also used as an excellent cover-up for liquor breath.

CAYENNE PEPPER:

Also, known as red pepper and is available in crushed, ground or whole form. Used in relishes, salsas, chili products, Italian foods, sausages, and dressings.

CELERY SEED:

Celery seed and celery salt are used in salad dressings, fish dishes, salads, pickling and many vegetable dishes. The supply comes mainly from India and France.

CELERY FLAKES:

Made from dehydrated leaves and stalks of celery. Made in the United States. Used in stews, stuffings, soups and sauces.

CHERVIL:

A French herb excellent for flavoring salad dressings. used similar to parsley.

CHILI PEPPERS:

To prepare them you must toast them with a long handled fork on top of the stove making sure that they blister on all sides. As soon as the skin is evenly blistered and puffed up away from the pulp, lay the pods on a cloth, sprinkle them with water and cover them with another cloth so that they steam. The skins will then pull away easily and the seeds and veins can be removed. All of the pulp can be used, but only use a few of the seeds.

Chili peppers and paprika are high in vitamin A. One teaspoon can supply up to 25% of your daily requirement.

CHILI POWDER:

The major ingredients are cumin seed, chili peppers, oregano, salt, cayenne pepper, garlic and allspice.

CHIVES:

Chives are a member of the onion family, but much milder. Used to flavor dips, sauces, spreads and ,of course, baked potatoes.

CINNAMON:

Obtained from the bark of the laurel tree, native to China and Indonesia. The cassia variety is used in the United States. In the whole form, it is used in preserving, flavoring puddings, pickling and hot wine drinks. Ground is used in sweet pickles, ketchup, vegetables, apple butter, mustards, and spiced peaches.

CLOVE

Comes from a tree which a member of the Myrtle family. First discovered in Indonesia. Whole cloves are used for pickling, ham roasts and spiced syrups. Ground cloves are used for making baked goods, puddings, mustards, soups, hot dogs, sausage, and barbecue sauces.

CORIANDER SEED:

Come from a small plant of the carrot family. They have a sweet musky flavor and are native to the Mediterranean area. Sold in seed and ground forms. Normally used in gingerbread, cookies, cakes, biscuits, poultry stuffing and is excellent if rubbed on fresh pork before roasting.

CUMIN SEED:

The flavor resembles caraway seed and it is native to Egypt. Sold in both seed and ground form. It is an essential ingredient in curry, chili powder, soups, stuffed eggs and chili con carne.

CURRY POWDER:

Curry powder is a blend of 20 spices, herbs and even some seeds. Some of the ingredients are chilies, cloves, coriander, fennel seed, nutmeg, mace, cayenne, black pepper, sesame seeds, saffron, turmeric, etc. The turmeric gives many of the dishes its yellow color.

DILL:

Used for pickling, soups, sauerkraut, salads, fish and meat sauces, green apple pie and spiced vinegar.

 Chef's Secrets

When making egg salad, try adding a small amount of dill to liven it up.

FENNEL:

Has a sweet anise-like flavor and is available in seed form. It is used in Italian sausage, sweet pickles, fish dishes, candies, pastries, oxtail soup and pizza sauce. Can be brewed as a tea and served hot.

FENUGREEK:

Has a similar aroma to curry powder and are bitter in flavor. It's main use is in imitation maple flavor.

GARLIC:

Grown in the United States and is a member of the Lily family. It is sold as garlic salt and garlic powder. Used in hundreds of dishes from pizza sauce to chicken pot pies.
Garlic has been used for centuries as a blood cleanser and in recent times to help lower blood pressure.

To peel garlic more easily, place it in very hot water for 2-3 minutes. Garlic cloves should be stored in a small amount of vegetable oil. They won't dry out and the oil can be used with a garlic flavor.

When peeling garlic, try rinsing the garlic in hot water first. The skin will come off easier.

To preserve garlic cloves after they have been peeled, try placing them in a sealed jar and cover them with olive oil. They will stay fresh for 3-4 months.

Before adding your salad ingredients to a bowl, rub a clove of crushed garlic on the sides of the bowl.

Garlic is more nutritious than onions.

Americans consume 250 million pounds of garlic annually.

Garlic salt may contain over 900mg. of sodium per teaspoon. Our average daily consumption should be no more than about 1500mg.

There are 300 varieties of garlic grown worldwide.

Elephant garlic has very large cloves, but is actually a form of leek and has a milder flavor.

Garlic will keep for up to 3 months if stored properly in a cool, dark, dry location. If the cloves sprout, the garlic is still usable and the sprouts can be used for salads.

If you nick a clove of garlic, it must be used or it will get moldy very quickly.

To make garlic vinegar, place 2-3 fresh cloves in each pint and let stand for two weeks before using. Works great for your oils too.

Never freeze garlic, it will destroy the flavor.

Garlic oil products should contain an antibacterial or acidifying agent such as phosphoric acid or citric acid or at least be kept under refrigeration.

Garlic butter should only be stored in the refrigerator for no more than 10-14 days for maximum safety.

Once garlic has been processed it is more perishable than most people realize.

"WITH TONGUE IN CHEEK"

Historically, garlic has been known to repel vampires providing it is no more than 1 month old, made into a circle, worn around the neck and each whole garlic separated by no more than 2 inches.

GINGER:

Has a pungent spicy flavor and is grown in India and West Africa. Sold in whole or ground form and is used in pickling, conserves, dried fruits and of course, gingerbread and pumpkin pies.

MACE:

Mace is a fleshy growth between the nutmeg shell and the outer husk. It is sold in ground form and used in pound cake and chocolate dishes. In it's whole form it is used in pickling, ketchup, baked beans, soups, deviled chicken and ham spreads and French dressing.

MARJORAM:

Has a sweet minty flavor and is an herb of the mint family. It is available in leaves and is imported from France, Chile and Peru. Usually combined with other herbs and used in soups, stews, poultry seasonings, sauces and fish dishes.

MINT FLAKES:

They are dehydrated flakes of peppermint and spearmint plants and have a strong sweet flavor. Grown in the United States and Europe. Used to flavor stews, soups, fish dishes, sauces, desserts and jellies. For an instant breath freshener, try chewing a few mint leaves.

MSG:

Monosodium glutamate has no taste of its own but helps to bring out the natural food flavors as well as helping foods blend better with one another. MSG has been implicated in enough adverse physical problems that it is recommended not to use it.

MUSTARD:

The yellow or white seeds produce a mild mustard, while the brown seeds produce the more spicy variety. Powdered mustard has hardly any aroma until mixed with a liquid. Has hundreds of uses and is one of the most popular spices worldwide.

NUTMEG:

Available in ground form and is imported from the East and West Indies. Used in sauces, puddings, as a topping for custards, eggnogs and whipped creams. Also, used in sausages, frankfurters, and ravioli. Best used in ground form only.

OREGANO:

A member of the mint family and also known as origanum and Mexican sage. Available in leaf or ground forms. Used mostly in Italian specialties such as pizza and a variety of spaghetti sauces.

Some oregano on a grilled cheese sandwich will really perk it up and you will probably never eat another one without it.

PAPRIKA:

Ground pods of sweet pepper. The red sweet mild type is widely used and grown in the United States. Used in a variety of dishes such as vegetables, mustards, dressings, ketchup, sausages and fish dishes and, of course, as a garnish.

PARSLEY:

Grown in the United States and Southern Europe. Used as a flavor in salads, soups, vegetable dishes, chicken pot pies, herb dressings and even peppermint soup. A favorite garnish and high in nutrients. makes your breath fresh since it is high in chlorophyll. When storing it should be kept in a plastic bag in the freezer.

Parsley can be dried in the microwave and frozen.

PEPPER:

Pepper is the most popular spice in the world. Sold in both black and white varieties and for the most part is imported from India, Indonesia and Borneo. Sold in whole or ground varieties. Used in almost every dish imaginable at one time or another.

POPPY SEED:

Have a nut-like flavor and are used in salads, cookies, pastry fillings and as toppings for numerous baked products.

POULTRY SEASONING:

The major ingredients are; sage, thyme, marjoram and savoy.

ROSEMARY:

A sweet fragrant spicy herb, imported from Spain and Portugal, used in stews, meat dishes, dressings and Italian foods. Great in gin drinks.

SAFFRON:

One of the most expensive of all herbs. It is derived from the stigma of a flowering crocus. It is imported from Spain and is used primarily in baked goods and rice dishes.

SAGE:

A member of the mint family and is available in leaf or ground form. Used in pork products, stuffings, salads, fish dishes and pizza sauces.

SALT:

In the purifying process of salt, the native minerals are stripped away and it is then enriched with iodine and dextrose to stabilize it, sodium bicarbonate to keep it white and anti-caking agents to keep it "free flowing." Morton's Special Salt is the only salt, to my knowledge that has no additives. Salt is used in almost every food in the food processing industry.

A simple barometer of your salt intake is to eat a slice of bacon–if it doesn't taste excessively salty, you are probably eating too much salt.

Your daily sodium intake per day should be no more than 230mg. per day, about 1/10 teaspoon. We consume about 25 times that amount.

Buy "Lite Salt" or a salt-free seasoning.

Mother's milk contains 16 mg. of sodium per 100 gr.

Canned baby food may contain 300 mg. of sodium per 100 gr.

Canned peas have 100 times the sodium of raw peas.

Sodium in Public Water Supplies:

Milligrams of Sodium In Public Water Supplies

Aberdeen, SD........48.0	Bismark, ND........14.4
Biloxi, Miss........55.2	Crandall,TX.......408
Galveston, TX.......81.6	Kansas City, MO....23.6
Los Angeles, CA.....40.1	Oklahoma City, OK..23.6
Phoenix, AZ.........25.9	San Diego, CA......12.0
New York, NY.........0.7	Reno, NV............1.1

40% of table salt is sodium.

Lite salt which is 50% table salt (nacl) is 20% sodium.

Excess amounts of dietary sodium places a burden on your kidneys, causing a possible malfunction, thus allowing extra amounts of sodium to build up in the bloodstream where it retains extra water, causing an increase in blood volume. This causes the heart to work harder, thus leading to an increase in blood pressure. Fast foods may use large quantities of salt to mask the offensive flavors of low quality foods.

Ground kelp can be used in place of salt. It contains only about 4% sodium. Try a kelp shaker at your table.

HIGH SODIUM FOODS

Food Item	Serving Size	Sodium mg.
Onion Soup (dry)	1 ½ oz.	3288
Pretzel Twists	3 ½ oz.	2370
Deviled Crab (frozen)	1 cup	2085
Dill Pickle	1 large	1935
Turkey Dinner (frozen)	1 large	1830
Saltines	3 ½ oz.	1794
Cream of Asparagus Soup	8 oz. can	1662
Dill Pickle	1 medium	1426
Lobster	1 pound	1359
Soy Sauce	1 Tbsp.	1320
Toasted Corn	3 ½ oz.	1307
Spaghetti & Meat Sauce	1 cup canned	1220
Puff Balls	3 ½ oz.	1190
Macaroni & Cheese (frzn)	1 cup	1090
Onion Soup	1 cup	1051
Chop Suey with Meat	1 cup	1050
Chicken Noodle Soup	1 cup	979
Pretzels	1 oz.	890
Sauerkraut (canned)	½ cup	880

Cinnamon Roll	1 reg.	805
Corned Beef (cooked)	3 oz.	800
Tuna Oil (packed)	3 ½ oz.	800
Corn Chips	3 ½ oz.	741
Sunflower Seeds	3 ½ oz.	721
Potato Salad (canned)	½ cup	660
Chicken Noodle Soup	5 oz.	655
Peanuts (roasted in oil)	1 cup	662
Creamed Corn (canned)	1 cup	671
Italian Dressing	2 Tbsp.	624
Salted Peanuts	3 ½ oz.	595
Pork & Beans (canned)	½ cup	590
Wheat Crackers	3 ½ oz.	566
Scalloped Potatoes	½ cup	540
Oyster Stew	5 oz.	510
Beef Hot Dogs	1 reg.	495
Chocolate Pudding	½ cup	490
Apple Pie	1/6 pie	486
Tomato Soup	5 oz.	475
Tortilla Chips	3 ½ oz.	468
Bologna	2 slices	450

MEDIUM SODIUM FOODS

American Cheese (slices)	1 oz.	447
Hash Browns (frozen)	1 cup	446
Mustard	2 Tbsp.	444
Pancakes (mix)	3 - 4" cakes	435
White Pudding Cake (mix)	1/8 cake	410
Cheese Cake (no bake)	1/8 cake	380
Mashed Potatoes(instant)	½ cup	375
Cheese Pizza (frozen)	1 med. slice	370
Wheat Crackers	16 small	370
Carrots (canned)	1 cup	366
Bran Flakes	3/4 cup	340
Cheese Crackers	10 small	325
Tomato Juice	½ cup	320

Cottage Cheese (creamed)	½ cup	320
Baking Soda	1 Tsp.	315
Italian Salad Dressing	1 Tbsp.	315
Worcestershire Sauce	1 Tbsp.	315
Ketchup	2 Tbsp.	308
Corn Flakes	3/4 cup	305
Corn Bread	2 inch square	283
Granola Snack Bar	One Bar	273
Buttermilk	1 cup	225
French Salad Dressing	1 Tbsp.	220
Muenster Cheese	1 oz.	220
Swiss Cheese	1 oz.	220
Doughnut	1 med.	210
Parmesan Cheese	1 oz.	210
Beets (canned)	½ cup	195
Cheddar Cheese	1 oz.	190
Bleu Cheese Dressing	1 Tbsp.	180
Oatmeal (cooked)	3 oz.	175
Tomato Ketchup	1 Tbsp.	155
Green Olive	1 Lg.	155
Celery (raw)	1 cup	151
Rye Bread	1 slice	140
Angel Food Cake	1/12 cake	130
Whole Wheat Bread	1 slice	130
Chocolate Candy Bar	3/4 oz.	115

LOW SODIUM FOODS

Graham Cracker	1 lg.	95
Brownie	1 reg.	90
Oysters (raw)	½ cup	90
Lima Beans (frozen)	½ cup	90
Mayonnaise	1 med.	70
Egg	1 med.	70
Turkey	3 oz.	70
Coffee (black)	1 cup	59
Margarine (salted)	1 tsp.	50

Cottage Cheese	½ cup	30
Oatmeal Cookie	1 med.	20
Fruit Cocktail	½ cup	7
Orange Juice	½ cup	2
Macaroni	1 cup	1

SAVORY:

Another member of the mint family that has a sweet flavor. Available in leaf and ground forms and primarily used to flavor meats, poultry and fish.

SESAME:

Has a nut-like flavor with a high oil content. Primary use is as a topping on baked goods and in halavah.

TARRAGON:

An anise flavored leaf that is a native of Siberia and imported from Spain and France. Used in sauces, meat dishes, salads, herb dressings and tomato casseroles.

THYME:

Belongs to the mint family and is available in leaf or ground form. Used in soups, stews, sauces, chipped beef (old army favorite), sausages, clam chowder, herb dressings and mock turtle soup.

TURMERIC:

A member of the ginger family and imported from India and Peru. Used in meats, dressings, curry powder, spanish rice, relishes and mustards.

VANILLA:

Beans:	Long, thin dark brown beans are expensive and not as easy to use as the extract. To use the bean, split it and scrape out the powder-fine seeds. The seeds from a single vanilla bean is. equal to 2-3 teaspoons of extract. Beans should be stored in a sealed plastic bag and refrigerated.

Pure Extract:	Comes from the vanilla bean, but the taste is less intense. Has excellent flavor, similar to the real bean.

Imitation Extract:	Made from artificial flavorings, tastes stronger and is harsher than pure vanilla. Should only be used in recipes where the vanilla flavor does not predominate the taste.

Mexican Extract:	A possible dangerous extract. This poor quality inexpensive product may contain coumarin, a blood thinning drug and banned in the U.S. due to possible toxic effects.

VINEGAR:

Produced from ethyl alcohol. A bacteria, acetobacter feeds on the alcohol, converting into acetic acid (vinegar). Vinegar can, however, be made from a number of other foods, such as; apples or grains. Distilled vinegar is best used for cleaning purposes and not for foods.

Balsamic vinegar produced in Italy is made from sugars that are converted to alcohol with the addition of boiled down grape juice are the best. They can be used for salad dressing and bring out the flavors in many vegetables.

Chapter 29

Food Additive Facts

"YUM, YUM"

Americans eat approximately 6-9 pounds of chemical food additives per year.

Today's foods contain over $500 million worth of additives.

"YOUR POOR LIVER"

Over 1 billion pounds of chemical additives are consumed every year. Your liver is in charge of detoxifying this garbage. The liver is the major organ that has the job of breaking down and disposing of all this material. In most cases it requires a number of nutrients to break them down, hopefully, they will be available.

The outside leaves of lettuce should be discarded. They may contain sulfites. Celery may also be guilty.

White bread may have as many as 16 chemical additives just to keep it fresh. Some of these may be in the wrapper.

BETA-CAROTENE: (pre-curser to vitamin A)

A natural substance found in all plants and animals. Has a yellowish-orange color and is especially prevalent in carrots and squash. Used as a food coloring agent in foods and cosmetics. Recent studies have shown beta-carotene to be an effective anti-oxidant. Best to take instead of vitamin A, has almost no toxicity.

BROMELIN:

Extracted from pineapple and used in meat tenderizers. A very effective protein-digesting enzyme. If a piece of meat is allowed to set in bromelin for a prolonged period, you will be able to drink your steak.

CITRATE SALTS:

Used in cheese spreads and pasteurized process cheeses. May tend to mask the results of laboratory tests for pancreatic and liver function and blood acid-base balances.

CITRUS RED #2:

Had been used for coloring Florida oranges, but in recent years has been discontinued. The dye remained in the peel and did not enter the pulp. However, if the dye is ingested in quantity, it could cause numerous serious visual, circulatory and urinary system problems.

COLORINGS:

The majority of the colorings presently being used are derived from coal-tars (carcinogens). As the years go on more and more of these colorings are being further tested and banned.

GELATIN:

Derived from boiling skin, muscle and hoofs of animals. Mainly used as a thickener and stabilizer for fruit gelatins. Also, helps strengthen fingernails.

METHYLENE CHLORIDE:

A gas used in the decaffeination of coffee. Residues may remain and coffee companies do not have to tell you their method of decaffeination on the label. Only drink decaf if you know the method used by the manufacturer. Water is the best method.

MSG:

Monosodium glutamate has no taste of its own but helps to bring out the natural flavors as well as helping foods blend better with one another. MSG has been implicated in enough adverse physical problems that it is recommended not to use it. When eating Chinese food always inquire whether MSG has been used in the food. If you find out that it has, refuse to eat it.

NITRITES:

One of the most dangerous additives used in our foods are the nitrites and nitrates. They are found in almost all processed meats,such as; luncheon meats, bacon, sausage, hot dogs, smoked fish and canned meats.

The chemical is mainly used for cosmetic purposes, to stabilize the color of the product. The industry also claims it is needed to retard bacterial growth and also reduce the possibility of botulism. Because of the risks involved with this chemical, the general consensus among scientists, is that companies should be researching a new and safer chemical compound instead of taking the easier and less expensive way out.

Nitrite studies have shown that in laboratory animals malignant tumors have developed in over 90% within 6 months, and death approximately afterwards. Other incidents have been reported and documented where high levels of nitrites in food have caused "cardiovascular collapse" in humans and even death from eating "hot dogs" and "blood sausage" that were produced by local processors in different areas of the U.S.

In Israel, studies on animals discovered problems related to brain damage when they were fed an equivalent amount of nitrites to heavy eaters of processed luncheon meats and hot dogs.

The biochemical changes that occur in the food take the following course: Nitrites are broken down into nitrous acid which combines with the hemoglobin of the meat or fish, forming a permanent red color.

In humans, there are two pathways that the ingested nitrites may take that could be harmful: (1) Nitrite is eaten and may react with the hemoglobin of the blood to produce a pigment called meth-hemoglobin which may seriously depress the oxygen carrying capacity of the red blood cell. (2) The possible cancer connection is when nitrites are biochemically altered to a substance called "nitrosamine."

This reaction usually occurs in the stomach and requires the presence of "amines" and "gastric juices." Amines are usually in adequate supply, since they are a product of protein metabolism, and protein foods often carry the nitrites. The end results are the formation of the "nitrosamines" which are classified as carcinogenic(cancer forming agents).

It is necessary, however, to clarify two points: (1) Just because you may eat meat containing nitrites does not mean that you will automatically produce nitrosamines. (2) If the nitrosamine is produced, your immune system may destroy it as soon as it is produced.

Vitamin C has been found to neutralize the reaction that takes place in the stomach, by interfering with the amine combining with the nitrite. Due to recent studies, relating to these neutralizing effects of vitamin C (ascorbic acid), some manufacturers are adding ascorbic acid to their products.

As a measure of protection it would be wise to chew a vitamin C tablet or drink a small amount of orange juice before consuming foods that contain nitrites.

NOTE:
Many countries have already banned nitrites from foods. However, the USDA and the FDA will not prohibit its use until a good substitute is found.

SORBITOL:

Extracted mainly from berries and some fruits. It is an alcohol that produces a sweet taste and is used in dietetic products as a replacement for sugar. Also, has numerous other uses as a food binder, thickener, texturing agent, humectant and food stabilizer.

SULFITES:

Three types may be used as an anti-browning agent, sodium, potassium and ammonium can be used on any food except meats or a high vitamin B content food. Used on salad bars to prevent fruits and lettuce from browning, also, to enhance their crispness. Physiologic reaction to sulfites are numerous with the most common taking the form of acute asthmatic attacks. My recommendation is to avoid any food that has been treated with sulfites.

SULPHUR DIOXIDE:

A chemical formed from the burning of sulphur. A food bleach, preservative, anti-oxidant and anti-browning agent. Its most common visibility is in golden raisins. Tends to destroy vitamin A and should not be used on meats or high vitamin A content vegetables.

Types Of Additives:

Flavorings -   There are approximately 1,100 to 1,400 natural and synthetic flavorings available to food processors. Scientists are most concerned regarding the toxicity of a number of the ones that are commonly used. Flavorings give foods a more acceptable taste, restore lost flavors due to processing and in some cases will improve natural flavors.

Stabilizers/Gelling Agents/Thickeners -
   These are used to keep products in a "set-state" such as jellies, jams and baby foods. They are also used to keep ice cream creamy. They generally improve consistency and will affect the appearance and texture of foods. The more common ones are modified food starch and vegetable gum.

Colorings - *Ninety percent are artificial and do not contain any nutritional value. Some foods have a tendency to lose their natural color when processed and must be dyed back to make them more appealing to the consumer. An example of this is banana ice cream which is dyed yellow and marachino cherries which are dyed red and green.*

Sweeteners -   The United States consumption of artificial sweeteners is estimated at approximately 6-9 pounds per person, per year. These are designed to make the foods more palatable.

Aroma Enhancers -   An example, is yellowish-green liquid diacetyl which is used in some cottage cheeses to produce an artificial butter aroma.

Preservatives - *Helps maintain freshness and prevents spoilage that is caused by fungi, yeast, molds and bacteria. Extends shelf life and protects the natural colors or flavors.*

Acids/Bases -   Provides a tart flavor for many fruits and is used in pickling as well as putting the "fizz" in soft drinks (phosphoric acid).

Antioxidants -   Reduces the possibility of rancidity in fats and oils. Natural ones are vitamins C, E, A, selinium and beta-carotene. Artificial ones are BHA and BHT.

Taste Enhancers -   Brings out the flavors of certain foods. MSG is a good example but is not recommended.

Improving Agents - Examples include:

(1) Humectants - Controls the humidity of a food.

(2) Anti-Caking Agents - Keeps salt and powders free-flowing.

(3) Firming/Crisping Agents - Used for processed fruits and vegetables.

(4) Foaming Agents - Used for whipped creams.

(5) Anti-Foaming Agents - Keeps pineapple juice from bubbling over a filled container.

Emulsifiers -   These help evenly mix small particles of one liquid with another, such as water and oil. Lecithin is a good example of a natural emulsifier.

NOTE:
Keep in mind that you are rarely aware of the quantity of additives you consume. Almost all these additives require vitamins and minerals to assist with their breakdown, so that they can be properly disposed of, usually by the liver. These additional nutrients must come from somewhere in the body that could probably use them more.

HEALTH HINTS: Processed meats (hot dogs, bacon, lunch meats, etc.) are so high in additives, artificial colorings and preservatives that they can deplete the body of many nutrients needed to break them down, especially our anti-stress fighting vitamin B's.

Pharmacies are now selling a "sulfite test strip" that can be used to test produce just by touching the strip to it. If the strip turns red, don't buy the produce.

Chapter 30

How Sweet It Is

"CONCENTRATED ENERGY"
Honey has twice the sweetness of granulated sugar.

Crystallized honey is easier to measure and spread, if you wish to liquefy it again, place it in the microwave for 30 seconds to 2 minutes depending on the size of the jar. Do not allow to boil.

"BELIEVE IT, ITS TRUE"
To produce a 1 pound jar of honey, bees have to forage over a flight path equal to three trips around the earth and burn only one ounce of honey for fuel, that's 7 million miles to the gallon.

If a product is labeled "maple sugar" it must contain a minimum of 35% "real" maple syrup. The lighter the color the better the quality. Store in refrigerator after opening, if it granulates just heat slightly.

"PERFORMING A LUMPECTOMY"
To soften brown sugar that has developed a case of "lumps." Place the sugar in a container in the microwave, then add a slice of bread or ½ of an apple. Cover the dish tightly and cook for approximately 15 seconds. The moisture from the bread or apple will produce steam which will soften the sugar.

To remove hard brown sugar from a box, just add a few drops of water to the box and microwave on full power for a few seconds.

Adults purchase over 50% of all chocolate sold in the U.S.

Dark chocolate is the most sought after by chocoholics.

Ghirardelli is the top rated chocolate bar.

Chocolate bars were invented by Fry & Sons in 1847 in England.

Blackstrap molasses is higher in nutrients than other types of molasses. It is high in iron, calcium and potassium.

"BALLOONING"

Candy and chewing gum cause the salivary glands to produce saliva at a higher than normal rate which causes more frequent swallowing. This may cause bloatiness and gas.

Milk chocolate must contain at least 10% chocolate liquor and a minimum of 12% milk solids.

Over 600 million dollars are spent each year on sugar related commercials.

Jams and jellies retain only a fraction of their vitamin C content after processing.

Most cough drops contain over 50% sugar.

Approximately 30% of all cough syrup contain over 25% sugar.

Pie, cheesecake and ice cream rank 1,2,3 as Americans favorite desserts.

"POP A CUBE"

If you have to satisfy a sweet craving, try eating a sugar cube. Only contains 10-16 calories, no fat and usually no preservatives or coloring agents.

Dark chocolate must contain at least 15% chocolate liquor and no more than 12% milk solids.

Brown sugar is chemically almost exactly the same as white sugar.

While honey is still a form of sugar, it still contains a number of trace minerals, which makes it healthier. Honey can be used in place of refined sugar, using only half as much as the recipe calls for.

"TIT FOR TAT"

Americans are finally consuming less sugar then they used to, however, they are now eating more foods containing corn syrup and similar sweeteners, increasing their total sugar intake to a level that is the highest ever recorded. We each consume 147 pounds of sweeteners each year, compared to 123 in 1970.

147 pounds of sweeteners equals 246,752 calories. This is enough calories to add over 68 pounds to a person's weight each year.

Americans consume approximately $3.4 billion worth of candy per year and 1.3 billion pounds of chocolate candy bars.

Candies are loaded with additives such as: Red Dye #3 and #40, Green Dye #3, Blue Dye #12, and #2, Yellow Dye #5, Glycerides and a long list of others.

Approximately $625+ million is spent on advertising junk food in the United States each year.

 Chef's Secrets

To improve the texture of your fudge, try adding a teaspoon of corn starch when you first start mixing.

If a dish is too sweet, try adding salt or a small amount of vinegar.

"SNIP, SNIP"
Marshmallows can be stored in the freezer, then just cut them with scissors when needed. Dip the scissors in hot water first.

When marshmallows become hard, try placing them into a plastic baggie with a slice or two of very fresh bread for a few days.

If your fudge won't set up, try returning it to the pot, add a teaspoon of water and continue cooking for a few more minutes.

If a candy recipe calls for water, always use hot water and your candy will be clearer.

Cane sugar should be used for candies. Beet sugar tends to foam too much.

Exercise helps to burn up excess sugar.

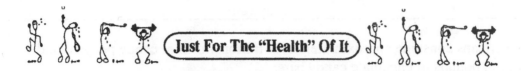

Just For The "Health" Of It

Monoglycerides used in some ice creams are a possible cancer causing agent in test animals.

ICE CREAM:

The best advice I can give to ice cream lovers is to make your own or purchase a non-fat yogurt that states "all natural" on the label. The ingredients in most commercial ice creams contain chemical substitutes for most of the good quality natural ingredients that are found in the "real" thing.

There are only a few manufacturers of a no-preservative, no-chemical "natural" ice cream. If you purchase ice cream from an ice cream shop, ask to see the list of ingredients from the top of the lid on the serving cartons. The law says that they must tell you what ingredients are in the ice cream.

The following is a comparison of homemade ice cream and the standard commercial ice cream:

Ingredient Comparison

HOMEMADE	MOST COMMERCIAL
Real Milk or Cream	Dry Milk Solids
Eggs	CARROGEENAN
Natural Color	Carboxymethyl cellulose
Natural Fruits	Yellow Dye #5
Weight Approximately	Ethyl Acetate
8 Lbs. per gallon	No less than 4 ½ Lbs.
	per gallon plus air
	to bring it to weight.

Carrogeenan - Has caused intestinal ulcers in test rabbits.

Yellow Dye #5 - Evidence related to rashes, swelling and allergic reactions.

Ethyl Acetate - Its vapors have been known to cause damage to lungs, heart and livers in laboratory test animals. It is also used as a cleaner and solvent for leather and plastics.

Carboxymethyl Cellulose - Used in printing inks and resin paints. In laboratory rats, the chemical compound produces tumors and arterial lesions.

Ice milk usually contains 6% fat and some contain eggs.

Ice cream, when made from whole milk contains 10-15% fat.

Imitation ice milk is usually made from vegetable oils and contains 4% fat.

"FAKIR"
Imitation ice creams must contain at least 6% fat and may be made from hydrogenated oils (high in saturated fats). Read the label and try to choose from ones made from safflower oil and non-fat milk.

Dietetic ice cream contains sugar substitutes, however, the fat is the same as regular ice cream 10-15%.

Sherbert has very little fat, but is high in sugar.

"BUYER BEWARE"
If the chemical Torutein is listed on the ingredients of ice cream cartons, don't buy it! This chemical has already been suspended in Utah, England and Japan due to evidence linking the oil-based protein to cancer in humans.

"A DEEP DARK SECRET UNVEILED"
Most ice cream is produced by a few major manufacturers. These manufacturers then supply the supermarket and ice cream chains with a pre-processed mix of dry milk solids, sugar, butterfat, emulsifiers and stabilizers. Most markets and ice cream store chains then run this mixture through machines which pump in air and

water and ,of course, their own special "unique" blend of flavorings and colorings. They sell this concoction to the public under new and strange names.

Purchase only jams and jellies made from the real thing and labeled "lite".

Bromine in chocolate may reduce the absorption of protein through the intestinal wall.

The commercial products usually only contain extracts of the real fruit.

"A COLD HARD FACT"
The first known recipe for ice cream was brought to Venice, Italy by Marco Polo after a journey to Japan. The Italians then introduced "Cream Ice" to Europe and later was renamed "Ice Cream" by our own Dolly Madison for a White House function.

Smokers tend to consume more sugar than non-smokers.

"WHOA"
Fluid movement in teeth is slowed to a crawl by a high intake of dietary sweeteners.

Studies are being conducted that may prove that sugar intake will raise cholesterol levels.

Nougat candy improves when frozen.

Never freeze clear hard candies, jellies, cereal, popcorn, candy, marshmallows, or candy dipped in chocolate. Hard candies may crumble, jellies get granular, and the rest lose their original consistencies due to the expansion of their liquids.

A "HONEY" OF A HONEY
Make sure you are purchasing "real" honey and not one that has been doctored with sugar or other ingredients.

Honey should be labeled "creamed" or "spun" for spreading on breads and muffins.

If you spoon your honey from a container, try running the spoon under hot water before placing it in the honey, it will flow off the spoon easier.

An easy way to soften brown sugar is to place 2 marshmallows in with the sugar and seal in a plastic container overnight.

Ice cream sales are approximately $2 billion a year in the United States.

We average almost 15 quarts of ice cream per person in the United States per year.

When you empty a jam or jelly jar, place it in the microwave for a few seconds or place the bottom of the jar in very hot water to melt the rest of the jam or jelly. Use another jar to save all the different ones until you make a ham, lamb or other food that needs to be basted with a sweet substance.

When defrosting candy, the temperature should be raised gradually. Place the candy to be thawed, that are still in their plastic wrappers in a brown paper bag. This will absorb the condensed moisture that collects during the defrosting.

IT'S NOT "THE REAL THING"
White chocolate isn't really chocolate. It is made of sugar, milk powder and cocoa butter. When cocoa butter is pressed from chocolate liquor it loses its chocolate flavor.

Sugar is a natural product and may be labeled as such.

Candies that are frozen when fresh, will taste better.

THE "NOSE" KNOWS
Candies tend to pick up foreign odors and should be stored properly in a closed container.

Sugar reduces the body's ability to destroy bacteria.

To keep sugar from caking up in your canister, try placing a few salt-free crackers in with the sugar to absorb the moisture.

If your candy tends to boil over, place a wooden spoon over the pan to break up the bubbles.

Children, as well as adults, are subject to personality changes and hyperactivity problems from high sugar intakes.

Sugar And Sugar Substitutes In Foods

Glucose	Sucrose	Maltose
Fructose	Lactose	Dextrose
Xylose	Levulose	Dextrim
Beet Sugar	Corn Syrup	Brown Sugar
Molasses	Maple Sugar	Mannitol
Xylatol	Hexatol	Invert Sugar
Sorghum	Honey	Turbinado Sugar
Nutrasweet	Equal	Aspartame
Saccharin	Sucryl	Malt

"Surprises Galore" Foods That May Contain Sugar

Packaged Cereals	Mustard	Ketchup
Salt	Canned Soups	Fudge
Tomato Sauce	Canned Fruits	Soft Drinks
Canned Meats	Rolls	Cookies
Ice Cream	Puddings	Lipstick
Lip Gloss	Breads	Jam/Jelly
Canned Veg. Juice	Bacon	Lemonade
Pancake Mixes	Waffle Mixes	Canned Beans
Cough Drops	Apple Butter	Breathe Mints
Breakfast Bars	Canned Fish	Potato Chips
Bread Mixes	Sherbert	Stewed Fruit
Soup Mixes	Peanut Butter	Baby Foods
Yogurt	Prepared Sauces	Condensed Mill
Dried Fruit	Egg Nog	Licorice
Protein Powd.	Laxatives	Vitamins
Red Wine	Crackers	Mouthwashes
Chewing Gum	Soy Sauce	Pickles
Relish	Tooth Paste	Meat

Tenderizers   Meat Sauces   Gravies
TV Dinners   Medications   Packaged Nuts
Condiments   Food Seas'n   Margarine
French Fries   Envelope Adh.   Pretzels
Stamp Adhesives   Chewing Tob.   Fast Foods
Breakfast Drink   Hamburger Buns   Snails

Sugar Content In A Few Goodies

CANDIES	%
Candy Corn	59.5
Nestles Crunch	47.4
Mr. Goodbar	42.2
3 Musketeers	41.0
Mars	40.3
Milky Way	36.4
Tootsie Roll	36.1
Baby Ruth	35.3
Butterfingers	33.5
Snickers	33.2
Milk Duds	30.7
Almond Joy	25.6
Mounds	21.7

COOKIES	%
Oreo	40.1
Vanilla Wafers	32.6
Lemon Snaps	31.7
Oatmeal and Raisin	18.8
Peanut Butter	16.4
Fig Newtons	11.6

Sugar In Common Foods   %

Food	%
Jello	82.0
Breakfast Cereals	up to 68.0
Cream Substitutes	up to 57.0
Shake & Bake	up to 51.0
Sara Lee Chocolate Cake	36.0
Russian Dressing	30.0
Ketchup	29.0
Ding Dong	25.0
Hamburger Helper	24.0
Cool Whip	22.0
Ice Cream	21.0
Libby's Peaches	18.0
Low-Fat Yogurt	14.0
Ritz Crackers	12.0
Most Peanut Butter	up to 12.0
Coffee	9.0
Ragu Spaghetti Sauce	6.0

SUGAR CONTENT OF BREAKFAST CEREALS

Product	Manufacturer	% Total Sugar
Honey Smacks	Kellogg	56.0
Apple Jacks	Kellogg	55.0
Fruit Loops	Kellogg	48.0
Super Sugar Crisp	General Foods	46.0
Cocoa Pebbles	General Foods	42.6
Lucky Charms	General Mills	42.2
Frosted Flakes	Kellogg	41.0
Cap'n Crunch	Quaker Oats	40.0
Bran Buds	Kellogg	40.0
Alpha Bits	General Foods	38.0
Trix	General Mills	35.9
Cocoa Puffs	General Mills	33.3

Fruit and Fiber	Kellogg	31.1
Post's Raisin Bran	General Foods	30.4
Golden Grahams	General Mills	30.0
Raisin Bran	Kellogg	29.0
Frosted Mini-Wheats	Kellogg	26.0
Just Right	Kellogg	25.7
100% Nat. Granola	Quaker Oats	21.5
All Bran	Kellogg	19.0
Life	Quaker Oats	16.0
Team	Nabisco	14.1
Grape Nuts Flakes	General Foods	13.3
40% Bran Flakes	General Foods	13.0
Product 19	Kellogg	9.9
Total	General Mills	8.3
Wheaties	General Mills	8.2
Rice Krispies	Kellogg	7.8
Special K	Kellogg	5.4
Corn Flakes	Kellogg	5.3
Kix	General Mills	4.8
Rice Chex	Ralston-Purina	4.2
Wheat Chex	Ralston Purina	3.5
Cheerios	General Mills	3.0
Shredded Wheat	Nabisco	0.6
Puffed Rice	Quaker Oats	0.1

Source: Analysis by the USDA in 1989 Manufacturer's   Information.

The above information does not take into consideration the actual nutrient content of the cereals. This is a more detailed study with Cherrios coming out as one of the all around best.

 Sucking on hard candy or lollypops causes a greater risk of tooth decay than consuming larger quantities of cake, ice cream or doughnuts. Hard candy dissolves slower and surrounds each tooth with a coating of sugar for a longer period of time.

Natural sugar has only 16 calories a teaspoon and may be less harmful when used in moderation than some of the artificial sweeteners.

Sugar requires B vitamins and minerals to enable the body to metabolize it into glucose, yet it contains none of these. Therefore, it must take the nutrients away from other bodily functions where they may be needed more.

Sugar may also increase the rate at which we excrete the mineral calcium, making bones more fragile and may also weaken the heart action.

Sugar robs the body of chromium, which is a crucial mineral for the regulation of blood sugar levels.

Fructose takes longer to break down to glucose, allowing more time to burn it up and for the body to prepare for the sugar load. This is especially helpful to a diabetic. It can also be directly absorbed from the intestinal tract without the need for excess insulin.

"BELIEVE IT OR NOT"
Finally, a chocolate bar that has good nutritional value. Barat Chocolates are made from real cocoa but they replace sugar with an organic granulated sugar called Sucanat. Sucanat is a complex carbohydrate that burns slowly and provides long-lasting energy. Instead of dairy products, Barat uses tofu for their creamy texture.

SWEETENERS

Corn Syrup - Produced from a mixture of refined sugars, water and partially digested starches. Corn syrup is artificially flavored and used for pancake syrups. Used in place of sugar in candy making and ice creams. Honey would be a better substitute.

Honey - The best honey will be labeled "100% pure unfiltered," "raw" or "uncooked." This honey will not be nutrient depleted by the heat of processing. To use honey as a spread, look for the labeling that says "creamed," "spun" or "granulated." Honey has many different flavors, depending where the bee obtained the nectar. Blended honey is the least expensive and lacks a unique flavor. Honey is one of the only foods in which bacteria will not grow. Honey should be stored at room temperature and has a very long shelf life.

Maple Syrup - Read the label well! Make sure it doesn't say "maple flavored," "maple-blended" or use the word "imitation." The real thing is rare and does contain an excellent blend of natural nutrients, especially iron and calcium.

Molasses - Made from sugar cane which goes through a complex processing which removes all of the nutrients resulting in a white sugar. The residue that remains after the processing, is the actual blackstrap molasses product. Unsulphured molasses is actually produced to make molasses and not the results of the processing to make sugar.

Raw Sugar (turbinado) - Refined sugar, almost exactly like refined white sugar, except with the addition of molasses for color. No advantage over normal refined sugar, don't bother to pay the extra price.

ARTIFICIAL SWEETENERS

ACESULFAME K:

A non-nutritive sweetener also called "Sunette" or "Sweet-One." It sweetens and does not breakdown in the body, but passes through and is excreted. Can also be used for high temperature cooking and baking unlike Nutrasweet. It is 200 times sweeter than sugar.

Used in chewing gums, dry beverage mixes, candies, puddings and custards. Received FDA approval in 1988. Has about the same sweetening power as Aspartame. Presently, approved in 20 countries. The Center for Science in the Public Interest tested the product, but the results were inconclusive.

Recent studies show that it may cause cancer in lab animals, and excess insulin secretion in rats.

ALLTAME:

A super-sweetener produced from two amino acids and is 2,000 times sweeter than sugar. It is metabolized by the body normally, with almost no calories. A good all around sweetener that may be used in almost any recipe and baked goods.

ASPARTAME: (Nutrasweet, Equal)

Two approved food additives, glutamate and aspartate (the two ingredients in Equal) have been implicated in testing related to a nerve disease. Testing is not conclusive, to date.

Aspartame may lower the acidity level of the urine causing a reduced susceptibility to disease.

When Aspartame is heated, a percentage may turn into methyl alcohol. Best if not used in baked goods and any drink that uses boiling water.

Recent study results by leading universities and the Arizona Department of Health Sciences were regarded by the FDA as "unfounded fears."

Symptoms are becoming more frequently reported relating to Equal consumption, these include; insomnia, headaches, vision changes, dizziness and nervous disorders.

A double blind study of diabetics using the products reported more adverse symptoms in the group consuming Aspartame. The study was conducted using a measured quantity of Nutrasweet equal to 14 diet drinks per day.

In 1980 when Aspartame was approved by the FDA, they set a maximum recommended amount at 34mg. per Kg. of body weight. This equates to a 140 pound person drinking 12 diet drinks per day or the equivalent in foods containing Aspartame, Nutrasweet or Equal. The World Health Organization recommended a maximum of 40mg. per Kg. of body weight for adults. A child in an average day consuming an assortment of cereals, gum, candy, puddings, ades, soft drinks, etc. could easily exceed the adult maximum amounts.

Future testing may prove very interesting.

CYCLAMATES:

The FDA has now decided to reverse its original decision that cyclamates are carcinogenic. It may very well be back on the market at any time and commercially used in baking goods. It would be best to read labels well and limit artificial sweetener intake.

L-SUGARS:

Contain no calories or aftertaste and may be used to replace a number of present day sweeteners. Can be substituted cup for cup for refined sugar in recipes. Still in the developmental stages.

SACCHARIN:

Has been used as a sweetener since 1879 and is 300 times sweeter than sugar. Used in mouthwashes and lipsticks. The FDA has proposed additional testing and recommended limiting intake. Products containing saccharin have a warning label stating that saccharin may be hazardous to your health.

SUCRALOSE:

Produced from common table sugar but is 600 times sweeter and has no calories. A very stable product in foods and carbonated beverages. Should be released for public consumption in 1991 after FDA approval.

Approved for use in Canada under the name "Splenda." No health risks have been associated with it as yet.

NUTRITIONAL COMPARISONS

Cocoa versus Carob

Cocoa	Carob
Real Chocolate Taste	Chocolate Flavor
Contains Caffeine	No Caffeine
Low In Fiber	Twice As High
Low In Calcium	Twice The Calcium
Lower In Vitamin A	Six Times Higher
Higher In Calories	One Third The Calories
Higher In Fat	Lower In Fat(1/16)
3x Higher In Protein	Lower In Protein
5x Higher In Potassium	Lower In Potassium
8x Higher In Phosphorus	Lower In Phosphorus
10x Higher In Iron	Lower In Iron

HEALTH HINT: Even though cocoa does contain certain minerals in higher
proportions than carob, carob is by far the healthier choice to
satisfy your sweet tooth.

However, when carob is processed into a coating for a
candy-type bar (health food variety) it increase its fat content
to a point where it equals the chocolate.

Oxalates, contained in chocolate, unite with calcium carrying it through the
intestines as an insoluble compound.

High sugar intake reduces the effectiveness of the body's healing mechanism,
causing a prolongation in the healing time. White blood cells which aid in the
healing process tend to stay in the bloodstream and "lap up" the glucose, which is
one of their preferred food sources, instead of going to work.

Chapter 31

The Travelers Food Facts

The best advise you can get where water is concerned in any foreign country is not to drink it, unless you are staying in a four or five star hotel. While water and food is relatively safe in Europe, Australia, New Zealand and Japan, the rural areas of these countries still have a problem.

When in small hotels it is recommended not to brush your teeth or eat any raw food that has been washed in the water. If you need water, then bring along an immersion heater to boil a small amount of water or use purifying tablets such as Halzone in the water. If necessary Tincture of Iodine can be used, three drops per quart if the water is cloudy, six drops if the water is clear, then allow the water to stand for 30 minutes.

Safe beverages are tea and coffee, providing you are sure that the water has been boiled first. Bottled wine, beer and canned soft drinks are usually safe. Locally bottled waters are sometimes no safer than tap water. Never drink from a bottle or can, always use a straw or wrapped plastic cup.

Raw vegetables may be contaminated with a number of pesticides. Only eat cooked vegetables and don't eat any fruit even after washing, if there are any breaks in the skin. Rinse all fruit with boiling water and if possible, skin them before eating.

Meat and fish should be thoroughly cooked and eaten when it is hot to avoid bacterial contamination. Fish should be cooked within 2 hours of being caught unless it is kept under refrigeration. Shellfish worldwide may carry hepatitis and should be cooked, never eaten raw.

Milk and dairy products have been known to cause many travelers a serious problem. If you have any doubts, don't eat them.

Never eat custards, whipped cream filled pastries, sliced meats, meat salads or other perishables unless they are sold from a refrigerated case.

Water in Mexico and many other countries are still not safe to drink for the most part. Ice cubes have been the cause of many a case of "Montezuma's Revenge."

Frozen water in tests performed by the University of Texas, School of Medicine, showed that water, containing bacteria even after being frozen at -20°F. for 1 week, still contained 10% of the active bacteria that could cause a disease. In fact, even after the ice cubes were placed into 86 proof tequila, one organism still survived that would cause diarrhea.

Chapter 32

Frosting and Topping Facts

One teaspoon of butter should be added to chocolate when melting it, to be used in an icing recipe. This helps the icing have a better consistency.

When frosting cakes or pastries, dip your knife frequently in cold water.

If you have a problem whipping cream, add a small amount of lemon juice or a small amount of salt to the cream.

Whipped cream will have an excellent flavor if you add a small amount of honey.

 Chef's Secrets

To glaze the tops of rolls before baking or browning, beat one egg white lightly with one tablespoon of milk and brush on.

To glaze cakes, try using one tablespoon of milk with a small amount of brown sugar dissolved in it.

In order to keep boiled icing from hardening, add 1/3 teaspoon of vinegar while it is cooking.

A quick frosting can be made by mashing a small boiled potato, then beating in confectioners sugar and a small amount of vanilla.

To prevent icing from running over the tops of cakes, try sprinkling a small amount of corn starch or flour on the top before you ice.

When making meringue pie topping, add no more then 2 tablespoons of sugar for each egg white. The meringue should be spread to the pastry rim, then cool the baked pie slowly and keep it away from drafts.

Before placing on the pic filling, be sure the filling is cool.

Chapter 33

Sauce and Gravy Facts

Spaghetti sauces should be homemade, store bought sauces are for the most part high in fat and calories. Prego, extra chunky with sausage and green pepper is 47% fat. Ragu, marinara is 40% fat. One of the best at the store is Newman's Own, its mushroom sauce is 22% fat.

A good method of removing fat from gravy or stew is to wrap a few ice cubes in a piece of cheesecloth, then pull it back and forth over the surface. The fat will become hard and stick to the cloth when it comes into contact with it.

Packaged sauces and gravies are all lower quality convenience items. They contain chemicals for flavor, coloring, freshness and texture.

"EDIBLE OFFAL AGAIN"
If you purchase spaghetti sauce, never buy the ones that already have the meat included. By law they only need to include meat that is 6% meat. Best to add the meat at home for a better quality sauce.

Use your blender to smooth lumpy gravy or sauces.

 Chef's Secrets

Add a teaspoon of peanut butter to cover up the burnt flavor of gravy. This will not alter the taste.

"ONE OF THE BIGGIES"
When using butter for sauteing, always use unsalted butter since the salt separates from salted butter when heated and may leave a bitter taste.

"OR USE A ROLLING PIN"
If you add a pinch of salt to flour before mixing it with a liquid, it will help keep the gravy from becoming lumpy.

To obtain a richer brown color to your gravy, spread the flour on a cookie pan and cook over a low heat, stirring occasionally until brown before using the flour or add a small amount of coffee to the gravy. You won't taste the coffee flavor.

Another trick to turn gravy brown is to add onion skins to the gravy while it is cooking, but only for a few minutes, then discard the skins.

When making a white sauce, add a dash of nutmeg for a great taste.

If your Hollandaise sauce has curdled, try beating a tablespoon of cold water into it and it will bring it back to smooth texture.

A high-fat gravy will have a better consistency if you add 1/4 teaspoon of baking soda to it.

Chapter 34

Soup and Stew Facts

"SHOE LEATHER, AU JUS"

When making stew, never add boiling water to the stew, if more water is needed, always use cold water. The boiling water may toughen the meat.

"JEWISH PENICILLIN"

When making chicken soup, use a quart of water to each pound of chicken.

Soups and stews when cooking should only simmer, never boil.

"TV DINNERS"

Place leftover stews into individual baking dishes or small casserole dishes, cover with pie crust or dumpling, mix and bake.

Store the liquids from canned mushrooms or vegetables, freeze it, then use it in soups or stews.

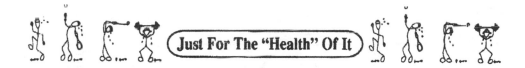

Just For The "Health" Of It

Refrigerate cooked or canned stews and soups overnight before serving. The fat will rise to the top, then you can just skim it off before heating and serving.

Read the label when buying soups. MSG and disodium inosinate and guanylate are favorite flavor enhancers.

Many vitamins are lost to the liquid when cooking vegetables. The liquid should be saved and frozen to be used when your making soups, etc.

One of the best commercial canned foods is Progresso. However, still watch out for the ones that have MSG.

Dry soup mixes are usually additive-free and only contain a few dried vegetables and seasonings.

Soup will go farther if you add pasta, rice or barley.

For an easy treat when making stews, take a stack of tortillas and cut into long thin pieces and add to the stew during the last 15 minutes of cooking. Corn tortillas are lower in fat than flour tortillas.

A good trick to avoid burning the peas in split-pea soup is to add a slice of white bread when you are cooking the peas and liquid together. Peas are an excellent source of protein.

When making stews, try adding a tablespoon of molasses for flavor.

If you add ½ cup of strong tea to the stew, it will help tenderize the meat and reduce the cooking time.

Leftover soups can be frozen in an ice cube tray and used in soups or stews at another time.

 Chef's Secrets

To thicken stews use a small amount of quick-cooking oats or a grated potato.

If your making vegetable soup, pour enough water into the pot to cover the vegetables by only 2 inches.

To reduce the saltiness of soups, add a can of peeled tomatoes, if feasible.

Another method of hiding the salty taste in soups, is to use a small quantity of brown sugar.

Oversalting soups and stews can be repaired by adding a piece of sliced apple or potato to the mixture for a short period of time, then remove and discard.

If you would like a sweeter taste in your soups or stews, try adding a small amount of pureed carrots.

Never use dark-colored bones in soups, they are too old and have deteriorated.

The best way to make stew or soup stock is to use a metal pasta cooker basket. Place it into your pot and cook all your ingredients, including any food containing bones. Remove the basket and it will have all the veggies or bones you don't want.

If you obtain too heavy a garlic flavor when cooking, place a few parsley flakes in a tea ball to soak up all the excess garlic.

To make soups or stews thicker, try adding a tablespoon or more of instant potatoes or ½ cup of rolled oats or wheat flakes.

When preparing tomato soup, always pour the tomato soup into the milk, this will prevent curdling. Low-fat milk works just as well.

To make a clear noodle soup, cook the noodles, then drain them before adding them to the soup.

When making a cream soup, try adding a little flour to the milk, it will make it smoother and will work with a low-fat milk.

Chapter 35

Food Canning Facts

When processing foods using the "open kettle" method, jars should still be sterilized.

When you cook the foods in the jars, the jars do not need sterilization, but should be thoroughly washed.

"EASY DOES IT"
Peas, corn, lima beans and most meats should be packed loosely, since heat penetration of these foods is slow. Fruits and berries should be packed solidly due to shrinkage and the fact that their texture does not retard the heat penetration.

Never use preservatives or any other type of artificial chemical substance in the product being canned.

"THE HIDEAWAY"
Canned products should always be stored in cool or cold dark locations. The excessive heat of a hot summer may cause a location to develop enough heat. Dormant bacteria will start growing.

When canned goods are frozen, then thawed, the texture may change but the food is still safe to eat. Be sure the seal is intact.

Canned foods will keep for an indefinite period of time as long as the seal is intact and they have been properly processed.

"MUSIC TO YOUR EARS"
After canning the food, tap the top, you should hear a clear "ringing note." If food is touching the top, this may not occur, but as long as the top does not move up and down, the food does not have to be reprocessed.
Black deposits that are occasionally found on the underneath side of the lid, are usually nothing to worry about (as long as the jar is still sealed) and are probably caused by tannins in the food or by hydrogen sulfide released by the foods during their processing.

Corn, lima beans and peas or any very starchy food needs to be packed loosely due to their expansion when processed.

Cloudy liquid in the jar probably means that the food is spoiled. Be very cautious, it probably should not be eaten or even opened.

When canning jellies or jams, it makes no difference whether you use cane or beet sugar, they are both the same.

 Chef's Secrets

The best vinegar to use when pickling is pure apple cider with 4-5% acidity

The outside of jars should be wiped with vinegar before storing to reduce the risk of mold forming on any food that wasn't cleaned off well.

Pickles will become soft if you use a brine or not enough vinegar or if the vinegar acidity is too weak.

To avoid hard water deposits on sealers, add vinegar to the water bath when canning.

Jars of frozen fruits should be thawed in the refrigerator. This will allow the fruit to absorb the sugar as it thaws.

Jelly jars should have a small piece of string placed on top of the wax before sealing the jar. This will make it easier to remove the wax.

Chapter 36

Substitution Facts

You can substitute ½ cup plain non-fat yogurt for the equal amount of mayonnaise. You will save approximately 90 grams of fat and almost 800 calories in a recipe.

2 teaspoons of baking soda to 1 cup of sour milk = ½ teaspoon of baking powder to 1 cup of sweet milk.

If Short This Item	You Can Substitute This
1 Teaspoon Lemon Juice	½ Teaspoon Vinegar
1 Tablespoon Cornstarch	2 Tablespoons of Flour
1 Cup Pre-sifted Flour Sifted Cake Flour	1 Cup & 2 Tablespoons
1 Cup Sour Milk / Buttermilk 1 Tablespoon Vinegar	1 Cup Sweet Milk plus
2/3 Cup of Honey	1 Cup sugar plus 1/3 Cup of Water
1 ½ Cup Corn Syrup	1 Cup Sugar plus ½ Cup Of Water
1 Whole Egg	2 Egg Yolks plus 1 Tablespoon of Water
1 Teaspoon of Oregano	1 Teaspoon of Marjoram
1 Teaspoon Allspice	½ Teaspoon Cinnamon plus 1/8 Teaspoon of Ground Cloves
Few Drops of Tabasco	Dash of Cayenne or Red Pepper

Chapter 37

Statistical Facts

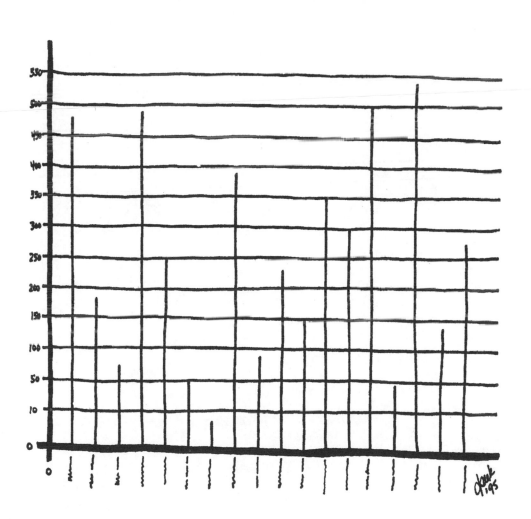

82% of the American public feel that a poor diet can increase their risk of cancer. Of these 82%, however, only 17% are willing to change their diet to reduce that risk.

A person consumes approximately 1600-2000 calories and 60-70 grams of fat in the average holiday dinner.

Almost 3 times the amount of synthetic pesticides are being used now than were used in 1965, over 800 million pounds annually.

"THE HIGH COST OF FOOD, AND WHY!"
By the time your food is picked, moved to a storage facility, then transported for processing and finally ends up in the supermarket, the food has traveled almost 1200 miles on the average.

According to the National Cancer Institute, diet is to blame for 30-35% of all cancer deaths.

Americans consume approximately 100 tablespoons of peanut butter annually.

The average American consumed 7.4 pounds of carrots, 4 pounds of green peppers, 3 pounds of cauliflower and 3 pounds of broccoli in 1993.

It takes up to 17 times as much acreage to produce 20 pounds of beef protein as it takes to produce 356 pounds of soybean protein.

Sales of "natural foods" exceeded 6 billion dollars in 1993, up 18% over 1992 according to the Natural Food Merchandiser.

"UP, UP AND AWAY"
A normal airline meal can cost the airline as much as $40 to produce and deliver to your seat.

The high-fat breakfast meal served on an airline of a cheese omelet and sausage is ordered over the healthier breakfast 70% of the time.

The average household in Honolulu spends $5,634 on food per year, Atlanta is only $4,187.

A supermarket has over 30,000 items.

The average amount of dollars spent in a supermarket in 1994 was $18.11 according to the Food Marketing Institute.

Top Grossing Restaurants

Tavern On The Green, New York City..............27 million
Rainbow Room, New York City.....................25 million
Windows On The World, New York City.............24 million
Smith & Wollensky, New York City................18 million
Bob Chinn's Crabhouse, Wheeling, IL.............16 million
Gladstone's For Fish, Pacific Palisades, CA.....13 million

Only 9% of all Americans eat enough fruit and vegetables according to the National Cancer Society.

23% of Americans don't even eat 1 serving of fruits and vegetables per day.

Each year Americans consume approximately 5 gallons of frozen desserts, most of which is ice cream.

Four out of five Americans own a microwave oven.

We spend 8.5 cents out of every dollar for food packaging.

Animal fat versus vegetable fat used in restaurants:

1989.....................62% used vegetable fat
1990....................89% used vegetable fat
1994....................93% used vegetable fat

In one year the average American consumes the following:

100 Pounds of Refined Sugar
55 Pounds of Fats and Oils
300 cans of Soft Drinks
200 Sticks of Gum
18 Pounds of Candy
5 Pounds of Potato Chips
7 pounds of Corn Chips, Popcorn & Pretzels
63 Dozen Doughnuts
50 Pounds of Cakes & Cookies
20 Gallons of Ice Cream

During the last ten years, over 10,000 new "convenience processed foods" have been introduced in the United States.

Approximately $50 million worth of Twinkies were sold in the U.S. in 1990.

More than 8,000 people in the U.S. die from food poisonings each year.

Americans drink 4,848 cups of coffee every second of every day.

It takes 10-14 ears of corn to produce 1 tablespoon of corn oil.

Food manufacturers spend $4 billion for advertising per year.
The average American teenager consumes approximately 1,800 pounds of food per year.

In a 24 hour period in the U.S., the following are consumed:

> 55 Tons of Caffeine (coffee, tea, soda)
> 985 Tons of Alcoholic Beverages

The average American consumes approximately 209 pounds of vegetables and 149 pounds of fruit per year.

The most favorite treat in the U.S. is ice cream. It is chosen first by 41% of women and 24% of men. In second place was cake/brownies, then chocolate and cookies.

Athletes prefer fresh fruit before a sporting event 25% of the time. In second place was fruit juice at 22% with water third.

More adults over 35 drink coffee than those under 35.

The most popular business lunch is now a salad by 43% over a meat dish 26%.

The choice meal of intimate dinners is lobster, 35% of the time.

Chapter 38

Dairy Facts

"LAST BUT WILL PROBABLY NOT BE LEAST"

Milk processed at high temperatures that has been sold in Europe for years will be available soon in the United States. UHT or ultra-high temperature milk is a process whereby the milk is sterilized while preserving its nutritional qualities. The process allows milk to be stored unopened without refrigeration for as much as 6 months.

"SLOWPOKES"

UHT milk has been sold in Europe for 30 years, we're not too far behind the times.

"OUI, OUI, SI, SI"

In France and Spain UHT milk accounts for 80-90% of all milk sold. Should be great for picnics or company trips.

California produces the most milk, 3 billion gallons per year.

"GOOD ALL-AROUND ADVISE"

When milking your cows, keep them calm and relaxed, they will "let down" and allow the milk to flow better. Talk to them in a low voice and play soothing music.

Wisconsin produces the most cheese, over 2 billion pounds per year.

Overall milk consumption in the United States is down 17% in the 1990's. One reason is the number of meals we eat out substituting soda and other beverages for the milk.

MILK FACTS:

When milk is discussed, the mineral calcium always seems to enter the conversation. While milk is a good source of calcium, so is cheese and dark green leafy vegetables. In fact, to obtain the same amount of calcium from 5 ½ pints of milk you need only to eat 2 ounces of cheese. This information is not being provided to discourage people from drinking milk, milk is an excellent source of vitamins, minerals and protein.

If milk is getting close to the curdling stage, try adding a teaspoon or two of baking soda to the milk. It will give you a few more good days.

While milk has been described in numerous nutrition publications as a "near-perfect food," there are two facts that should be taken into consideration:

> - Milk quality is dependent on the feeding habits
>   of the cows. Poor feeding habits with
>   insufficient green feed produces a lower
>   nutrient milk.
>
> - Many cows will receive large doses of
>   antibiotics, traces of which have shown up in
>   milk.

 # Chef's Secrets

Thin cream can be whipped by adding 1 tablespoon of unflavored gelatin that is dissolved in 1 tablespoon of hot water. If you add this to 2 cups of cream, it will whip up as good as heavy cream and will keep in the refrigerator for 3-4 hours.

Heavy cream will whip faster if you add 6-8 drops of lemon juice per pint, which will make 2 cups of cream.

"WHIPPET"
Cream whips and milk doesn't! The reason being the higher fat content, whole milk is only 3.3% fat while heavy cream is 38% fat. During the whipping process the fat globules break open causing them to stick together in clumps. Also, air is trapped between the fat globules.

Milk that has been pasteurized and homogenized may be frozen for up to 2 weeks, but be sure to pour off a small amount to allow for expansion.

Fresh milk will stay fresher longer, if you add a pinch of salt to each quart.

After you open a can of evaporated milk, place a wad of wax paper in the holes to keep it fresh longer and to stop the milk from crusting in the holes.

"WELL I'LL BE"
Cottage cheese will last longer if you store it upside down.
Spores get into the cottage cheese and live on the oxygen layer when closed up. When you turn it upside down, you eliminate a percentage of the available oxygen and the spores can't grow as fast.

Cottage cheese only retains 25-50% of the calcium from the milk it's made out of.

"BE AWARE"
There are no federal regulations regarding frozen yogurt, many are closer to ice milk in nutrient content than real yogurt, especially where calcium is concerned. While this may not be bad, watch out for the sugar content.

Yogurt consumption in the United States has risen from 1 pound per person annually in 1970 to 4 pounds per person in 1994.

When boiling milk, you can prevent it from sticking to the pot if you rinse the pot in cold water before starting.

Sour cream can be homemade by adding 3-4 drops of pure lemon juice to every 3/4 cup of whipping cream. Let sit at room temperature for 30-40 minutes.

Sour cream contains about 18% milk fat; light sour cream has 10-12% milk fat.

Many brands of frozen yogurt have as many calories as ice cream. All they do is substitute sugar for fat.

Commercial ice cream must contain at least 10% milk fat.

Powdered milk should always be kept on hand, especially if you run out of milk.

If skim milk is too thin and watery for you, try adding a tablespoon or two of non-fat dried milk to it. It will become thicker and richer as well as having a higher calcium and protein content, with no added fat.

To avoid freezer burn on ice cream, cover the top of the container with a plastic bag.

Lower price ice creams are usually lower in fat and calories due to their higher levels of air and water.

When whipping cream, place the bowl in the sink for less mess.

"I AIN'T GOT NO BODY"
Whipped cream will not hold its shape well unless the label says "heavy." The cream will have a butterfat content of 40% which gives it the body.

"KEEPING IT UP"
If you have trouble keeping your whipped cream up, try adding a small amount of gelatin when whipping it.

To avoid milk from boiling over, rinse the pot in cold water first.

Buttermilk was named for the product left over after cream was churned.

Buttermilk today comes from skim milk which has been cultured. This milk has a rich flavor and almost no fat.

A cow is more valuable for its milk, cheese, butter and yogurt than for its beef.

Evaporated milk can be used in place of whipping cream if you first place the can in the freezer until almost frozen, then pour it into a pre-cooled bowl and add 1 tablespoon of lemon juice and 2/3 cup of milk. Should whip up nicely.

When you are whipping cream, the bowl and the beaters should be placed in the refrigerator for 30 minutes before they are used. When whipping, place the bowl into a larger bowl filled with ice cubes, with a light layer of salt on top to make it even colder.

Imitation milk contains no real milk. It is made from water, sugar and vegetable fat. Usually contains only 1% protein compared to 3.5% in whole milk.

Filled milk is a combination of skim milk using vegetable oil to replace the milk fat. Sometimes contains coconut oil.

Milk will not burn if you sprinkle a teaspoon of sugar on top of the milk, before starting to cook. However, if you stir it, it may still burn.

Cottage Cheese

Creamed — Contains 4.2% fat or 9.5 grams per cup. Not recommended for dieters.

Low-Fat — Contains 1% or 2% low-fat milk.

Uncreamed — Similar to low-fat and is often sold salt-free and can be used in recipes calling for cottage cheese. Usually, it will need more seasoning than standard cottage cheese.

Milk can retain its freshness for up to 1 week after the expiration date on the carton.

Buttermilk contains only 1% milk fat.

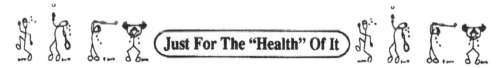

Just For The "Health" Of It

The pasteurization process has been related to the following:
* Milk allergies in children.
* The loss of calcium/phosphorus supplies, which may affect the metabolism of calcium, phosphorus and nitrogen.
* Destroys 50% of the vitamin C content.
* Destroys 25% of the vitamin B1.
* Destroys 9-15% of the vitamin B2.

Whole milk is the highest source of saturated fatty acids in the American diet.

"GOING UP"
Americans are now drinking 16 gallons of low-fat milk per person annually. In 1970 they were drinking only 6 gallons per person.

"GOING DOWN"
Americans were drinking 26 gallons of whole milk per person annually in 1970. In 1994 the annual consumption is only 9 gallons.

"NOSY SUBJECT"
New studies from Australia have shown that the milk-mucous controversy has proven to a degree that milk products did not produce an increase in mucous production.

"ZZZZZZZZZZZZZZZ"
A glass of warm milk before bedtime can be a very soothing drink containing the amino acid trytophan, which can reduce anxiety and stressful feelings.

Chocolate milk may interfere with calcium from the milk. The chocolate contains the chemical oxalate, a calcium neutralizer which affect the absorption.

Throw out any milk product that has mold on it.

Warm milk can cause insomnia in persons who have a milk lactose intolerance.

Calcium in milk stimulates the secretion of stomach acids that may irritate ulcers. Antacids with high buffering qualities are better. Food will also act as a buffer.

MILK ALERT
Milk is better purchased in paper cartons which block 98% of the harmful effect of the light. The plastic containers in just four hours of store light, can destroy 44% of the vitamin A in low-fat and skim milk containers. Some markets have installed light shields to avoid the problem.

Cream cheese has a higher percentage of saturated fat than any other cheese. Two tablespoons contain approximately 10.6 grams of fat and only 0.3 grams of polyunsaturated fat. 90% of its calories are fat.

The homogenization process, may allow an enzyme xanthane oxidase to be released into the bloodstream and reduce the effectiveness of important body chemicals that protect the small coronary arteries.

The pasteurization process has also related to a number of potential health problems:

> Milk allergies in children and adults destroys 50%
> of the vitamin C content.
> Destroys 25% of the vitamin B1 content.
> Destroys 9-15% of vitamin B2 content.
>
> Whole milk contains 3.5% fat.
> Low-fat milk contains 2% fat.
> Skim milk contains no fat.

Certified raw milk is the best milk, but you need to be sure the product is pure.

Whole milk contains 65% saturated fatty acids.

Many people do not have the proper enzyme (lactase) to break milk down, thus causing digestive problems and diarrhea.

BGH (Bovine growth hormone) is used to help cows increase milk production, it is not banned by the FDA and according to the latest studies and tests, traces have not been found in milk.

CALCIUM RICH FOODS

FOOD	SERVING SIZE	MG. CALCIUM
Milk Products		
Chocolate Milk	12 fl. ozs.	506
Low-Fat Milk	1 cup	298
Whole Milk	1 cup	288
Yogurt	½ cup	146
Condensed Milk	½ cup	393
Ice Cream	½ cup	131
Instant Breakfast	1 cup	407
Egg Nog	1 cup	330
Sour Cream	1 oz.	31
Evaporated Milk	½ cup	252
Non-Fat Milk Powder	½ cup	388
Ice Milk	½ cup	140

FOOD	SERVING SIZE	MG. CALCIUM
Cheese		
Cheddar Cheese	1 oz.	209
Swiss Cheese	1 oz.	255
Cottage Cheese	½ cup	105
Mozzarella	1 oz.	145
Ricotta	½ cup	337
American Cheese	1 oz.	195
Seafood		
Shrimp	1/4 cup	68
Lobster	3 ½ oz.	29
Sardines	3 ½ oz.	449
Salmon (canned)	½ cup	196

Beans, Nuts, Seeds

Sesame Seeds	½ cup	808
Soy Beans	½ cup	226
Garbanzo Beans	½ cup	150
Sunflower Seeds	3 ½ oz.	120
Peanuts	½ cup	88
Beans, Pinto	½ cup	70

Vegetables/Fruits

Prunes	8 lg.	90
Greens (all types)	1 cup	340
Kale	1 cup	170
Spinach	1 cup	180
Figs (dried)	5 med.	126
Watercress	1 cup	120
Broccoli	1 cup	115
Orange	1 med.	96
Dates	10 med.	59
Cranberries	1 cup	100

Grain Products

Oatmeal	3/4 cup	151
Cream Of Wheat	3/4 cup	142
Farina	3/4 cup	125
Wheat Germ	3 ½ oz.	72
Cornbread	3 ½ oz.	28

Combination Foods

Omelet/Cheese 2 oz.	1 serving	470
Macaroni & Cheese	½ cup	204
Pizza	1med. slice	140
Tostada	1 reg.	190
Cheeseburger	1 small	158
Vegetable Bean Soup	8 oz.	95

Desserts

Banana Split	1 reg.	350
Bread/Raisin Pudding	3/4 cup	210
Coconut Custard Pie	1/6 pie	145
Vanilla Pudding	½ cup	146
Rice Pudding	3/4 cup	142
Cake/Made With Milk	3 ½ oz.	130
Blackstrap Molasses	1 tbl.	116
Custard	½ cup	163

Chapter 39

Vegetarian Facts

GENERAL OVERVIEW

An ever-increasing segment of the American public is choosing not to eat meat. Approximately 12 million Americans consider themselves vegetarians, or at least ovo-lacto vegetarian (one who eats milk and eggs). This food trend is pursued for a variety of reasons, such as considering it wrong to kill animals, a waste of natural resources by using large quantities of grain to feed beef and hogs, to religious beliefs and just the belief that it is healthier.

While vegetarianism is way of achieving a healthier diet for most of the public, it is a radical change and one that is not easily adhered to. There are sufficient studies and evidence that do provide us with the proof, that even a modified vegetarian diet is beneficial and results in a healthier longer life.

One of the major concerns among non-vegetarians who wish to consider changing to vegetarianism is that they will lack protein. There are of course, many excellent vegetable sources that are capable of supplying all your amino acid (protein) needs.

One of the best plant sources of protein is soybean, which contains 30-40% protein and is closer to meat protein than vegetable when examined under amino acid pattern analysis.

The question also arises regarding the lack of B12 in a vegetarian diet, but most vegetarians do eat some form of dairy products eliminating that problem.

If you are planning to change your dietary patterns to vegetarianism, it would be wise to purchase a book on vegetarianism and learn to do extensive meal planning, especially for the first 6 months.

Types Of Vegans

True Vegetarians
Eats nothing from an animal, fresh or processed.

Lacto-Vegetarian
Includes dairy products in their diet.

Ovo-Vegetarian
The only animal product is eggs.

Pesco-Vegetarian
Includes fish, chicken, eggs and dairy products, no red meat.

Meat is not necessary for a healthy diet.

B12 is usually taken as a supplement, since it is found only in sufficient quantities in animal products.

Most vegetarians have lower cholesterol levels than meat eaters.

Vegetarians have fewer cases of colon cancer and digestive problems.

They have a lower overall incidence of cancer.

Soy products contain high levels of phytoestrogens which scientists now think will reduce the risks of breast and prostate cancer.

Tofu products may vary significantly regarding nutritional content, best to read the labels.

Tempeh is a chunky, chewy soybean product that has been mixed with rice or millet.

Miso is a combination of soybeans and a grain. Has very little fat and usually used as a seasoning for soups, dips and stews.

Iron and zinc are not as easily absorbed by true vegetarians and may have to be supplemented.

Beans and rice are one of the best combinations to acquire all the essential amino acids.

A good source of calcium is dark green leafy vegetables.

Vegetarian products made from soybeans have a lower fat content and still provide an excellent source of protein.

Most vegetarian foods contain too much sodium. When preparing vegetarian foods, try to omit the soy sauce which seems to be the high sodium source.

Chapter 40

Water Facts

Approximately 75% of Americans are concerned about the quality of their drinking water according to a 1994 survey.

Approximately 97% of the Earth's water is in the oceans as salt water. Desalinization is becoming more popular and cost effective.

2/3 of all rural households are drinking water that is in violation of EPA standards.

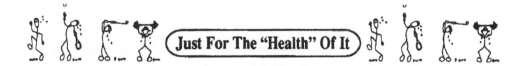

Just For The "Health" Of It

Water, the most abundant and most important nutrient in the body is as essential to life as the air we breathe. Since all body functions are dependent on water, it is evident that water is important for general physical fitness. Thus, the quality of the water we consume becomes of more than just academic interest to us all.

Alcohol, tea, coffee, and colas are not ideal as a water source, because they tend to have a diuretic effect on the body.

Medical experts agree that a water with a good mineral balance is the best bet for you. A good quality still water or a sparkling water labelled from a "natural" source would be the healthiest choice.

Copper excesses have been found in tissues of schizophrenic patients and have been traced to soft water eroding away copper pipes.

Water filters are only good if they remove the particular problem in your area and are serviced properly, this includes changing the filters on a regular basis.

According to the National Cancer Institute, nine recent studies correlated water quality and cancer with the drinking water in Pittsburgh, New Orleans, and various cities in Ohio, New York, and New Jersey.

Private wells, as a result of using soft water for drinking may be the cause of mental illnesses in one out of every 10 families.

Ice water may be harmful to persons with cardiovascular disease. Sudden drops in tissue temperatures are a shock to the system and cause a strain on the heart.

The colder the water we do drink with meals, the slower the digestive process works.

Drinking water with meals is not beneficial, since we have the tendency to wash foods down instead of adequately chewing them up.

Hot water is more dangerous than using cold water and heating it. Hot water is more corrosive and can contain larger amounts of dangerous debris.

If you consume 15-23 eight ounce glasses of water in a one hour period, it could be dangerous to your health.

Homes with copper plumbing that have no soldered joints may be hazardous to your health.

If it were not for the water secreted by the salivary gland in the mouth, we would be unable to swallow and then digest the foods we eat.

Water in our bodies dissolves the foods, carries nutrients to various parts of the body, leaves the body as perspiration, helps maintain the normal body temperature, cleanses our systems of wastes, and is then eliminated through the kidneys at the rate of 3-8 pints per day.

Americans are spending over $2.4 billion dollars on bottled water annually and are purchasing almost that dollar amount in home purifying equipment.

A family consisting of five people, uses approximately 326,000 gallons of water a year.

There are over 50,000 water contaminants and only 100 are subject to regulation. These include organic compounds, biological, heavy metal salts, inorganic compounds, gases and suspended solid particles.

In the United States each year about 30 outbreaks of diseases are traced to bacterial or chemical contamination of water supplies.

Most all filter systems only remove large particles. They still leave the small ones, such as viruses, etc.

There are 55,000 chemical dump-holes across the United States according to the EPA that can leak contaminants into the water supplies in those areas.

All water is mineral water except distilled. Even rain water contains many impurities.

A study of 969 water systems in the United States showed that 41% had impure water that was being delivered to 2.5 million people.

Rinsing vegetables in a sink filled with water will save approximately 200 gallons of water per month.

Waiting for water to get hot wastes 200 gallons per month. Try saving the water for the plants or a refrigerator bottle.

To grow one pound of meat, it requires 2,500 to 6,000 pounds of water.

You will use one gallon of water to just brush your teeth.

If you weigh 150 pounds, your body contains approximately 90 pounds of water.

Humans are 60-70% water by weight.

Brain	-75%	Kidney	-83%
Heart	-75%	Bone	-22%
Muscle	-75%	Blood	-83%
Lungs	-86%	Saliva	-95%
Liver	-85%	Perspiration	-95%

An earthworm is 80% water.

A carrot is 90% water.

Salt used to give you better traction on roads in the winter can raise the sodium content of your tap water.

Mineral water from famous name spas have no particular health benefits.

When water is called for in a recipe it should between 60-80 degrees for the best reasons.

Soft water is the best for most cooking if available. Real soft water, not artificially softened.

Let your water run in the morning before using it, there may be lead from pipes in the first water that comes out.

If the recipe calls for water by weight, remember 1 tablespoon = 1/2 oz., 2 cups = 1 pound.

Sugar lowers the boiling point of water.

The average person requires about six pints of water per day to replace losses.

A runner may lose 7-9 pints of fluid during a marathon.

The body absorbs cold water more quickly.

It takes 100,000 gallons of water to produce 1 auto.

To print 1 copy of the Sunday paper it takes 280 gallons of water.

It takes 5 gallons of water to produce 1 gallon of milk.

1 out of 12 household in the United States use bottled water as their main source of drinking water.

A laundromat with 10 washing machines, uses 1,800 gallons of water per day.

A carwash, handling 24 cars per hour, uses 8,000 gallons of water per day.

47% of our nation's water supply goes for food production.

To feed one person in the United States for a year, it requires approximately 1,726,000 gallons of water.

> 1 average baked potato requires 12 gallons of water to grow.
> 1 pat of butter takes 100 gallons of water to produce.
> 2 dinner rolls require 26 gallons of water before they
> make it to your table.

If you are on a well, have your water tested every six months.

It takes 325 gallons of water to make one gallon of alcohol.

It takes 375 gallons of water to produce a one pound sack of flour.

Every person drinks approximately 16,000 gallons of water in their lifetime.

WATER QUALITY:

The quality of water we consume is as diversified as the sources from which it is derived. Most tap water comes from streams, rivers, and lakes. If the water has flowed down a mountainside, for example, it may very likely come in contact with, and carry a variety of impurities in suspension.

Surface water may contain pollutants and agricultural wastes. Fertilizers and insecticide residues are frequently found when water is tested. Air pollutants and lead from automobiles and industrial exhausts may all end up in our drinking water supply.

Other chemicals, such as chlorine, fluorine, phosphates, alum, sodium aluminate, and others are frequently added to drinking water for purification. Fluoridation is considered by some to be the most dangerous of all methods of treating water. Sodium fluoride, one of the most poisonous of all chemical compounds, is the active ingredient in rat poisons and moth control preparations.

Water should not be relied upon as a healthy source of minerals. Frequently, it may contain inorganic minerals which cannot be assimilated by the body, but rather are deposited in various parts of the body, with the end result of arthritis, calcium-hardened arteries and stones.

It cannot be taken for granted that the water we drink is beneficial to our health. A home filtering device or purchasing a quality bottled water may be the best bet.

Water Treatment Methods

Filtration: Units that contain carbon usually in the from of activated charcoal. Very effective in removing odor, chlorine, pesticides, and organic compounds. Not as effective for bacterial removal or heavy metals and hard minerals. Attracts particles from the water until it reaches the saturation point.

Chlorination: Designed to kill bacteria with chlorine. Has a tendency to leave an objectionable taste and odor. It also may form a potentially dangerous element.

Microstrainers: Capable of removing bacteria and some chemicals from water, but cannot remove nitrates.

Reverse Osmosis Systems: Contains a sediment filter and an activated filter. Effective in removing 60-90% of most minerals and inorganic compounds. Does not produce a large amount of water in a 24 hour period.

Distillation: Boils water to produce steam, which is then cooled to produce a relatively clean water. However, this method will usually not clean the water of gases.

Aeration: The best method to remove radon gas which is one of the worst environmental hazards to man. The EPA estimates that over 8 million people may be at risk in the United States from high radon levels in their water.

Sediment Filters: Screen that filter out suspended particles such as detergents.

Ultraviolet Radiation Purifiers: Effective for the removal of bacteria. Usually installed on wells with other types of filters.

Electrohydrolysis Units: Demineralizes the water by passing a current of electricity through it to remove inorganic minerals. This method is not very effective in removing organic substances or bacteria.

Ozonators: Utilizes a highly activated form of oxygen to burn up bacteria.

Water Softeners: Removes hard minerals such as calcium or magnesium and replaces them with sodium through a process of ion-exchange. The addition of the sodium softens the water and makes it more effective for washing clothes, bathing, and doing dishes. The high salt content does not make it recommended for drinking.

Ultra Filters: Uses membranes similar to those used in reverse osmosis units, but utilizing a different method of operation. The membrane is designed to collect relatively large organic molecules as they remove dissolved inorganic solids or bacteria.

Types Of Water

Sparkling Water: Carbonated water obtained either through natural underground springs or made by dissolving CO_2 gas in water. Carbonation lasts longer in naturally carbonated waters.

Mineral Water: Contains dissolved minerals. Various brands will contain different levels of minerals. Some mineral waters are made from tap water, then minerals are added or removed as desired.

Club Soda: Usually tap water that has been filtered and carbonated. Minerals and mineral salts are added. Club soda will also take tomato juice stains out of your carpet.

Seltzer:	Usually tap water, filtered and carbonated. No mineral or mineral salts are added.
Soft Water:	Low mineral content water. Usually comes from deep in the earth with its principal mineral being sodium. Will dissolve soap better, and won't leave a ring around the bathtub. Will dissolve minerals such as lead from pipes.
Hard Water:	High mineral content water. Usually comes from shallow ground that has high concentrations of calcium and magnesium. Hard water leaves a residue of rock-like crystals
Spring Water:	Water without gas bubbles, usually tap water or natural spring water. Bottled "bulk" water falls into this category. When purchasing bottled water, try buying it in glass bottles labeled "natural."

There are more than 64 rare and different formulas for water utilizing hydrogen and oxygen isotopes. We still have a lot to learn about water.

97% of all water on earth is in the ocean. Only 3% is fresh water, which concerns all of us. 3/4 of the fresh water is frozen in glaciers.

The average person uses 75 gallons of water each day in their home, and another 100 gallons outside of their home.

43% of our water is used commercially.

Safe drinking hotline 1-(800) 426-4791

FOOD TERMINOLOGY
From A to Z

"A"

A la mode   Means the addition of a food item to another food item. Pie a la mode is pie which includes the ice cream.

Allemande   A thick sauce made from meat stock with egg yolks and lemon juice.

Angelica   Refers to a candied leafstalk, part of a European herb. Used for cake and dessert decorating.

Anglaise   A typical English dish that is boiled or roasted.

Antipasto   An Italian word for an assortment of appetizers, such as cold cuts, olives, pickles, peppers, and vegetables.

Aspic   Gelatin made from concentrated vegetables and meat stocks. Usually contains tomato juice.

A buerre   Either "with" or "cooked in butter."

Au gratin   Usually refers to a dish that has a browned covering of bread crumbs, usually mixed with cheese or butter.

"B"

Baba   A rum or fruit juice flavored French cake made with yeast dough.

Bake   To use dry heat, such as in a oven when cooking.

Barbecue	Using hot coals to cook meats on a grill while basting it with a seasoned sauce.
Barquette	A pastry in a boat shape.
Bar-le-duc	A French jam made with currants and honey. The French variety is best with the seeds removed. The American version leaves the seeds in.
Baste	A process of moistening foods while they are cooking, usually by spooning liquid over them.
Batter	A combination of a liquid and flour or other ingredient and thin enough to pour. Mainly used to coat other foods.
Bavaroise	A creamy custard that is set with gelatin.
Beat	To vigorously mix in order to have the food become smooth or increase the air in the food.
Beignets	Any food that has been dipped in batter, then deep fried in fat.
Beurre noir	A butter sauce that is browned.
Bigarade	Foods cooked in orange juice.
Bisque	A rich creamy soup made from fish or game or a frozen ice cream dessert.
Blanch	Plunging a food into boiling water usually to remove the skin off of fruit and vegetables.
Blend	Mixing thoroughly.

Bombe	A dessert made using a melon-shaped mold and filling one layer of ice cream with another.
Bordelaise	A brown sauce made using Bordeaux wine as one of its main components.
Borscht	A soup made from beets and sour cream.
Bouillabaisse	A soup made from a variety of fish, usually containing many fish parts such as the heads.
Bouillon	A clear soup made from meat broth.
Bouquet garni	Combines herbs in a cheesecloth and then used to season soups and stews.
Braise	Lightly browning the exterior of meats.
Bread	Applying a coating of bread crumbs, flour and eggs.
Brioche	A sweet French breakfast yeast bun.
Broil	Placing the food directly under a heating element.
Brunoise	A generic term referring to a food that contains finely diced vegetables.
Brush	To apply a coating thinly over a food surface.

"C"

Cafe au lait	Coffee with hot milk added.
Canape	A small piece of toasted bread topped with a variety of foodstuffs.

Capers   The unopened flower buds of the caper
plant usually preserved in a vinegar solution.

Capon   An emasculated male chicken.

Carmelize   Melting granulated sugar over a medium
heat forming a brown syrup.

Caviar   Fish eggs (roe). May be red, black, or
gold. Caviar is obtained from a variety
of fish such as the sturgeon. The finest
is called Beluga Caviar.

Chantilly   A name derived from a castle near Paris
which refers to a dish that contains
whipped cream.

Chapon   A small crust of bread that has been
flavored with garlic.

Charlotte   A dessert made from whipped cream lined with
lady fingers or sponge cake, and served in a
gelatin mold.

**Charlotte
Russe**   Sponge cake in a small cardboard cup with a
whipped cream topping and a cherry.

Chill   Allowing food to become thoroughly cool.

Chop   To cut foods into pieces, large or small.

Chorizio   A heavily seasoned Mexican pork sausage.

Chowder   A very thick creamy soup usually made from
fish, clams, vegetables, potatoes, and onions
then cooked in milk.

Chutney   A sweet relish made from a combination of
fruits and vegetables.

Coat   To cover the food with a thin film of
sugar, bread crumbs, icing, crushed nuts, etc.

Coddle   A gentle simmering in liquid for a short period.

Compote   Usually refers to a stew of mixed fruits
cooked at a slow temperature in a syrup
allowing the fruits to remain in their
natural from.

Condiment   A substance to make a food more appetizing
such as; ketchup, mustard, chutney.

Consomme   A clear broth usually made from chicken or veal.

Cool   To allow a dish to set at room temperature
until it is no longer hot.

Coquille   A dish cooked in a scallop shell.

Cracklings   The crisp remains of fat after lard has been
cooked out of food.

Cream   To blend shortening and sugar against the
sides of a bowl or with a beater until creamy.

Creole   A heavily seasoned food containing a blend of
pepper, onions, bell peppers, and tomatoes.

Crepe   A very thin pancake of French origin.

Croquette   A crisply fried, chopped meat patty made with
a white sauce and coated with crumbs and egg.

Croutons	Very small pieces or cubes of bread that have been toasted until they are crisp. Usually served with soups and salads.
Cube	Cutting foods into pieces with six equal sides.
Curry	A dish that is cooked and flavored with curry. Usually a stew.
Cutin	The process of adding fat into a flour mixture with a pastry blender or other utensil.
Cutlet	A piece of meat cut from the leg or ribs and usually fried or broiled. Most popular is the veal cutlet

"D"

Daube	A piece of braised meat.
Demitasse	A small cup of after dinner coffee.
Devil	A preparation made with spicy seasoning or sauce.
Dice	Cutting into very small cubes of food.
Dough	A combination of flour, liquid and other ingredients used to prepare pastries and breads.
Dredge	To place a thick coating of a flour mixture on a food.
Drippings	Meat juices or fat that collects in the bottom of cooking pans.

"E"

    Eclair   An oblong shaped pastry, filled with whipped cream or custard and usually topped with a chocolate icing.

    En Brochette   To be cooked on a skewer.

    Entree   A dish that is served between heavy dishes at a formal meal.

"F"

    Fillet mignon   A small round-cut piece of meat from the beef tenderloin.

    Fillet   A thin boneless strip of lean meat or fish. Usually a choice piece.

    Flake   To break up a food into small pieces.

    Flambe   Setting a food aflame.

    Fold In   The process of cutting into the center of a batter with a wooden spoon or spatula and adding ingredients then stirring them in gently and slowly.

    Fondant   A sugary syrup that is cooked to a soft ball stage (234°F.) then cooked and kneaded to a creaminess.

    Fondue   A Swiss Cheese dip for small pieces of bread.

    Frappe   Frozen, diluted, sweet fruit juice that has been made into a "mushy" consistency.

French Fry	Cooking foods in a deep fat until they are able to float.
Fricassee	To cook a meat by braising, and chicken by stewing.
Frizzle	The process of pan frying until the edges curl.
Fromage	French for cheese.
Frost	The process of covering a food with icing.
Fry	Cooking a food in a pan with a small amount of fat.

"G"

Garnish	To use colorful foods to decorate with.
Glace	Coating a food with a sugar syrup then cooking it to "crack" stage.
Glaze	Coating a food with a sugar syrup or jelly to add luster. The food can then be heated or chilled.
Gnocci	A very light dumpling made from flour, or potatoes and eggs.
Goulash	A thick, beefy stew flavored with paprika, and vegetables.
Grate	Shredding food either manually or with a machine.
Grind	To crush foods through a grinder.
Grits	Coarsely ground corn that has been hulled.

Gumbo	A thick soup usually made with okra and a combination of other vegetables and seasonings. A Creole dish.

"H"

Hache	Hashed or minced foods.
Haricot	A term used to describe a thick meat stew.
Herbs	Plants used for seasoning, garnish, and also used for medicinal purposes.
Hollaindaise	A sauce made from egg yolk, butter and seasonings. Usually served hot over vegetables and fish.
Hors d'oeuvres	A selection of different canapes and appetizers.

"I"

Ice	Usually referred to as a frozen dessert made of fruit juice, sugar and water.

"J"

Julienne	Foods are cut into long, thin strips.
Junket	A sweet milk dessert coagulated by rennet and flavored.

"K"

King, a la	A food served in a rich, creamy sauce.
Kisses	Very small dollops of meringue.
Knead	Working dough with a downward pressing motion with occasional folding and stretching.

"L"

Lard   The fat made from swine.

Leavening   Placed in baked foods to make them light and porous by releasing gas during baking.

Leek   A pungent onion-like vegetable.

Legumes   Beans, peas, lentils.

Lyonnaise   Usually means a dish that has been seasoned with onions and parsley.

"M"

Macaroons   Cookie-like pastry made from egg whites, sugar, almond paste and coconut.

Macedoine   A mixture of vegetables and fruits.

Maigre, Au   A dish prepared without meat.

Marguerites   A baked salty cracker covered with frosting and nuts.

Marinade   Usually referred to as a meat tenderizer or flavor enhancer. An oil acid mixture sometimes utilizing pineapple or papaya.

Marinate   The actual process of allowing a meat to stand in the marinade mixture for a period of time.

Marzipan   A candy made with the paste of almonds and sugar and usually shaped into miniature fruits and vegetables.

Meringue	A stiffly beaten mixture of egg whites and sugar that is used for pies, or made into small kisses.
Mignon	The most tender cut of meat.
Mince	The process of cutting foods into very small pieces.
Minestrone	A very thick Italian vegetable soup.
Mix	Combining ingredients by stirring.
Mocha	A coffee flavoring.
Mornay	A rich, cheesy sauce.
Mousse	A frozen dessert usually made from whipped egg white or cream.

"N"

Navarin	A lamb stew.

"P"

Panada	A thick sauce containing bread or flour.
Pan-Broil	Cooking in an uncovered, lightly greased pan and removing excess fat as it accumulates.
Pan-Fry	Also called "saute". Cooking in a small amount of fat.
Parboil	Partial cooking of food in boiling water and then completing the cooking by another method.
Parch	Browning with dry heat.
Pare	Removing the outer skin from apples or potatoes.

Parfait   Either an ice cream sundae or a frozen
                     dessert made from whipped cream and eggs then
                     cooked with syrup and flavored.

Patty   Puffed pastry shell filled with a creamed
                     chicken, meat or fish dish.

Peel   The process of removing the outer covering of
                     a fruit or vegetable.

Petits fours   Small fancy cakes made by cutting a square
                     sheet cake into different shapes then
                     decorating each differently.

Pilaf   A rice that has been specially seasoned and
                     used as a bed under meat, chicken or fish dishes.

Piquant   Having a sharp flavor.

Poach   Cooking foods by surrounding them with
                     boiling water to retain their form.

Poivrade   A strongly peppered flavored dish.

Polenta   A corn meal or farina mush , to which
                     Italians usually add cheese.

Potage   A thick Soup.

Puree   To press fruits or vegetables through a small
                     sieve to reduce them to almost liquid form.

"Q"

Quenelles   Meat that is finely ground, mixed with eggs
                     and shaped into ovals then poached.

"R"

Ragout	A very thick meat stew heavily seasoned.
Ramekin	Individual baking dishes.
Ravioli	Small square pasta shapes filled with cheese or meats.
Relish **Render**	A flavored blend of spices and sweet pickles. The process of removing fat from meat usually over a low heat.
Rissole	A mixture of meats encased in a pastry shell and deeply fried.
Roast	Meat cooked in the oven or over a dry heat.
Roe	Fish eggs.
Roux	A special cooked mixture of flour and butter usually used to thicken sauces and stews.

"S"

Saute	Browning or cooking in a pan using a small amount of fat.
Scald	Heating a semi-liquid until a skin forms on the top. Usually to a point just before the boiling point.
Scallop	A sea food baked in a sauce.
Score	Cutting narrow gashes partially through the outer surface of a fruit or vegetable to prevent curling.
Sear	A quick browning of the surface of a food.

Shortening	A fat used for baking or frying.
Shred	The process of tearing or cutting foods into small, narrow pieces.
Sift	To pass through a sieve to remove lumps.
Simmer	Cooking just below the boiling point.
Skewer	A long metal stick to which food items are attached for cooking.
Soubise	A food that is strongly flavored with an onion puree.
Souffle	A custard that is delicately baked and contains cheeses, meats, vegetables or fruits.
Sponge	A light cake with air and steam.
Steam'bake	A dish baked in the oven in a "dish set" in a larger dish of boiling water.
Steep	Allowing a food to cook just below the boiling point in order to extract flavor.
Sterilize	Using boiling water to kill microorganisms.
Stew	Cooking a combination of meats and vegetables in a small amount of liquid for a long time.
Stir	Mixing, using a fast rotary motion.
Stock	A liquid in which meats and poultry have been cooked.

"T"

Tartare   A sauce made from mayonnaise, capers, pickles and mustard.

Timbale   A custard or white sauce, unsweetened, with vegetables, meats, fish or poultry baked in individual dishes.

Torte   A cake made from crumbs, nuts and eggs.

Tortilla   A thin round Mexican flat bread either corn or flour.

Toss   To mix a number of ingredients without squashing them.

Truss   To tie a poultry or roast for cooking so that it won't fall apart.

Tutti-frutti   A combination of fruits.

"U"

Until set   The time it takes to set a liquid such as gelatin or custard.

"V"

Veloute   A rich sauce that is made with cream and a fish or chicken stock.

Vinaigrette   A dressing made from vinegar, oil, salt, pepper and herbs.

"W"

Whip   Beating a food to increase its volume by aeration.

"Z"

Zest   The oil found in the outer yellow or orange rind of a citrus fruit.

Zwieback   A variety of toasted bread.

REFERENCES

American Medical Association, Department of Drugs
American Heart Journal
American Journal of Clinical Nutrition
American Journal of Public Health
Archives of Biochemistry
Archives of Environmental Health
British Heart Journal
International Journal of Vitamin and Nutrition Research
Journal of Agriculture and Food Chemistry
JAMA
Journal of the Dietetic Association
Journal of Nutrition
Journal of Occupational Medicine
National Institute of Health
New England Journal of Medicine
United States Center for Health Statistics

Index

"A"

Abalone, 208
Acids, 31, 96, 142, 145, 147, 174, 182, 201, 220, 228, 237, 239, 289, 291, 380, 398, 443, 451
Aging, 66, 76, 105, 143, 263
Alcohol, 5, 6, 12, 99, 105--106-, 195, 225, 228, 229, 252, 312, 322, 323, 357, 371, 378, 398, 455, 457, 459
Allspice, 32, 357, 359, 427
Anchovy, 51, 211
Angel food cake:, 123, 283, 369
Angler, 212
Anise, 358, 358, 361, 370
Antibiotics, 105--106-, 196, 301, 323, 438
Antioxidants, 83, 114, 380
Apples, 28--30-, 32, 34--35-, 59, 70, 85, 94, 135, 371, 476
Aroma enhancers:, 380
Arthritis, 55, 460
Artichokes, 62--62-
Asparagus, 62--63-, 78, 86, 367
Aspirin, 103, 106, 107, 269
Avocados, 63, 63--64-, 139

"B"

Bacon, 12, 51, 85, 99, 142, 172, 176, 179--180-, 182, 186, 290, 294, 376, 382, 392
Bagels, 215, 255, 256
Baked potatoes:, 92, 360
Baking powder:, 92, 275--277-, 286, 427
Baking soda:, 5, 9, 11--12-, 30, 39, 57, 99, 252, 255, 286, 307, 310, 347, 369, 414, 427, 438
Bananas, 29, 30, 51, 262
Barbecuing, 73, 303, 311
Barracuda, 212, 212
Bases, 142, 380
Basil, 1, 30, 86, 233, 243, 353
Bay leaf:, 358
Beef, 13, 21, 31, 66, 132, 145, 151, 170, 172, 175--178-, 180, 182, 184, 190, 200, 292, 370, 431, 440, 449, 471
Beer, 13, 170, 178, 203, 225, 227, 324, 405
Beets, 21, 51, 85, 102, 369, 467
Berries, 38, 38--41-, 43, 135, 234, 378, 423
Beta carotene, 37, 37, 56
Beverages, 13, 225--226-, 239, 263, 265, 266, 323, 331, 358, 400, 405, 434, 437
Biotin, 99, 106, 227
Blue Fish:, 212
Blue(Bleu) cheese:, 369
Bonita, 201, 201

Bread, 8, 10, 11, 13, 21, 68--69-, 71, 79, 84, 110, 131, 133, 140, 144, 178, 182, 191, 192, 242, 247, 249, 251, 253, 255--256-, 273, 275, 279, 284, 302, 311, 341, 358, 369, 375, 387, 392, 418, 446, 465, 467--471-, 476, 479, 480
Brick cheese:, 163
Broccoli, 51, 56, 60, 336, 431, 445
Bromelin, 49, 337
Brown sugar:, 67, 132, 386, 391, 392, 409, 418
Bugs, 1, 2, 6
Bulgar wheat:, 246
Burns, 11, 100, 396
Butter, 10, 13, 21, 30, 41, 58, 60, 64, 78, 91, 121, 123, 131, 133, 135, 139, 144, 146, 148--150-, 156--157-, 185, 192, 206--207-, 236, 237, 274, 278, 284, 301, 307, 340, 341, 345--347-, 360, 362, 380, 393, 394, 409, 431, 440, 459, 466, 473, 477
Butterfish, 204, 212, 215
Buttermilk, 94, 192, 311, 335, 369, 427

"C"

Cabbage, 51, 56, 58, 69--70-, 72, 85--86-, 100, 169, 358
Caffeine, 260, 260, 263--264-, 267, 322--324-, 434
Cakes, 8, 13, 30, 121, 146, 163, 273--275-, 279, 280, 282, 285, 294, 360, 368, 409, 433, 476
Calcium, 9, 31, 39, 56, 60, 66, 68, 69, 71, 144, 186, 241, 323, 352, 385, 396, 397, 401, 437, 439, 442, 444, 451, 460, 462, 463
Candies, 337, 358, 361, 393, 398
Candle holders:, 13
Canned foods:, 108, 131, 315, 417, 423
Cantaloupe, 27, 40, 46, 51, 60
Caraway seeds:, 358, 358
Carbonated beverages:, 13, 400
Cardamon seed:, 358
Carob, 147--147-, 401
Carp, 202, 219
Carrots, 51, 56, 58--60-, 71, 85, 103, 317, 349, 352, 368, 375, 419, 431
Catfish, 206, 219
Cauliflower, 51, 71, 431
Cayenne pepper:, 359, 359
Celeriac, 72
Celery, 51, 58, 65, 86, 180, 225, 226, 359, 369, 375
Celery flakes:, 359
Celery seed: , 359, 359
Celtuce, 72
Cereals, 110, 235, 246, 392, 395, 399
Champagne, 20, 22, 44
Cheddar cheese:, 135, 145, 155, 292, 369, 444
Cheese, 6, 20--21-, 51, 84, 135, 141, 145, 150, 153, 156, 161, 163, 180, 185, 228, 303, 311, 312, 317, 358, 364, 367, 370, 375, 431, 437, 439, 441, 444, 465, 471, 472
Chervil, 359
Chewing gum:, 15, 142, 386, 393
Chicken, 13, 150--151-, 173, 176, 182, 183, 186, 189, 191, 196, 229, 284, 292, 294--295-, 302, 331, 361, 363, 365, 367, 368, 450, 468, 469, 472, 480

Chili peppers:, 80--81-, 359

Chili powder:, 233, 359, 360

China, 37, 219, 259, 312, 360

Chives, 61, 86

Chocolate, 22, 56, 99, 102, 266, 268, 282, 293, 296, 341, 363, 368, 369, 387, 394, 396, 401, 409, 434, 444, 471

Choline, 106

Cigarette burns:, 11

Cigarette smoke:, 311

Cinnamon, 9, 19, 32, 266, 357, 360, 368, 427

Citrate salts:, 375

Citrus red #2:, 376

Clams, 202--203-, 206, 208--209-, 468

Cloves, 1, 357, 360, 427

Cocoa, 147, 221, 266, 268, 340, 396, 401

Coconut, 29, 37, 145, 150, 241, 441

Cod, 31, 204, 214, 215, 218

Coffee, 3, 4, 6, 9, 11, 15, 102, 105, 144, 263, 266--267-, 322, 324, 331, 335, 369, 394, 405, 433--434-, 455, 467, 470, 475

Coffee grounds:, 9, 266

Coffee stains:, 6, 11

Coleslaw, 51, 61

Colorings, 142, 296, 376, 379, 382, 390

Cookies, 8, 13, 23, 125, 148, 274, 276--277-, 279, 284, 358, 360, 365, 392, 393, 433, 434

Cooking, 10, 11, 28, 30, 33, 34, 39, 45, 52, 55--56-, 60, 73--75-, 77, 95, 100, 102, 105, 113, 121, 123, 124, 126, 133, 139--140-, 147, 149, 157, 170, 171, 174--176-, 178--180-, 183, 185, 190--192-, 200, 202, 205, 210, 211, 213, 229, 234, 238--239-, 241--242-, 247, 253, 299, 343, 345, 349, 351, 353, 387, 398, 409, 414, 419, 458, 465, 466, 470, 472, 477

Cookware, 6, 121, 147, 350, 351

Copper, 91, 99, 101, 108, 111, 227, 308, 352, 456

Coriander seed:, 360

Corn, 70, 73--74-, 107, 139, 141, 143, 176, 193, 220, 221, 236--238-, 280, 281, 292, 338, 346, 367, 386, 387, 392, 393, 395, 409, 418, 423, 424, 427, 433, 473, 477, 479

Corn oil:, 96, 141, 281, 433

Corn syrup:, 176, 338, 386, 392, 427

Corned beef:, 132, 368

Cottage Cheese:, 20, 51, 86, 157, 158, 161, 164, 180, 369, 370, 439, 441, 444

Crab, 205, 206, 209, 367

Cracked wheat:, 234, 234, 237, 251

Cranberries, 39--39-, 41, 445

Crayfish, 209

Crayon marks:, 12

Cream, 10, 10, 13, 22, 27, 86, 123, 125, 133, 140--141-, 156, 160--161-, 163, 209, 215, 228, 247, 277--278-, 284, 286, 289, 327, 331, 332, 367, 386, 388, 390--392-, 395, 405, 409, 419, 432--434-, 438, 443--445-, 465, 468, 469, 471, 475--476-, 480

Cream Cheese:, 20, 156, 443

Crisco, 15

Croaker, 213, 213

Crock pot:, 349

Cucumbers, 19, 51, 59, 75, 303

Cumin seed:, 359, 360

Curry powder:, 360, 360, 361, 370
Cusk:, 213

"D"

Decals, 5, 307
Dehydrated foods:, 108, 113, 315, 317
Dinner rolls:, 21, 459
Dips, 19, 19, 20, 65, 360, 450
Dogs, 99, 135, 172--173-, 175, 176, 179, 180, 357, 360, 368, 376--377-, 382
Dough, 125, 243, 251, 255, 256, 273, 275--276-, 278, 280, 282, 465, 470, 474
Doughnut, 281--281-, 283, 369
Drains, 55
Dried foods:, 316, 316

"E"

Easter eggs:, 119
Edible offal:, 173--173-, 175, 181, 293
Eel, 213
Eggplant, 55, 55, 75, 78, 86
Eggs, 5, 21, 22, 51, 66, 85, 110, 119, 126--127-, 133, 135, 144, 178, 216, 219, 237, 243, 274--275-, 283, 300, 335--337-, 360, 388, 389, 449--450-, 467, 468, 472, 476--477-, 479
Enzymes, 28, 102, 147, 159, 201, 252, 315
Espresso, 266--267-

"F"

Fast food:, 113, 196, 287, 290, 294, 299
Fat substitutes:, 147
Fats, 64, 106, 139, 142, 144--145-, 147--148-, 150, 152, 274, 295, 301, 338, 380, 389, 433
Fennel, 67, 75, 177, 360, 361
Fenugreek, 361
Fertilizer, 9, 122, 133, 299
Fingernails, 7, 376
Fish, 31, 42, 51, 85, 100, 104, 135, 145, 150, 151, 172, 177, 186, 197, 199, 201, 206, 211, 213, 215, 218--219-, 229, 293, 294, 357, 359, 364, 366, 370, 376, 377, 392, 432, 450, 466, 468, 471, 473, 477, 479, 480
Flavorings, 30, 160, 357, 371, 379, 390
Fleas, 308
Flounder, 204, 213, 218
Flour, 1, 2, 91, 110, 124, 133, 146, 171, 178, 179, 220, 221, 240, 243, 247, 251, 255--256-, 276, 277, 284--285-, 292, 337, 409, 413--414-, 418, 419, 427, 457, 459, 466, 467, 470, 472, 476, 477, 479
Foaming agents:, 381, 381
Folic acid:, 100, 106
Food additives:, 375, 398
Food discolorization:, 30
Food safety:, 132, 297, 304

Fowl: , 175, 187, 191, 194--196-
Freeze dried foods:, 316
Freezer, 13, 46, 49, 57, 66, 70, 134, 142, 190, 202, 235, 251, 362, 365, 387
Freezer containers:, 13
French fries: , 91, 92, 95, 150, 289, 291, 293, 393
Fresh food:, 302, 315
Frosting:, 277, 277, 407, 474
Frozen food:, 131
Fructose, 338, 392, 396
Fruit:, 3, 4, 19, 29, 40, 45, 46, 48, 55, 74, 83, 84, 87, 225, 227, 234, 239, 243, 247, 275, 336, 357, 370, 376, 390, 394, 395, 424, 432, 434, 465, 466, 472, 473, 476, 478, 480
Furniture, 9, 311

"G"

Garbanzo beans:, 445
Garlic, 30, 85, 233, 243, 246, 357, 359, 361, 363, 468, 478
Gelatin molds:, 13
Ginger:, 51, 91, 321, 358, 363, 370
Glasses, 10, 14, 20, 331, 456
Glue:, 15, 309
Grain, 169, 169, 178, 180, 231, 234, 236, 239--240-, 246--247 , 252, 234, 280, 293, 445, 449, 450
Grapefruit, 42--43 , 50
Grapes, 20, 43, 44, 51, 182, 226
Grater, 6, 6, 14, 312
Gravy, 133, 178, 194, 302, 411, 414
Grease, 4, 4, 5, 10, 13, 15, 92, 95, 283, 284, 311
Green beans:, 65, 65
Greens, 57--58-, 60--61-, 67, 71, 85, 445
Ground meat:, 172, 172, 185
Grouper, 204, 213

"H"

Haddock, 204
Hake, 204, 213, 218
Halibut, 202, 204, 206, 214
Ham, 135, 171, 179, 220, 243, 360, 363, 391
Hamburger, 134, 141, 151, 172, 174, 176--178-, 180, 181, 184, 190, 263, 289, 294, 331, 393, 394
Hard candy:, 20
Herring, 201, 204, 214, 216
Hiccups, 7
Honey, 103, 282, 338, 390--392-, 394, 397, 409, 427, 466
Hot dog:, 13, 13, 151, 173, 180
Hot water bottle:, 4
Humectants:, 381
Hydrogenation, 144

"I"

Ice, 7, 9--10-, 14, 20, 62, 63, 70, 92, 131, 135, 141, 178, 190, 206, 207, 210, 253, 259, 265, 273, 274, 283, 285, 289, 293--294-, 386, 390--392-, 394, 395, 397, 405, 406, 409, 413, 418, 432--434-, 439--440-, 456, 465--467-, 473, 476
Ice cream cone:, 10
Ice cream:, 10, 10, 133, 135, 289, 327, 386, 389, 392, 394, 395, 432--434-, 440, 444, 465--467-, 476
Ice cube trays:, 20, 133, 190, 265
Ice cubes:, 9, 13, 14, 20, 132, 227, 259, 283, 405, 406, 413, 440
Iced tea:, 259, 259, 260
Ink stains:, 308
Insects:, 1, 2, 58, 71, 76, 335, 337
Iron, 7, 68, 71, 99, 103, 108, 127, 227, 239, 260, 283, 351, 385, 397, 450

"J"

Jams, 30, 303, 379, 386, 390, 424
Jellies, 30, 303, 358, 363, 379, 386, 390, 424
Jewelry:, 309, 309
Jicama, 51, 75
Juices, 28, 29, 46, 170, 171, 176, 179, 195, 225, 273, 378, 470

"K"

Kiwi, 45--45-, 48, 51

"L"

Label terminology:, 328, 337
Lamb, 134, 145, 177, 180, 182, 185, 186, 215, 391, 475
Langostinos:, 209
Lard:, 4, 139, 142--143-, 149, 254, 346, 469, 474
Leeks, 76
Leftovers:, 9, 131, 302
Lemon, 3, 3, 30, 46, 59, 71, 72, 78, 176, 192, 195, 207, 208, 242, 246, 251, 266, 267, 273--274-, 277, 278, 311, 393, 409, 427, 438--440-, 465
Lettuce, 51, 77, 86, 141, 180, 292, 303, 353, 375, 378
Lima beans:, 65--67-, 369, 423, 424
Limburger Cheese:, 220
Liver, 31, 103, 135, 173, 179, 220, 225, 261, 375, 381, 458
Lobster, 151, 212, 367, 434, 444

"M"

Mace, 360
Mackerel, 201, 204
Magnesium, 99, 100, 102, 104, 111, 227, 228, 462, 463

Mahi Mahi:, 214

Manganese, 99, 101, 176, 227

Mangos, 46--47-

Maple syrup:, 278, 385, 397

Margarine, 96, 133, 135, 139, 142, 143, 147, 149, 150, 234, 274, 307, 346, 370, 393

Marjoram, 73, 177, 363, 365, 427

Marshmallows:, 13, 279, 390, 391

Mayonnaise, 11, 124, 133, 147, 148, 290, 302, 307, 331, 369, 427, 479

Meat, 13, 21, 27, 29, 42, 110, 132, 133, 167, 169, 171, 176, 179, 182, 186, 191, 193--194-, 200, 218, 227, 243, 290, 300, 302--303-, 307, 311, 327, 331, 338, 347, 361, 365, 370, 377, 378, 417, 418, 434, 450, 457, 467, 469, 472

Meatballs, 178, 185

Meatloaf, 178--179-

Meringue, 121, 275, 277, 285, 474, 475

Mice:, 1, 261

Mildew, 14, 309

Milk, 3, 3, 8, 13, 20, 22, 58, 69, 74, 92, 94, 103, 104, 133, 141, 142, 144, 156, 160, 162, 174, 178, 179, 185, 201, 220, 225, 236, 241, 267, 268, 283, 299, 311--312-, 323, 324, 340, 353, 366, 386, 389, 391--393-, 405, 437, 440, 442, 446, 449, 459, 467, 468, 473

Millet, 238, 239, 450

Mint flakes:, 363

Mirrors, 12

Mold, 5, 13, 49, 62, 71, 157, 162, 237, 309, 424, 442, 467, 468

MSG, 77, 238, 376, 380

Mullet, 204, 214

Mushrooms, 51, 77--78-, 99, 417

Mussel, 210

Mustard, 8, 60, 93, 169, 308, 364, 368, 392, 469, 479

"N"

Nail polish:, 11

Nectarines:, 47--47-

Niacin, 68, 99, 105, 227, 236, 255, 349

Nitrites, 99, 171--173-, 175, 176, 377--378-

Nutmeg, 261, 357, 360, 363, 364, 414

Nutrasweet, 322, 392

Nuts, 30, 51, 139, 234--235-, 237, 242, 243, 247, 284, 301, 393, 395, 445, 469, 474, 479

"O"

Ocean Perch:, 204

Odors:, 9--9-, 58, 69, 120, 146, 391

Oils, 106, 107, 139, 141, 142, 144, 147, 149--150-, 152, 241, 254, 274, 293, 348, 357, 362, 380, 433

Okra, 78--78-, 473

Olive oil:, 30, 58, 139, 146, 211, 217, 242, 243, 246, 281, 309, 362

Olives, 5, 20, 30, 51, 85, 139, 465

Omelcts, 123, 124, 146

Onions, 3, 20, 51, 79, 362, 468, 469, 474

Oranges:, 19, 29--31-, 47, 48, 50, 51, 113, 274, 376
Oregano, 233, 359, 427
Ovens, 345, 346
Oxalic acid:, 56
Oysters, 82, 151, 200, 206, 369

"P"

Paba, 102
Pancakes, 134, 143, 144, 251, 252, 276, 278, 282, 284, 368
Pantothenic acid:, 99, 236, 255
Paprika, 55, 178, 359, 364, 472
Parmesan Cheese:, 243, 243, 369
Parsley, 56, 58, 60, 82, 87, 177, 246, 359, 419, 474
Parsnips, 56, 58, 79
Pasta, 228, 238, 243, 245--246-, 347, 418, 419, 477
Peaches, 28, 30, 45, 336, 360, 394
Peanut butter:, 13, 236, 237, 301, 307, 341, 392--394-, 413, 431
Pears, 28--30-
Peas, 51, 55, 59, 65, 67, 79--80-, 109, 221, 418, 423, 424, 474
Pectin:, 29, 29
Pepper, 2, 7, 48, 80--81-, 85, 86, 246, 321, 322, 359, 360, 364--365-, 413, 427, 469, 480
Peppers, 51, 59, 60, 80--81-, 87, 169, 359, 431, 465, 469
Perch, 204, 219
Persimmons, 49, 49
Pets, 7, 345
Pickles, 51, 60, 290, 358, 360, 361, 393, 424, 465, 477, 479
Pies, 36--36-, 134, 184, 274--275-, 277, 278, 284, 361, 363, 365, 475
Pike, 219, 219
Pineapple, 30, 49, 176, 229, 262, 337, 375, 381, 475
Ping pong balls:, 10
Pinto beans:, 292
Pizza, 20, 256, 294, 295, 341, 351, 358, 364, 366, 368, 446
Plants, 1, 2, 9, 55, 56, 62, 85, 86, 104, 133, 189, 202, 363, 375, 457, 473
Plastic wrap:, 11, 13, 61, 131, 195
Playdough, 10
Plums, 30
Pomegranates:, 50
Pompano, 204, 212, 215
Popcorn, 96, 234, 239, 282, 336, 351, 390, 433
Poppy seed:, 365
Porgy, 201, 215
Pork, 134, 151, 169, 172--173-, 177--178-, 180, 182, 200, 220, 300, 360, 366, 368, 468
Postage stamps: , 15
Pot Cheese:, 164
Potato, 6, 48, 59--60-, 63, 70, 75, 91, 93, 96, 113, 133, 141, 142, 147, 150, 157, 180, 194, 233, 280, 282, 310, 312, 348, 368, 392, 409, 419, 433, 459
Potato Chips:, 95--96-, 141, 146, 147, 150, 233, 392, 433
Potato salad:, 60, 91, 93, 368
Pots, 3, 6, 13, 307, 351--352-

Poultry seasoning:, 365
Preservative:, 218, 379, 388
Pressure cooking:, 348
Protein, 49, 49, 56, 64, 66, 85, 99, 111, 121, 122, 144, 148, 155, 161, 169, 172, 174, 182, 201, 206, 215, 220, 235, 239, 240, 244, 256, 280, 312, 375, 389, 390, 392, 401, 418, 437, 439, 440, 449, 451
Prunes, 31, 50, 103, 445

"R"

Radishes, 51, 81
Raisins, 30--32-, 50, 51, 85, 103, 379
Rapeseed oil:, 145
Raw Sugar:, 397
Red pepper:, 2, 85, 243, 359
Red Snapper:, 204
Refrigerator, 9, 9, 11, 14, 20--23-, 30, 38, 40, 59, 63--66-, 70--72-, 76, 79, 93, 103, 120, 122, 123, 157, 171, 173, 178, 179, 186, 190, 199, 212, 234, 235, 240, 246, 303, 308, 357, 362, 385, 424, 438, 440, 457
Restaurants:, 109, 147, 185, 192, 216, 289, 294, 299, 432, 433
Rice, 4, 13, 110, 132, 220, 234, 236, 243, 246--247-, 280, 365, 370, 395, 418, 446, 450, 451, 476
Rockfish, 215
Rosemary, 177--178-, 353, 365

"S"

Sablefish, 215
Saffron, 360, 365
Sage, 1, 87, 177, 364--366-
Salad, 5, 5, 22, 27, 42, 59, 61, 72, 76, 85, 91, 93, 125, 139, 143, 148, 149, 196, 218, 237, 290, 293, 294, 301--302-, 310, 331, 352, 358--359-, 361, 362, 368--369-, 371, 378, 434
Salad dressing:, 5, 5, 133, 139, 143, 147, 193, 301, 302, 371
Salmon, 151, 199, 201, 204, 215--216-, 220, 243, 341, 444
Salt, 3--6-, 8, 11, 14, 23, 43, 46, 57--60-, 62, 72, 73, 78--79-, 96, 99, 119, 121--124-, 142, 159, 161, 164, 172, 178, 179, 182, 189, 191, 195, 201, 207--208-, 233, 240--242-, 246, 253, 265, 279, 280, 282, 284, 290, 292, 308, 350, 357, 361, 362, 366--367-, 381, 387, 391, 392, 409, 419, 438, 440, 441, 455, 458, 462, 480
Sandwiches, 13, 13, 19, 131, 218, 286
Sardines, 104, 444
Sausages, 143, 182, 359, 370
Savory, 69, 353, 370
Scallops, 210, 210, 217, 290
Sea Bass:, 213, 216
Sea Trout:, 201, 216
Seafood, 51, 200, 201, 221, 444
Serotonin:, 240
Sesame, 220, 360, 370, 445
Shad, 216
Shark, 204, 205, 208

Shellfish:, 100, 105, 135, 200, 202, 204, 206, 208, 405
Shortening, 119--119-, 139, 140, 147, 256, 469, 478
Shrimp, 51, 85, 110, 135, 208, 218, 293, 444
Silverware, 331
Sinks, 236
Smelt, 219
Smoked meats:, 173
Snow shovel:, 8
Sodium, 83, 143, 176, 201, 240, 289, 292--293-, 302, 323, 335, 337, 362, 366--369-, 378, 458, 463
Soft drinks:, 268, 323, 324, 380, 392, 399, 405, 433
Sorbitol, 378
Souffle, 276, 478
Soup, 13, 15, 41, 65, 227, 347, 358, 361, 365, 370, 392, 415, 418--419-, 446, 466--468-, 473, 475, 477
Soy beans:, 237, 445
Spaghetti, 83, 237, 245, 273, 351, 364, 367, 394
Spinach, 51, 56, 58, 60, 70, 82, 85, 87, 102, 110, 239, 243, 445
Squash, 55, 56, 82--83-, 87, 348, 358, 375
Squid, 201, 205
Stabilizers:, 379, 389
Statistics, 170, 481
Steaming, 69, 74, 348
Stew, 349, 357, 368, 413, 415, 419, 469, 470, 472, 473, 475, 477, 479
Sturgeon, 219, 468
Sugar, 1, 1, 2, 13, 19, 20, 23, 37, 41, 47, 52, 58, 62, 74, 91, 92, 99, 101, 104--106-, 123, 132, 147, 157, 171, 177, 238, 239, 242, 252, 254, 274, 275, 277, 278, 282, 309, 321--323-, 337--338-, 352, 378, 387, 389, 393, 396, 399--401-, 409, 418, 433, 440, 441, 458, 468--469-, 473
Sulfites:, 29, 375, 379
Sulphur dioxide:, 379
Supermarkets, 37, 42, 95, 113, 186, 191, 193, 205, 327
Sushi, 201, 201, 216
Sweet potatoes:, 91--91-, 95
Swiss Cheese:, 162, 220, 369, 444, 471
Swordfish:, 201, 205, 217
Syrup, 14, 14, 50, 176, 278, 296, 338, 385--386-, 392, 397, 427, 468, 469, 471--472-, 476

"T"

Tarragon, 177, 177, 370
Taste enhancers:, 380
Tea, 2--4-, 6, 7, 12, 100, 257, 260, 268, 309, 311, 324, 331, 361, 405, 418, 419, 434, 455
Tennis balls:, 11
Thyme, 87, 365, 370
Tomato Juice:, 179, 226, 307, 336, 369, 462, 465
Tomatoes, 34, 48, 51, 58--59-, 70, 85, 109, 243, 246, 292, 303, 351, 418, 469
Tooth decay:, 29, 395
Tooth enamel:, 29, 323
Triticale:, 237, 240
Tropical oils:, 147
Trout, 143, 151, 201, 202, 206, 216
Tuna, 13, 51, 85, 172, 201, 202, 205, 217--218-, 237, 290, 358, 368

Turkey, 85, 135, 172, 173, 176, 186, 193--194-, 367, 369
Turnips:, 56, 60

"U"

Ugli fruit:, 50

"V"

Vanilla, 9, 281, 284, 296, 308, 311, 371, 393, 409, 446
Veal, 145, 151, 172--174-, 177, 469, 470
Vegetables, 12, 53, 55, 57, 60--61-, 63, 64, 69--71-, 81, 104, 109, 110, 113, 133, 174, 246, 299, 301, 303, 315, 316, 346, 360, 364, 371, 379, 381, 417, 418, 434, 437, 445, 451, 457, 466--469-, 472--475-, 477
Vegetarian facts: , 447
Venison, 179, 182, 184
Vichyssoise, 93
Vinegar, 2, 4--5-, 58, 61, 70, 74, 79, 80, 122, 123, 139, 155, 157, 179, 182, 206--208-, 273, 277, 285, 299, 307, 309--311-, 357, 361, 362, 371, 387, 409, 424, 468, 480
Vitamin B1:, 40, 441, 443
Vitamin B12, 106, 260
Vitamin B2, 255, 441, 443
Vitamin B6, 99, 255
Vitamin C:, 29, 32, 45, 50, 65, 68, 69, 73, 75, 77, 81, 83, 84, 99, 100, 103--104-, 108, 110, 114, 144, 241, 252, 378, 386, 441, 443
Vitamin D:, 104, 105, 110, 201
Vitamin E:, 103, 106, 110, 143
Vitamin K:, 29, 71, 106
Vitamins, 28, 49, 57, 62, 63, 67, 80, 83, 99, 101, 108, 109, 114, 143, 146, 225, 227, 228, 244, 315, 322, 347, 348, 380, 381, 392, 396, 417, 437
Vitamins A:, 49, 80, 104
Vodka, 22, 226

"W"

Waffles, 134, 252, 283
Water, 2, 4, 7, 9, 11, 13, 20, 27, 30--33-, 38, 39, 43, 46, 48, 49, 52, 58, 61, 65--67-, 69, 71, 75, 77, 79--80-, 85, 86, 93--94-, 101, 121, 123, 133, 134, 140, 144, 146, 173, 177--179-, 193, 202--204-, 207, 210, 212, 217, 236--238-, 244--245-, 251, 254, 255, 276, 282, 285--286-, 292, 299, 307, 310, 311, 316, 324, 335, 349--350-, 352, 359, 367, 376, 381, 385, 390--391-, 397, 398, 405--406-, 409, 414, 417, 418, 427, 434, 438, 440, 453, 456, 461, 463, 466, 473, 476, 477
Watermelon:, 23, 51, 220
Whipping cream:, 274, 409, 439--440-
White chocolate:, 391
Whitefish:, 219
Whiting:, 218
Whole wheat flour:, 236--236-, 240, 254, 255, 273
Wine, 2, 2, 4, 13, 20--22-, 44, 100, 140, 190, 225, 229, 243, 260, 283, 299, 307, 360, 392, 405, 467

Wine bottle:, 4, 21
Woodwork: , 6, 12, 310, 311

"Y"

Yams, 91--91-, 95
Yeast, 125, 132, 220, 255, 308, 380, 465, 467

"Z"

Zinc, 99, 100, 104, 109, 111, 227, 228, 264, 450

1st NATIONAL RELEASE
from the National Cherry Festival
Held each year in July

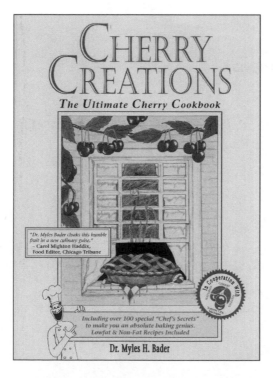

For Cookbook information and shipping call 1-800-717-6001.

For Festival information call 616-947-4230.

$15.95
plus shipping